TAKEOVER

TAKEOVER

*How the Left's Quest for Social Justice
Corrupted Liberalism*

✳   ✳   ✳

Donald T. Critchlow and
W. J. Rorabaugh

Wilmington, Delaware

Library of Congress Cataloging-in-Publication Data

Critchlow, Donald T., 1948–
  Takeover / Donald T. Critchlow and W. J. Rorabaugh.
    p. cm.
  Includes bibliographical references and index.
  ISBN 978-1-61017-059-8
  1. Liberalism—United States—History—20th century. 2. Liberalism—United States—History—21st century. I. Rorabaugh, W. J. II. Title.
  JC574.2.U6C75 2012
  320.51'30973—dc23
                          2011052575

Published in the United States by

ISI Books
Intercollegiate Studies Institute
3901 Centerville Road
Wilmington, Delaware 19807-1938
www.isibooks.org

Manufactured in the United States of America

Contents

Introduction

The New Progressives

How did liberals get to be the way they are today?

This book answers that important question. It is a question more and more Americans began asking as they witnessed the ascent of Barack Obama, the most left-wing Democrat to be nominated for president since George McGovern in 1972 and arguably the most progressive president ever elected.

Searching for answers, many commentators have looked back to the progressive movement of the early twentieth century. To observers such as talk radio host Glenn Beck, author Jonah Goldberg, and historian Ronald J. Pestritto, modern liberalism is of a piece with the progressivism that President Woodrow Wilson embodied a century ago.[1] To be sure, today's liberals, many of whom embrace the label *progressive*, share the older progressive faith in using governmental power to address societal ills. But this focus on the similarities between modern liberalism and early-twentieth-century progressivism overlooks a sharp break in the history of liberalism that began in the 1960s. Only by understanding that break—and the radicalism that accompanied it—can we fully understand our current political situation.

The older progressive tradition primarily aimed to address the ills of industrial capitalism. Progressive reformers such as Theodore Roosevelt and Woodrow Wilson sought strict regulations on business to protect the rights and health of workers and citizens and to deal with the problem of corporate monopoly. They proposed an associative order in which

1

civic and business organizations cooperated with government at the municipal, state, and federal levels to promote the general welfare. In the 1930s, Franklin Roosevelt's New Deal built on this reform tradition by providing a "safety net"—old-age pensions, unemployment benefits, and welfare payments. Lyndon Johnson's Great Society went further in the 1960s, extending grants and loans to college students, establishing the Jobs Corps, creating Medicare and Medicaid, and declaring war on poverty. But this progressive tradition did not seek to dismantle capitalism itself. Even the New Deal, for all its statist sympathies, refused to nationalize banks or ailing industries during the worst global economic crisis in history.

The liberal agenda today is much more radical and encompassing. It is no coincidence that upon taking office, President Obama pushed for government control of nearly every aspect of American life—through nationalized health care, environmental regulation, caps on energy use, financial regulation, and a range of other governmental intrusions. The roots of this radicalism lie in a strategy that emerged in the 1960s and 1970s to challenge the American corporate order.

Infiltrating the Establishment

The New Left that came of age in the 1960s was not an extension of Roosevelt-Wilson progressive reform. Nor, for that matter, was it a continuation of New Deal or Great Society liberalism. Indeed, these activists denounced mainstream liberalism as the enemy of reform. Influenced by a rekindled interest in Marx, they saw the New Deal regulatory state as benefiting large corporations, and the New Deal welfare state as only an ameliorative measure designed to maintain class privilege. Where earlier progressives were concerned mostly with the failings of industrial capitalism, the new activists of the 1960s addressed the problems of a postindustrial order, which were related more to affluence than to scarcity. The range of concerns thus expanded beyond poverty and inequality to include corporate greed, toxic waste, unsafe consumer products, environmental abuse, overpopulation, and many other issues. These radicals disparaged consumption and corporate capitalism. They espoused what they called community control and direct democracy, though leaders of this movement generally came from elite backgrounds and aimed to impose their visions of "social justice" on the rest of society. This emergent Left was a new political phenomenon.

By the early 1970s, the New Left's anti–Vietnam War protests and other street activism had faded away. But the radicalism remained. The activists simply changed their tactics for remaking American society. After fighting against the establishment, radical leaders discovered that they could achieve much more by working within the system. They learned to harness politics and the courts to pursue what they thought of as social justice. Becoming lawyers, professors, journalists, consumer advocates, union leaders, and even politicians, left-wing activists morphed into a new movement—the "New Progressives."

This book examines how the New Progressives colonized many areas of American life in creative and powerful ways. They achieved their two most significant successes in rewriting the Democratic Party's presidential nominating rules and in remaking the legal profession. In the first case, New Progressive activists got their opportunity following the disastrous 1968 Democratic National Convention. Antiwar activists were outraged that Vice President Hubert Humphrey had won the Democratic nomination despite earning a small percentage of primary votes. The Democratic Party responded by appointing a commission, headed by antiwar senator George McGovern, to revise the party's process for selecting delegates. Reformers on the commission—especially young staffers who came out of the antiwar movement—quietly rewrote the rules to give much greater power to left-wing activists, including peace protesters, feminists, environmentalists, community organizers, homosexual-rights advocates, and ethnic-minority leaders. These rules changes have had long-term consequences for the Democratic Party, enshrining identity politics and pushing the party much further to the left. As this book will show, Barack Obama almost certainly could not have won the 2008 Democratic presidential nomination without the McGovern Commission's changes favoring progressive activists.

Still, New Progressives maintained an uneasy alliance with the Democratic Party. Left-wing activists wanted to radically transform American society—by pursuing militant environmentalism; tearing down corporate power; crusading for population control, abortion, and euthanasia; pushing for nationalized health insurance; and more. But electoral politics meant compromise, working with lobbying interests, and trusting politicians interested only in winning elections. Often, too, New Progressives found that voters did not embrace their radical agenda. They needed to find a way to impose their vision on the country. That is where the second notable achievement, in the field of law, proved so consequential.

New Progressive legal activists practically invented the field of public interest law. Growing out of the rights revolution of the 1960s and especially the anticorporate crusading of Ralph Nader, a left-wing legal movement took advantage of liability law and class-action suits to go after businesses, physicians, civic organizations, government agencies, and any number of other groups. By the mid-1970s, leading New Progressive legal thinkers had laid out the strategy for taking down corporations in the name of giving power to the people. One prescient essay outlined how class-action suits could be used to exact hundreds of billions of dollars from tobacco and liquor companies, the pharmaceutical industry, food manufacturers, and other groups—exactly what activist lawyers would do in the succeeding decades.

The courts also became the place to seek social transformation, especially in the area of abortion rights. The appeal of circumventing the normal democratic process was not lost on New Progressives. According to the lawyer who argued for the right to abortion in *Roe v. Wade*, she and her fellow activists recognized that "around the nation, the big advances seemed to be coming from the courtrooms, not legislative halls."[2]

The story of the New Progressives is one of radicalism tied up with elite power. Well-heeled foundations provided extensive financial support to the New Progressive judicial activism. Most notably, the Ford Foundation funded public interest law and legal clinics at the country's leading law schools, helping make these elite institutions training grounds for left-wing legal activism. Both the legal professoriate and the student body shifted increasingly leftward. An October 1967 survey at Harvard Law showed that 31 percent of the students identified as Republicans; by 1972 those voting Republican had dropped to a mere 11 percent—this at a time when McGovern the Democrat was losing in a landslide. Similarly, in a 1956 survey at Yale Law School, 56 percent of entering students described themselves as "liberal" or "far left"; by 1972, this aggregate figure had risen to 80 percent, with fully 32 percent describing themselves as "far left."[3]

The Ford Foundation also funded a host of public interest law firms that reflected the wide-ranging agenda of the New Progressives. Among the groups the foundation helped establish were the Center for Law in the

Public Interest, the Public Advocates, the Education in Law Center, the International Project, the Mexican American Legal Defense and Education Fund, the Native American Rights Fund, the ACLU Women's Rights Project, the Natural Resources Defense Council, the Environmental Defense Fund, the Sierra Club Legal Defense Fund, the Citizens Communication Center, the Georgetown Institute for Public Interest Representation, and the League of Women Voters Education Fund.[4]

Public-sector unions such as the Service Employees International Union (SEIU), as well as key industrial unions, contributed crucially to this radical matrix by providing funds and personnel to activist causes, including community organizing, voter registration drives, and political campaigns. They cooperated with organizations such as the Association of Community Organizations for Reform Now (ACORN) in campaigns for low-income housing development, health-care reform, political mobilization, and other causes. Funding for these activities often came from philanthropic foundations as well as wealthy corporate backers. By the 1990s, for example, hospital associations and large private insurance corporations backed national health insurance reform. Industrial unions such as the United Auto Workers (UAW) joined with hard-pressed corporations to shift long-term pension and health-care benefits to the American public.

New Progressives involved themselves in an astounding variety of causes. Fears of overpopulation and environmental degradation, for example, led activists to oppose nuclear power and to promote animal rights, regulations for food packaging, use of mass transportation, construction of low-income housing, and restriction of population growth. One of the leading figures in the population-control movement was John D. Rockefeller III, heir to the oil fortune. Rockefeller supported abortion on demand, family planning, sex education in schools, immigration restrictions, and more.

Given the array of issues it has pursued, the New Progressive movement is diffuse and fluid. Its goals are sometimes ambiguous. Causes have appeared, disappeared, and then reappeared. For a time, the leading issue was nuclear development, followed by suburbanization, unsafe drinking water, food additives, McDonald's Styrofoam containers, a nuclear weapons freeze, the destruction of rain forests, and nationalized health care.

What unites these disparate causes is the rallying cry of social justice. Radicals have never defined the exact meaning of "social justice." The concept appeals to the heart and to good intentions. It has allowed New Progressives to form alliances, at various times, with concerned Americans who would resist being called radicals. Even some activists drawn to the New Progressive banner have been well-intentioned reformers who sought answers to legitimate problems related to poverty, environmental pollution, health care, and corporate abuse. Yet their mistrust of corporations and their ignorance of, and hostility to, free markets led them increasingly toward solutions that relied on big government and technocratic and legal elites.

That reliance on governmental power, the faith in elites to determine the collective good, and the suspicion of free markets are all hallmarks of the New Progressives. Indeed, only by examining how the New Progressives emerged and the radical departure they represent can we see the close connections among seemingly unrelated issues. Modern liberalism can appear to be a grab bag of causes: radical environmentalism, class warfare, abortion rights, nationalized health care, feminism, regulations on the free market, assisted suicide, sex education, caps on energy, and on and on. To these new-style liberals, the breadth of the agenda is the very point. They call for new standards of public morality to be built on a foundation of social justice in which individual rights are subsumed in the collective interests of the community—with the New Progressives defining those collective interests, of course.

Such public morality does not stop at determining how government treats the needy and how much leeway businesses are given to operate. It involves how all citizens live their lives: how much energy they consume, the health-care plans they purchase, the cars they buy, the lightbulbs they use, and even the food they eat and drink. Big corporations, New Progressives suggest, manipulate consumers with sophisticated advertising campaigns, often targeting children, the poor, or ethnic minorities. To these activists, health warnings, public education campaigns, and common sense are not enough to ensure that consumers make the right choices; the state must step in to restrict those choices.

In short, this leftist agenda is intent on transforming America into a European-style social democracy, run by a governmental elite from the top down. If the public and corporations cannot be cajoled by the argument of social justice, then coercion through new legislation or court rulings is necessary. With an electorate that has remained stubbornly center-right through the decades, such coercion has often proved necessary.

Into the White House

Progressives did, however, finally achieve their long-sought electoral triumph when Barack Obama won the presidency in 2008. Sickened by the centrism of Democrats such as Bill and Hillary Clinton, progressives had long looked for a new leader. After flirting with John Edwards, they found that person in Barack Obama, who had come directly out of New Progressive circles. The son of a Kenyan father and an American mother who had worked for the Ford Foundation in Asia, Obama had been educated at Columbia University and Harvard Law School. He had worked as a community organizer on Chicago's South Side, devoting himself to the cause of social justice and to activist methods. Most important, he shared progressive concerns, opposing the war in Iraq, calling for nationalized health insurance, proposing new energy and environmental policies, urging the end of corporate greed, and advocating arms control and the reduction of nuclear weapons.

In 2008, Obama stepped forward to harness progressives into a well-organized political movement. Once in office, he proposed transformative change: a sweeping national health insurance program, an extensive "cap and trade" energy policy, unprecedented regulation of finance and banking, and a government purchase of a big chunk of America's largest automobile company. In 2009, the government invested heavily in the takeover of General Motors, the insurer AIG, the student loan program, and many of the nation's home mortgages. If the president got his way, the New Progressive elite that ran the government would control health care, automobiles, energy use, nutrition, and banking. There would be top-down control, oversight, and regulation from cradle to grave. In Obama's America, the nanny state had become the nanny-to-granny state.

1

Legacies of the Sixties

Like many changes in American life, the transformation of liberalism began in the 1960s. Until that crucial decade, liberals could be found in both major political parties, although the Democratic Party, as the majority party, contained more liberals. At the beginning of the sixties, liberals, suspicious of big business, influenced by the social gospel, hopeful that an informed public would make enlightened decisions, and confident that increased governmental power and regulation could cure all ills, were still close to the economic and social reform ideas of Theodore Roosevelt, Woodrow Wilson, and Franklin Roosevelt. To these tenets, Harry Truman had added support for civil rights and strong anticommunism.

The sixties rattled liberals, challenged their premises, and turned liberalism to the left. John F. Kennedy used money, television, and primaries to destroy the boss-led convention nomination system, while Lyndon Johnson completed the New Deal agenda. Meanwhile, the civil rights revolution introduced moral politics, participatory democracy, egalitarianism, and voting rights. Young radicals emerged, while African Americans, women, and other groups embraced identity politics. Then the Vietnam War brought antiwar protesters into the Democratic Party. In 1972, George McGovern cultivated identity politics and ran for president on progressive principles. Although McGovern lost in a landslide, he pushed the Democrats permanently leftward. By the eighties the Democrats were increasingly a party of New Progressives devoted to elite control of governmental power in pursuit of social justice.

Kennedy and Johnson: Old-Style Liberals

In the early 1960s, Americans innocently embraced the present as prelude to a better tomorrow and imagined easy successes. The sixties were the "go-go" years. The stock market rose, and the jet set cavorted in Capri. The government planned to send an American to the moon (outer space), while others plotted to turn America on to psychedelic drugs (inner space). No one affirmed the country's optimism more than President John F. Kennedy.[1] "We were guys of the fifties," one of Kennedy's advisers later recalled, "who thought there was nothing we, or America, couldn't do."[2] Presenting himself as a dynamic, can-do guy, Kennedy was nevertheless only a moderate liberal. This cautious liberalism along with a mastery of television style, sex appeal, charm, and wit enabled him to enjoy unusual popularity, even though he accomplished little as president.

Traditionally, the Democrats had been an umbrella party that included liberals, moderates, and conservatives. Big-city party bosses, who ran the party until the late 1960s, tended to be pragmatic. They were less interested in whether a candidate was liberal or moderate than in who could win. Although Kennedy had cultivated the bosses, he invented a new nomination method that employed money, television, and primaries. This new system gave liberal candidates an edge in gaining nominations. Liberal Democrats were more likely to give money to candidates, to work on campaigns, and to vote in primaries. The old system produced Franklin Roosevelt and Harry Truman, who won and governed successfully, as well as Adlai Stevenson, a shrewd choice to hold the party together in an inevitable loss to the popular Dwight Eisenhower. The new system led to Jimmy Carter, who could not govern, and George McGovern and Michael Dukakis, neither of whom could win a national election.[3]

After Kennedy's assassination, the presidency fell to Lyndon Johnson, a thirties New Dealer who had survived in Texas politics by keeping his liberalism to himself.[4] Johnson broke a southern Senate filibuster to pass the Civil Rights Act.[5] After winning a landslide election in 1964, Johnson moved to complete the New Deal agenda. He pushed successfully for the Voting Rights Act and Medicare, the government health program for senior citizens that promised to end the nightmare by which elderly Americans lost their homes in an effort to pay high medical bills. He expanded Social Security, Aid to Families with Dependent Children, urban renewal, and funding for public education and for colleges, including the new federal student loan program. Johnson's War on Poverty included the Jobs Corps for unemployed youths as well as neighborhood job training programs.[6]

Johnson's domestic social programs were impressive in breadth and scope. In effect, all the New Deal proposals from the thirties, except national health insurance, were enacted. He had to skip universal health care because there were not enough votes in Congress to pass it, but he saw Medicare as a first step. In 1966, Johnson said, "Medicare need not just be for people over sixty-five. That is where we started." An incrementalist, he believed that Medicare would lead inevitably to national health insurance. Expressing a view common among New Deal liberals of his generation, Johnson always thought that half a loaf was better than nothing.[7]

Johnson's completion of the New Deal agenda, except for national health insurance, suggested that the old-style liberalism of Kennedy and Johnson had reached its natural limit. These liberals had always imagined, as had Theodore Roosevelt, Woodrow Wilson, and Franklin Roosevelt, that the government's role was to provide a helping hand. The purpose of social programs was to make it possible for average people or the poor to enjoy the same opportunities that the upper middle class or the wealthy were able to provide for themselves. Hence, government-aided home ownership, freeways, mass transit, college loans, job training, and health care for the elderly (Medicare) and the needy (Medicaid). Capitalism was affirmed, and the social order went unchallenged.

Old-style liberalism meshed poorly with the upheavals of the 1960s. Kennedy's death in 1963 marked the decade's first shock. That murder shattered the country's equilibrium, challenged liberal confidence, strained the political structure, disillusioned youthful idealists, and ultimately energized emerging radicals. Alas, Kennedy's assassination would not be the last. The murders of Martin Luther King Jr. and Robert Kennedy less than five years later would complete a trilogy. The civil rights movement, college student protests, and peace marches increasingly filled the streets and appeared on the evening television news. Peaceful black demonstrations ("Freedom Now") turned into riots in Watts and across the country ("Black Power"), and radical opponents of the Vietnam War brought chaos at home ("Ho, Ho, Ho Chi Minh, the NLF is gonna win"). Violence escalated. At the end of the decade, H. Rap Brown, a black militant, called violence as "American as cherry pie."[8]

The Civil Rights Revolution

In the last half of the twentieth century the civil rights movement was the most consequential social movement in the United States. While important for the rights of African Americans, the movement also transformed politics in both obvious and subtle ways. Ever since slavery ended in 1865, black Americans had remained second-class citizens. In the South, they were subjected to a formal legal system of racial separation and white supremacy. In the North, informal segregation was the norm, but there was access to the ballot. As a result of the Great Migration to the North, especially during and after World War II, black voters by 1948 proved pivotal in carrying such key states as New York, Pennsylvania, and Illinois. Black migration, in many ways, put civil rights onto the national agenda.[9]

Martin Luther King Jr., a Baptist preacher and the son of a prominent Atlanta clergyman, saw that principles of nonviolent protest could be applied to the racial problem in the United States.[10] Nonviolent protest enabled African Americans to confront the role that violence had played in southern society. White supremacy in the South depended heavily on violence to crush black resistance. A devout Christian, King believed that black nonviolent protest both occupied the moral high ground and created political opportunity. Whites who attacked peaceful protesters revealed their own degradation against a moral challenge and mocked the claim that they were guardians of virtue. If whites avoided violence, they lacked the means to defeat the protests. Once black nonviolence claimed the moral high ground and neutralized white violence, the civil rights movement would prevail.

King and other movement participants sought to win rights for African Americans, who faced widespread discrimination in jobs, housing, and education. To help unlock opportunities, blacks needed to vote in large numbers. Voters could then push for social change. In the late 1960s rights activists, including King, became increasingly interested in poverty, which was seen as an issue of social justice.[11] Most civil rights groups shared the same vision. The Congress of Racial Equality (CORE) had practiced nonviolent protest since the 1940s. In 1960 southern black college students who admired King's principles founded the Student Nonviolent Coordinating Committee (SNCC). While King, CORE, and SNCC provided inspiration and advice, the civil rights movement took place at the local level, where the grassroots did the organizing. The movement was a bottom-up, self-help operation.[12]

The civil rights movement reshaped politics in four distinct ways. First, the movement believed in and practiced *moral politics*. Unlike Lyndon Johnson, participants in the civil rights movement believed in the primacy of moral principles. Accordingly, adherents pursued politics in the name of social justice. Although this moral dimension was important to the movement's essence and drive to success, it proved problematic when applied to electoral politics. Politics is often about old-fashioned horse trading and compromise. Infusing the political system with moral fervor had a cost.[13]

Many young white liberals—they mostly thought of themselves as liberals at that time—embraced the civil rights movement in the early sixties, and as they did so, they attached themselves to the movement's moral principles. By the midsixties, even before the Vietnam War, these liberals increasingly wanted to take moral stands on political issues. This is not the way to get Congress to build an interstate highway or a dam, nor does it lead to a "half-loaf" law like Medicare, which helped the elderly but ignored everyone else. Instead, young liberals wanted to use governmental power to pursue social justice with transforming legislation that would end all war, stop racism, and save the planet. Liberal moral enthusiasm made such liberalism less flexible. For a brief time, Todd Gitlin, Mary King, and Tom Hayden thought along these lines.[14]

The second contribution of the civil rights movement to the new politics was *participatory democracy*. The phrase was first widely used by young white activists, including Tom Hayden, who helped organize Students for a Democratic Society in 1962, but the concept actually dates to the creation of SNCC in 1960 and, arguably, to CORE in the 1940s. Because nonviolent protest forced participants to risk arrest, group solidarity was important.[15] Leaders, of course, had a say. After all, leaders were required to conduct negotiations. But when negotiations seemed futile, and activists believed that the time had come to "put your body on the line," then the rank and file made the decision, because they were the ones who would face arrest. No one, in a moral movement, could tell another person when to protest. The movement was not an army managed from the top. It was a bottom-up, grassroots movement of ordinary people making extraordinary efforts to gain their own rights.[16]

Movement participants learned that narrow majorities could not make effective decisions. Instead, the entire group had to participate in meetings that lasted for hours. The grass roots, not leaders, made important decisions. Each person had an equal chance to take part, and the group hashed out all possible reasons for or against a particular course of action. At the end of the meeting, consensus would be reached. Only through this laborious process could the group be kept together. In practice, leaders learned to outwait enemies and spring proposals on a tired group that had been thrashing around aimlessly for hours. A prepackaged proposal could be sold to a rump meeting. In theory, participatory democracy meant the absence of leaders, but in practice it favored the most guileful. These leaders were also usually educated, aggressive males who liked to talk a lot—and had sex appeal.[17]

Democratic Party liberals—they increasingly called themselves progressives—embraced the civil rights style to impose participatory democracy on party structures. Liberals called for broad voter participation inside the party, discouraged the role of leaders at all levels, and demanded precinct caucuses to pick presidential candidates. Caucuses were arguably the least democratic form of democratic politics ever invented. They attracted far fewer voters than did primaries. Those who attended rarely represented public opinion. And a small number of activists could rig meetings. Caucuses were unfair in another way: women with children found it hard to attend.

Caucuses embraced "persons of the people" who rose mystically from the mud, like Jimmy Carter rising from the Iowa caucuses all the way to the White House (to the ultimate embarrassment of millions of Americans). Of course, Carter was no man of the people but instead a shrewd and often devious politician who propelled his campaign forward in the Iowa caucuses largely through artful dodges. ("On a range of issues," wrote journalist Jules Witcover in his account of the 1976 presidential race, "he showed all the elusiveness of a scatback.")[18]

The third contribution of the civil rights movement to the new politics was *egalitarianism*. Since the movement's goal was to tear down segregation and white supremacy, it is understandable that the movement was egalitarian. The movement accepted Thomas Jefferson's line "All men are created equal," assuming that "men" could be read to include all people. In the sixties, the egalitarian ethos percolated throughout the liberal community. For example, in 1962 the U.S. Supreme Court in *Baker v. Carr* declared that the federal courts had a right to control legislative districting. In a subsequent ruling, the court's liberal majority held that all apportionment had to be based on "one man, one vote." This egalitarian concept of proportionality in representation can be seen as rooted in the ideology of the civil rights movement. "One man, one vote" became a guiding phrase for the egalitarianism of the new liberalism.[19]

Liberals used governmental power through statutes, executive orders, agency regulations, or the courts to impose their own particular brand of egalitarianism in numerous situations. In the name of equality and fairness, colleges and employers were forced to adopt racial, ethnic, and gender quotas, despite promises from Hubert Humphrey that the Civil Rights Act (1964) did not impose quotas. Many Jews, who had been subjected to quotas in Europe, were livid. Quotas were also forced on banks. The government eventually wrecked the mortgage industry by forcing lenders to give loans to unqualified borrowers in the name of promoting equality of home ownership.[20]

In another sign of egalitarianism, progressive campaigns were waged to allow felons to vote, even if they were in prison. (Do the felons get to vote for the warden?) Liberal judges extended many rights to felons under the guise of equal treatment, ignoring the fact that hardened criminals had been locked up because they were dangerous to other people. Thus, the liberal governor of Massachusetts Michael Dukakis famously furloughed convicted murderer Willie Horton, who fled the state and ended up raping a woman and beating and binding her fiancé.[21]

Fourth, the civil rights movement pushed for African American *voting rights*, a cause the Democratic Party quickly adopted. In the early sixties, Attorney General Robert Kennedy encouraged voter registration drives in the South. Increased black registration would make southern senators more pliable on racial issues and might help John Kennedy in 1964. Much of the civil rights campaign in Mississippi from 1960 to 1964 focused on voter registration.[22] Because few blacks in Mississippi were allowed to register at that time, the movement decided to organize a private registration system and hold a mock election, called the Freedom Vote. The main idea was to show that a lot of African Americans wanted to vote. The Freedom Vote quickly led to the organization of the mostly black Mississippi Freedom Democratic Party (MFDP). The MFDP petitioned the 1964 Democratic National Convention to be seated in place of the regular all-white Mississippi delegation, which was pledged to segregation.[23]

In 1964, Lyndon Johnson wanted to avoid racial politics. The Democratic Party platform committee heard Fannie Lou Hamer's testimony about being evicted from her home, fired, and beaten for trying to register to vote. Hamer's televised performance was so powerful that Johnson called a sudden press conference to knock her testimony off the air. Johnson offered the MFDP two seats at the convention. The MFDP delegates rejected the proposal. This compromise seemed like half a loaf in violation of moral principle, participatory democracy, and egalitarianism. The Democrats promised the MFDP that the 1968 Mississippi delegation would be integrated and forced to pledge support for the national platform.[24]

For many on the Left, the Democratic National Convention's treatment of the MFDP in 1964 was outrageous. This was the moment when morally sensitized leftists split with liberals, and when disillusioned young liberals began to call themselves radicals. They did not care that Lyndon Johnson calculated that he could win a landslide against Senator Barry Goldwater, a conservative Republican, by keeping the racial issue under wraps. Johnson planned to use his landslide and the numerous Democrats whom he pulled into Congress on his coattails to pass unprecedented liberal legislation. Johnson's victory matched his hopes, and in 1965 Congress passed major bills. By then, young radicals, influenced by the civil rights movement, were moving away from liberalism.

Young Radicals

During the conservative 1950s, political radicalism waned. The postwar consumer boom that lifted almost everyone's living standard replaced the anticapitalist despair of the 1930s, and the Cold War discredited the Communist Party. Americans found it hard to ignore the postwar Soviet threat to Europe, the North Korean invasion that started the Korean War, and the Soviet invasion of Hungary in 1956.[25] Then, too, Senator Joseph McCarthy and others had harassed leftists or scared them into silence. Eisenhower's presidency suggested political moderation, stability, and tranquillity in what some called the Age of Consensus. Challenges to orthodoxy tended to be more cultural than political.[26]

In the early 1960s the idea of the New Left was rooted in cultural and political restlessness, as well as inspiration from the civil rights movement. While young radicals showed contempt for middle-class values by embracing sexual freedom and tolerating drugs, their two main ideas were enthusiasm for civil rights and opposition to the Cold War. Anti-anticommunism distinguished the New Left from anticommunist liberals.[27] These young radicals, small in numbers at the time, also insisted that the country needed structural reform, a point the influential radical sociologist C. Wright Mills had made. *Studies on the Left*, a serious scholarly journal published at the University of Wisconsin, provided additional assistance in the birth of the New Left.[28]

Although the New Left was always loosely organized, it was often identified with Students for a Democratic Society (SDS), which a small group of radical college students founded in 1962. Tom Hayden largely wrote the Port Huron Statement, SDS's declaration of principles. In that document, the University of Michigan newspaper editor laid down a vision for a national radical student movement. Attacking the Cold War as dangerous and morally wrong, SDS claimed to be "anti-anti-communist." SDS had no ties to the Communist Party, although a few members' parents had been communists. Mostly, SDS looked askance at the old-style liberalism of Kennedy and Johnson.[29]

Young radicals moved into the New Left from three main directions. One strand was composed of veterans, mostly white, of the southern civil rights movement. They had begun as opponents of racism, but exposure to the South had converted them into radical critics of the American system.[30] A second strand was composed of the children of white, middle-class liberals or left-liberals. Unlike their parents, these young radicals did not accept the Cold War. "The present student generation," wrote Hayden, "was born on the brink of war and has never seen their country at more than wobbling peace." Kennedy's saber rattling left them weary of the Cold War and fearful of nuclear annihilation.[31] A third strand were the "red-diaper babies," the children of communists, who retained their parents' dislike of the Cold War and support of civil rights.[32]

The name New Left is itself interesting. Young radicals adopted the label to set themselves apart as a generation from communists and other leftist groups, whom they collectively called the Old Left. But the phrase New Left also suggested some continuity.[33] Unlike anticommunists, New Leftists did not reject everything about the Old Left. They denounced the sectarian factions that had splintered the Old Left, and they opposed top-down parties that tried to tell members what to think or do. They did not consider SDS essential, and many young radicals never belonged to that organization. Because they were rooted in moral fervor, young radicals were more interested in leftist issues than in building any political structure. In the long run, the inability to construct and maintain organizations limited the New Left's capacity for political success.

New Leftists had four main goals. First, they sought global peace through a conciliatory foreign policy ("Kumbaya," sang Joan Baez). Second, they embraced the civil rights movement's agenda. Third, they wanted the government to create vast new programs to build housing, create jobs, and expand education. They were especially interested in ending poverty, which they saw as the root cause of America's racial problems. Fourth, they wanted to change the economic system to redistribute wealth. While some were orthodox Marxists who wanted government ownership of the means of production, others favored a Swedish-style welfare state with private ownership, steeply progressive taxes, and vastly expanded government services. In either case, they wanted more governmental power in pursuit of social justice.[34]

At the same time, young radicals held existing liberal-controlled government in contempt. New Leftists believed that special interests, usually wealthy capitalists, had captured and corrupted elected officials, government bureaucracies, and regulatory agencies. They blamed liberals, who held power in the sixties, for being pressured or co-opted by powerful forces into unwise compromises that sold out the public and, especially, the poor. Young radicals believed liberal co-optation thwarted the will of the larger community. Disliking compromise, these moralists were especially outraged at the idea of accepting half a loaf.[35]

Radical complaints were part of an assault on hierarchical authority. Young leftists, borrowing from the civil rights movement, sought empowerment for the poor, advocated greater government intervention, and urged massive redistribution of wealth. Taken as a whole, these three positions posed contradictions. All three policies would have required additional large bureaucracies, which the New Left attacked for being unresponsive. Heavily influenced by nonviolent protest, they believed that effective politics was morally based and required both personal action and direct participation. This grassroots, bottom-up approach, which came out of civil rights, clashed with the demand for government action and redistribution, which was top-down and required bureaucracy for implementation.

Young radicals borrowed a lot from the civil rights movement, including the idea of participatory democracy. They failed to see that the unstructured format and temporary passion that breathed life into a social movement were problematic for stable governance in a democratic political system. Participatory democracy formed an important part of the New Left's search for community.[36] Despite, or maybe because of, this strong desire for community, politics meant personal action.

Finding inspiration in the moral fervor of the civil rights movement, SDS urged a massive overhaul of the domestic economy. SDS was radical in that it rejected the status quo, accepted the technique of the sit-in to force change, and imagined a society remade socially, economically, and politically. Several early members of SDS, including Hayden, had aided the southern civil rights movement. When visiting the South, they had been shocked by massive southern black poverty. Similar poverty could be found in northern cities. Accordingly, SDS in 1964 set up the Economic Research and Action Project (ERAP), whereby students worked to change poor communities by living in the midst of the poor. Almost all these community-based organizing programs failed, either because students tried to tell the poor what to do or because the projects collapsed when the students left. The programs did, however, influence some of Johnson's War on Poverty legislation.[37]

By embracing participatory democracy and presenting students as an identity group worthy of representing itself politically, SDS inspired the broader student movement of the 1960s. Much of the movement had ties to SDS, especially at Columbia University in 1968.[38] That was the year young radicals erupted in a fury over the Vietnam War. Some moved further left to become Maoist or Castroite revolutionaries. Others admired the Black Panthers, a militant African American group that talked about "picking up the gun."[39] In 1969, SDS splintered into factions and disintegrated. During the 1970s, radicalism faded, and in the more conservative 1980s it all but disappeared, except in certain enclaves such as Madison, Wisconsin, or Berkeley, California, where radicals successfully entered local politics. When they did so, they infused the Democratic Party with New Left ideas about participatory democracy, community-based decisions, civil rights, identity politics, expanded government programs, hostility to the military, progressive taxation, antibusiness policies, and economic redistribution. Over the long run, the radical legacy helped reshape the Democratic Party along New Progressive lines.

The Rise of Identity Politics

While the civil rights movement included persons of all races, the heart of the movement was black. Primarily about African Americans' demanding rights for themselves, the movement necessarily asserted black identity. Once blacks had gained the right to vote in the South, rights activists, considered heroes in their own communities, often were elected to office. Marion Barry, active in the Nashville movement, won election as mayor of Washington, D.C., and Andrew Young and, later, John Lewis went to Congress from Atlanta. Charles Evers, half brother of the slain Medgar Evers, became mayor of Fayette, Mississippi, a predominantly black small town.[40]

Most civil rights leaders were Democrats. The national Democratic Party seemed more welcoming, many white liberal Democrats had supported the movement, and polls showed that Democrats supported nonviolent sit-ins much more strongly than did Republicans. After Barry Goldwater, the Republican candidate for president in 1964, voted against the Civil Rights Act on constitutional grounds, blacks overwhelmingly backed Lyndon Johnson. Goldwater's vote cost black votes, but he carried five Deep South states and laid the groundwork for the Republican Party among whites in those states.[41]

Democrats in the North had long practiced ethnic politics, and African Americans in the South could be seen simply as a new ethnic group. Movement participants, however, had a different take on their own importance. They pushed the Democratic Party to adopt a rights-based, egalitarian agenda: affirmative action set-asides for federal contracts, proportional racial representation in appointive political or governmental bodies, and judges who would enforce black rights.[42] This new kind of rights-based politics replaced traditional ethnic politics and became known as identity politics. Some civil rights leaders believed that all politics was about race and rights. They expected African Americans to stick with Democrats, even if they preferred Republican policies on taxes, defense, or abortion.[43]

For African Americans, identity politics worked. Not only were a large number of new black leaders elected as Democrats, but also the Democratic Party took African American demands about rights seriously. For Democrats, moral politics and egalitarianism mattered. As black influence grew, the party embraced the concept of using governmental power to advance social justice. By 2000, African Americans accounted for close to 20 percent of all Democratic votes and were far more important in many states. The result in 2008 was the election of Barack Obama as America's first black president. Whenever Democrats held power, they advanced the rights-based agenda that identity politics demanded.

A second powerful form of identity politics that emerged in the sixties came from feminists. Ties to the civil rights movement were strong. In the early sixties, women who worked in the movement noticed that male leaders consistently ignored women. Expected to make coffee, wash dishes, answer phones, and type letters and memos, women did the movement's grunt labor but got little credit. Change, however, was in the air. In 1963 Betty Friedan published *The Feminine Mystique*, a bestseller that challenged stereotyped women's roles and especially the role of the suburban housewife. That same year Congress passed the Equal Pay Act, a law that required employers to pay men and women the same money for the same work. This was the first federal law ever passed against gender discrimination.[44]

Inside the civil rights movement, a number of women came to recognize that women, as well as blacks, had issues about their rights. Casey Hayden (then the wife of Tom Hayden) and Mary King, both white women who did a lot of office work, decided to take a stand. At a civil rights conference in Waveland, Mississippi, in 1964, Hayden and King issued an anonymous manifesto attacking movement men for ignoring, patronizing, and humiliating movement women. Stokely Carmichael dismissed the complaint by telling the conferees, "The position of women in SNCC is prone!" While he got a big laugh, early feminists noted the condescension and sexism.[45]

In 1964 the Civil Rights Act prohibited gender discrimination. Representative Howard W. Smith, a conservative southern Democrat, put the provision in the bill either in the hope that the gender clause would sink the bill or because he wanted to protect southern white women. By 1966, Friedan and other self-proclaimed feminists had created the National Organization for Women (NOW), which organized politically for women's rights by seeking passage of new federal and state laws. They were an elite that wanted to use increased governmental power to advance their agenda. Eventually, NOW split over abortion rights (a minority opposed abortion) and lesbian rights (many women declined to equate feminism with lesbianism).[46]

Feminists, like black civil rights activists, became closely tied to the Democratic Party and quickly entered politics. Shirley Chisholm went to Congress in 1968, Bella Abzug in 1970, and Geraldine Ferraro in 1978. Ferraro became the Democratic nominee for vice president in 1984. Democrats gave feminists a chance to embrace identity politics, and the party gained votes from women, opening up a "gender gap" among voters. On rights grounds, Democrats appealed for women's votes, even among women who might have had good reasons to vote Republican. For example, a wealthy woman who feared high taxes might naturally favor the Republicans, but if she thought of herself primarily as a feminist defending women's rights, then she might vote Democratic. Or a devout woman who considered abortion immoral might vote Democratic, even for a candidate who favored abortion, to advance other women's issues, including job opportunities.[47]

By the late sixties identity politics spread in new directions. Hispanics, Asian Americans, and Native Americans joined with African Americans to form multiracial nonwhite political alliances. First-generation college students played a major role in these activities, which tended to be campus based. Calling themselves Persons of Color, they launched "Third World" movements to protest and bargain over group rights. According to these activists, the United States and its allies were the First World, communist nations were the Second World, and emerging nonwhite nations were the Third World. They believed that nonwhites inside the United States belonged to the Third World.

At San Francisco State University in 1968, and at the University of California, Berkeley, a year later, Third World strikes led to the creation of ethnic studies programs on campus. Within a few years, Persons of Color ran for and won political office in large numbers. In most cases, they supported new governmental policies and programs that advanced their own version of a social justice agenda.[48]

Another identity politics movement that emerged by the end of the sixties was the American Indian Movement (AIM). Prior to this time, most Native Americans had self-identified only as members of a particular tribe, which had weakened political power. By the sixties, a younger generation of better-educated Indians understood that if they acted as a single group, they would have enough numbers to win rights. A group's influence, in other words, depends on numbers, and the most effective political identity might be one that is artificially constructed. Dennis

Banks and Russell Means, among others, founded AIM. Federal policies among the Lakota Sioux in South Dakota spurred the movement, but AIM's most interesting pan-Indian event was the occupation of Alcatraz Island, an abandoned federal prison in the middle of San Francisco Bay.[49]

In 1969 homosexual men at the Stonewall Tavern in New York rioted against the local police. They were tired of being arrested and harassed because they were gay. This sudden explosion of gay identity marked yet another arrival of identity politics. So long as gays and lesbians were in the closet, as they were throughout the fifties and most of the sixties, gay identity politics was impossible. Coming out of the closet meant that gay men and lesbians could organize politically, vote as a bloc, and try to elect candidates favorable to rights issues. San Francisco supervisor Harvey Milk became the first openly gay elected official in a major American city. Gays, too, were part of the Democratic Party's emerging identity politics.[50]

Racial minorities, women, and homosexuals had been powerless inside a political, economic, and social structure controlled by straight white men. Identity politics produced a new political dynamic in which government resources were to be redistributed according to group political strength and in which government rules were to force the private sector to behave in a similar way. Practitioners of identity politics spoke in terms of oppression and rights, and they invoked moral principles when making demands. In reality, the leaders were members of elite groups seeking to use governmental power to advance their own agendas for what they called social justice. Leaders wanted more power for themselves, and they also wanted the groups they led to gain resources.

The Liberals' War: Vietnam

When John Kennedy ran for president in 1960, he campaigned as a Cold War hard-liner. As a Catholic, he had strong anticommunist credentials, and Kennedy's campaign was designed to position him to the right of Richard Nixon on foreign policy. The promise of a more robust policy to combat global communism, by arms if necessary, was set forth in Kennedy's inaugural address. In this saber-rattling speech, which drew enthusiastic support, he promised that the United States would "pay any price, bear any burden" to promote the cause of freedom around the world.[51]

Within a few months, Kennedy launched the failed invasion of Castro's Cuba at the Bay of Pigs, and a year later the Cuban Missile Crisis pushed the world to the brink of nuclear war.

In late 1963 the administration sponsored the military coup that overthrew Ngo Dinh Diem, the president of South Vietnam. Three weeks later, Kennedy was murdered. In mid-1964, President Lyndon Johnson and Kennedy's militantly anticommunist advisers, all still in place, began to plan the Vietnam War, to be launched in 1965. Meanwhile, Johnson ran against Barry Goldwater for president as the "peace" candidate. Johnson successfully demonized his opponent as a warmonger, and fear of Goldwater's accidentally starting a nuclear war helped Johnson win in a landslide.[52] Having won the election pledging peace, Johnson then expanded the Vietnam War in 1965.

From 1965 to 1968, Johnson's escalating war gradually divided public opinion. Early opponents of the war included pacifists, communists, other radicals who objected to the war on grounds of capitalist or imperialist expansion, and young anti-anticommunists, such as members of Women Strike for Peace, the Committee for a Sane Nuclear Policy (SANE), and SDS. Whereas peace marches in the early sixties usually attracted only hundreds of people, the SDS-sponsored march in Washington on April 17, 1965, amazed organizers by drawing fifteen thousand or more people.[53]

When Johnson expanded the Vietnam War in mid-1965 by sending in American ground troops, military draft calls rose. The draft and increasing casualties explain a lot of the growing opposition to the war on the part of the young. College students worried about losing draft deferments. One failed exam could be fatal. Many also felt guilty about having deferments while less fortunate youths were sucked into battle, although they seldom acknowledged this aspect. The death of a high school classmate could be traumatic. Threatened by the liberal government whose election they had applauded, they felt betrayed by Johnson's deception in making a war after winning as the peace candidate in 1964. Fear and betrayal pushed students toward protest and political radicalism.[54]

By late 1965, with more than one hundred thousand troops in Vietnam and deaths running more than one hundred per week, youthful antiwar protests exploded. In Berkeley the Vietnam Day Committee held public events and marches that rallied tens of thousands of people to the antiwar cause. Although some demonstrators came from the civil rights movement, many of these people had never before engaged in political protest.[55] The rights movement, however, provided leaders, grassroots organizing skills, belief in self-help, and the idea of mobilizing in defense of moral principles (against the evil of war), rights (not to be drafted), and social justice (peace).

In 1966 antiwar activists turned to electoral politics and challenged a number of pro-war incumbents in Congress. In most of the country, a majority supported the war, but in liberal pockets, especially college towns, the war drew strong, passionate criticism. In Berkeley, Robert Scheer, a radical journalist (later an investigative reporter for the *Los Angeles Times*), challenged Jeffery Cohelan, the sitting pro-war Democratic member of Congress, in the Democratic primary. Cohelan was a strong domestic liberal but also a staunch anticommunist. Scheer openly urged antiwar activists to register as Democrats to vote in the closed Democratic primary. Many did so, and Democratic registrations soared in Berkeley from 35,911 to 42,571 in three months. Although Scheer lost the primary, he won 45 percent of the vote. Carrying the Berkeley portion of the district as well as black neighborhoods in both Berkeley and Oakland, he lost only because Cohelan won Oakland's white working-class precincts.[56]

All over the country, the antiwar movement showed strength, but it lost even in very liberal districts. The movement then split. Some radicals argued that they should continue to work through the Democratic Party and build a left-liberal coalition around issues of a peaceful foreign policy, racial advancement, and economic justice. Scheer's strong showing in Berkeley suggested that radicals, if they had Democratic Party support, could be elected to the city council. In 1967 a white radical-black coalition elected the African American Ron Dellums to the council, and three years later he defeated Cohelan for Congress in the Democratic primary, largely by registering many new black voters in Oakland. The antiwar Dellums became one of the first left-liberals in Congress. Later, he called himself a progressive.[57]

Other radicals, including Scheer, concluded that a left-liberal coalition inside the Democratic Party would always be pulled to the right by the nonradical nature of liberals. Liberals might give lip service to radical principles about racial equality or peace, but in Scheer's eyes they were always too willing to compromise, too eager to accept Lyndon Johnson's idea that half a loaf was better than nothing. To true radicals, it was immoral to compromise with evil in this way. Only a leftist party could be pure and uncontaminated by the corporate capitalism and imperialism that, in the radical analysis, explained the racial exploitation and overseas adventurism that infected American society. Power, as the civil rights movement had shown, had to be confronted head-on. Once radicals gained power, their elite control (a vanguard) could use governmental power to impose social justice (destroying capitalism, racism, and imperialism).[58]

In 1967, Scheer helped organize the Peace and Freedom Party (PFP) in California. The party planned to run local candidates throughout the country in places where there seemed to be leftist support and youthful grassroots energy. Scheer's campaign had drawn thousands of student volunteers who registered new voters, licked envelopes, and canvassed door to door. PFP might cooperate informally with Democratic Party candidates, like Dellums, who were sufficiently on the left. It helped that city council elections in California were nonpartisan, so Dellums did not have to disclose any party identity when he ran for the council, and PFP-registered voters could vote for Dellums in a nonparty contest.[59]

A sister radical organization, the National Conference for New Politics (NCNP), emerged at this same time. The NCNP national council included Paul Booth of SDS, Stokely Carmichael of SNCC, the Reverend William Sloane Coffin of Yale, and Warren Hinckle of the radical *Ramparts* magazine.[60] In 1966 a leftist group in Chicago closely affiliated with NCNP issued a formal electoral platform. It proposed putting the poor in charge of poverty programs (community-based participatory democracy), providing Medicare to all (universal health insurance), replacing all sales taxes with progressive income taxes (redistribution), setting up a government-run mortgage company to serve low-income people (a role later taken on by Fannie Mae and Freddie Mac), and establishing public employee unions with the right to strike. As radical influence inside the Democratic Party grew, the party adopted many of these proposals.[61]

The main idea behind both NCNP and PFP, however, was to nominate a strong antiwar candidate for president in 1968. From the beginning, leaders in both groups hoped to persuade Martin Luther King Jr. to run. King's nonviolence could be understood as Christian pacifism, and he had privately detested the Vietnam War from the outset, considering it both an imperialist adventure and a distraction from the racial issue at home. But he had declined to antagonize Lyndon Johnson, whose backing he needed on civil rights. By 1967, however, King felt that the war was tearing the country apart. In April he publicly denounced the war, and PFP and NCNP took notice.[62]

Given growing disenchantment with the war, PFP might mount a stronger than usual third-party challenge for the presidency in 1968, but few believed that PFP could win the election. Indeed, the main consequence of a PFP candidate might be to cause Johnson, the presumptive Democratic nominee, to lose to a conservative, pro-war Republican. Radicals hated Johnson, the peace candidate of 1964 turned war maker of 1965, so much that they were willing to see this result to oust a man they considered a liar and hypocrite. At the same time, some radicals who despised electoral politics believed the country was trending hard left at the grass roots. "We're saying to people," wrote Terry Robbins and Bill Ayers in late 1968, "that youth is the revolution." In the revolutionary scenario, elite (activist) control would lead to governmental power and (radical) social justice.[63]

Other radicals had a more strategic vision and a long-term political strategy. Convinced that no third-party candidate could win the presidency in 1968, these leftists stayed out of electoral politics. But they still saw a way to advance a socialist revolution. At a meeting of socialist scholars, the radical sociologists Richard Cloward and Frances Fox Piven laid out a strategy to cause the country to implode. The key was to push welfare recipients to demand higher benefits in order to bankrupt cities. Then the federal government would be forced to take over soaring costs, impose higher corporate taxes, and eventually go bankrupt. Government bankruptcy would lead inevitably to socialist revolution.[64]

A year later, Michael Harrington, a democratic socialist, told another conference of socialist scholars that the poor by themselves were inadequate in numbers or sophistication to launch a socialist revolution in the United States. An advocate for bringing socialism through elections, Harrington wanted to build a cross-class coalition for socialism at the polls.[65] One leftist at the conference denounced Lyndon Johnson's War on Poverty as a fraud, except for the jobs that it provided to community organizers. The crowd laughed. It was well known among radicals that many poverty program employees were leftists.[66]

If Cloward, Piven, and Harrington were correct, then the best way to promote radical change—sometimes called "stealth socialism"—in the United States was to burrow deep inside existing institutions. Some radicals chose to work at the local level inside the Democratic Party, where they increasingly set themselves apart from liberals by calling themselves *progressives*. Others entered academe, and still others, like

Paul and Heather Booth, became community organizers, after learning effective techniques from Saul Alinsky, who in 1971 published the manifesto *Rules for Radicals*. Settling in Chicago, the Booths and their radical friends later cooperated in various organizations with a younger community organizer, Barack Obama, when he was entering local politics.[67]

Eugene McCarthy and the 1968 Democratic Convention

As 1967 waned, the war expanded, and so did the antiwar movement. The political situation grew tense and traumatic. President Johnson could scarcely visit any city without being mobbed by antiwar protesters, and Vice President Hubert Humphrey, the quintessential liberal, found that the war had poisoned relations with his own formerly ardent followers. Among the first to understand the huge scale of the Democrats' problem was Allard Lowenstein, a liberal lawyer and civil rights supporter, who believed that the Democrats would be crushed at the polls in 1968 if Johnson were the nominee. He decided to dethrone Johnson.[68]

For Democrats, presidential politics took strange and dramatic turns in 1968. The issue of governmental power was very much in the air. Disgusted with Johnson's war, antiwar liberal Democrats looked for a credible candidate to challenge Johnson for the nomination. The most obvious choice was Robert Kennedy, who loathed Johnson, but in the fall of 1967, Bobby declined to run. The New York senator doubted that a sitting president, who had control over the party, could be deprived of the nomination, and Johnson would do anything to make certain that Kennedy was not the nominee. Senator George McGovern of South Dakota also said no. A liberal who hated the war, he wanted to run for reelection to the Senate that fall.[69]

Offended by the war, Senator Eugene McCarthy, a liberal Minnesotan known for dry wit and political laziness, agreed to challenge Johnson.[70] McCarthy's main goal was to prod the political system to stop the war. He wanted to show that the war was unpopular. Realistically, he doubted that he would be the Democratic nominee, but he set great store on getting the 1968 party convention to adopt an antiwar platform. A former college professor, he also saw the campaign as educational. He wished to overcome media and White House spin and inform the country about the war's destructive, brutalizing effects on society and espe-cially on young people.[71]

McCarthy declared the Vietnam War to be primarily neither a political question nor a policy choice but a moral issue. By embracing moral politics, he appealed to young Americans who had been influ-enced by the civil rights movement. He also avoided a policy debate. McCarthy's insight was that if the war were seen merely as a political problem subject to debate, the administration might be willing to debate its policy but then assert that in a democracy people had a right to dif-ferent policy preferences. Policy would go unchanged. By framing the issue in moral terms, McCarthy made it harder for the administration to defend the war.

McCarthy's moral argument was rooted in his own religious back-ground. As a devout Catholic, McCarthy, unlike Martin Luther King Jr., could not oppose war on pacifist grounds. He could oppose a particular war only if it failed to pass the Catholic test of being a just war. By calling the war immoral, McCarthy, a former seminarian, was asserting that the war was unjust.

Turning the war into a moral issue also allowed young antiwar activ-ists to try to avoid military service by claiming conscientious objector sta-tus. If antiwar youths objected to the war on political grounds, they risked incarceration for refusing to be drafted. But if these youths opposed the war on moral grounds, the government was on shakier ground trying to lock up youthful apostles of morality.

McCarthy followed John F. Kennedy's strategy to seek the nomina-tion. In 1968 party leaders picked a majority of the delegates. For exam-ple, Mayor Richard Daley of Chicago personally chose most Illinois delegates. McCarthy could gain these delegates only in an indirect fash-ion. Like Kennedy, he had to demonstrate extraordinary popular sup-port—that is, he needed to win primaries. If the war was as unpopular as McCarthy believed, then he would carry many primaries, and party lead-ers, forced to recognize the politically suicidal nature of the war, might dump Johnson, whom they had never especially liked, and replace him with McCarthy. At the least, party leaders might force a renominated Johnson to run on an antiwar platform.

The Minnesotan started his campaign with limited money and was less successful on television than Kennedy had been. On the other hand, his quiet, scholarly demeanor appealed to educated voters, many of whom were independents or Republicans. In some states these voters could vote for McCarthy in open primaries. In other states it was necessary to persuade them to reregister as Democrats to vote against the war. McCarthy's secret weapon, as in Scheer's campaign in Berkeley in 1966, was to use students to mount an unprecedented grassroots effort. The first primary was in New Hampshire, and thousands of students from all over New England donned long skirts or coat and tie to be "neat and clean for Gene" and sell McCarthy's antiwar candidacy door to door. Johnson did not campaign, and although the president narrowly won, the media portrayed McCarthy's loss as a victory.[72]

Robert Kennedy then jumped into the race. He did not intend to allow McCarthy to take the nomination. Kennedy had money, most of his late brother's staff, impressive polls, and popularity among the poor and working class, both white and black, that eluded McCarthy. But he entered the race too late to be on the ballot in the second primary state, Wisconsin. There, in a state where the Vietnam War was especially unpopular, McCarthy ran all-out against the president. Using students, McCarthy's grassroots organizational effort overwhelmed the feeble Johnson campaign. Polls predicted a huge McCarthy victory in Wisconsin.[73]

Two days before the primary, Lyndon Johnson announced on television that he would not seek reelection. McCarthy had driven Johnson out of the race. While McCarthy and Kennedy fought in the remaining Democratic primaries to establish who was the most popular antiwar candidate, Vice President Humphrey entered the contest and collected most of the nonprimary delegates who had been previously pledged to Johnson. All spring Kennedy and McCarthy dueled, and although Kennedy won all the contests, he could not persuade McCarthy to drop out. Then, in Oregon, McCarthy upset Kennedy. It was the first election that any Kennedy had ever lost. The Kennedy staff complained that there were not enough poor people or African Americans to win there. A week later blacks and Hispanics helped Kennedy win California, but Kennedy was assassinated moments after his victory speech.[74]

Meanwhile, Humphrey had locked up the nomination by collecting most of the delegates from the nonprimary states. He did so despite the fact that Kennedy and McCarthy had won 80 percent of the vote in the primaries, with Johnson, Humphrey, and others sharing only 20 percent. In California, a winner-take-all state where the victor would gain more than a sixth of the total delegates needed to be nominated, a delegation informally pledged to Humphrey got just 12 percent of the vote; Kennedy bested McCarthy, 46 to 42 percent.[75]

To many people, there was something galling about Humphrey, the self-styled original liberal, gaining the Democratic Party nomination mainly through the support of party bosses, who dared to ignore the voters' preferences. Many Democrats believed that had Kennedy lived, he would have become the nominee. Yet *Newsweek*, *Time*, and *U.S. News & World Report* all agreed in issues that went to press before Kennedy died that Humphrey essentially had the nomination locked up, "a bare whoop and a holler from nomination," according to *Newsweek*.[76] In any case, to many Democrats the 1968 nomination process showed that the political system needed to change.

After Kennedy's death, some of his delegates backed McCarthy on antiwar grounds, but other delegates backed Humphrey, whose record as a domestic liberal was strong. Many of the remaining Kennedy delegates voted for George McGovern, a close friend of Robert Kennedy who agreed to run as a last-minute surrogate. McGovern calculated that he would gain televised stature for future national use and might also benefit from the prestige of showing popularity at the convention in his reelection campaign in South Dakota.[77]

With Humphrey's nomination at the 1968 Democratic National Convention certain, the main issue inside the convention hall in Chicago was the party's platform plank on the war. Humphrey desperately wanted a compromise peace plank that would attract McGovern and McCarthy supporters, but Lyndon Johnson refused to allow any whiff of peace to enter the platform. The pro-war plank won a narrow majority. Antiwar delegates despaired, knowing that while primary voters had selected them, those delegates who supported the war were appointed party hacks elected by nobody. If the party could not run a democratic convention, how could it be trusted to pursue social justice?[78]

The convention results did not surprise the raucous radicals on the streets of Chicago. Contemptuous of youths who dressed in coat and tie to beg for votes for McCarthy, and equally sneering at the Peace and Freedom Party's attempt to build an electoral Left, the marauders in the streets saw themselves as the tough-minded and hard-bodied revolutionary vanguard. Some were Marxists, ranging from theoretical neo-Marxists to orthodox Stalinists, Maoists, and romantic Castroites.

Among those present was the once idealistic and now radicalized Tom Hayden. Others felt that militant protest was the only way to stop an obscene war that had now killed more than twenty thousand young Americans. By 1968 more than five hundred thousand American troops were in Vietnam, and deaths were running more than two hundred per week. Still others were hippies who saw protesting in Chicago as the best way, other than wearing long hair and smoking pot, to thumb their noses at society.[79]

Other militants on Chicago's streets included Abbie Hoffman and Jerry Rubin, founders of the Yippies, best described as a guerrilla theater group that kept the media entertained with pranks that conveyed an anarchist or libertarian political message. In Chicago, while the Democrats nominated Humphrey, the Yippies held their own political convention and nominated a pig named Pigasus for president. The Yippies debated whether the candidate should be sent to an animal shelter or roasted and eaten. Announcing that Pigasus was illegal because the Yippies possessed livestock inside the city without a permit, the humorless Chicago police seized the Yippie candidate for president.[80]

The Chicago police made their own plans. Ordered by Mayor Daley to keep the protesters away from the Democratic Convention at all costs and to break up any mass demonstrations, the cops charged the long-haired protesters in Grant Park and shot tear gas at the demonstrators alongside the delegates' hotels facing Michigan Avenue. The police also raided the McCarthy headquarters inside one of the hotels. On the sidewalk in front of the convention hotels, police pushed delegates into plate-glass windows, arrested reporters, and manhandled protesters. It was a police riot. Protesters chanted to the television cameras, "The whole world is watching." And it was. Instead of boring speeches from Humphrey's convention, the networks broadcast the police attacking the kids.[81]

Hubert Humphrey won the nomination, but the "happy warrior" was not happy. The Democratic Party was divided about the war, and the country was on the verge of a nervous breakdown. The radicals had planned the protest in Chicago when Johnson was still presumed to be the nominee. They had calculated to give the incumbent a black eye. Instead, they had made the Democratic nomination all but worthless. How could the party govern the country when it could govern neither its divided self at the convention nor Chicago's riotous police? Hayden declared "a confrontation between a police state and a people's movement." Polls, however, showed that the public sided with the police, not long-haired protesters. The backlash was on.[82]

Tom Hayden, Abbie Hoffman, Jerry Rubin, and other radical leaders who organized the Chicago demonstrations were arrested and charged with conspiracy. The sensational "Chicago Seven" trial ultimately ended in an appellate court that dismissed charges after disclosure of government misconduct.[83] Hayden moved to Berkeley to live in a radical collective and issued a manifesto calling for a five-year plan in communist fashion. (Creedence Clearwater Revival's John Fogerty mocked the plan in the song "Who'll Stop the Rain?") Later, Hayden was thrown out of the collective as a male chauvinist and moved to Los Angeles, where he eventually married the actress Jane Fonda and entered Democratic Party politics as a progressive in Santa Monica.[84]

In the aftermath of the Chicago turmoil, the New Left suffered an angry breakdown. In 1969 the largest radical organization, SDS, disintegrated into four factions, one of which, the Weatherman group, turned to bank robberies, bombings, and other forms of violence.[85] Weatherman, which took its name from a line in a Bob Dylan song, went underground, and members, including Bernardine Dohrn and Bill Ayers, turned to violence. Years later Ayers, by then a respected but still radical college professor, would help Barack Obama launch his political career.[86]

Like the civil rights movement, the antiwar movement profoundly remade the Democratic Party, which gained a large middle-class and intellectual base. Opposition to the war brought unprecedented numbers of educated people into the party. Many were middle-class parents whose sons were of or near draft age. They found the war and the slaughter that it brought appalling. Others were college youths. Some, like Howard Dean, hailed from strongly Republican families. Their moral fervor about the war, parallel to the fervor about civil rights, gave the party a more moral (or moralistic) tone. The Democratic Party also became linked, not always happily, to the Left. Many Democrats were committed to policies of elite control and governmental power in pursuit of social justice (peace and freedom).

At the same time, the antiwar movement spawned radicals who rejected the existing political system. Militants were disorganized and disagreed among themselves about long-term goals, strategy, and tactics. They perhaps evinced more frustration than a coherent rejection of American society and politics. Their hatred of liberals, however, had political implications for years, perhaps decades. Radical contempt for conservatives was so complete that when conservatives were in power, radicals were usually withdrawn and sullen. Liberal political success, on the other hand, brought forward radicals determined either to push liberals to the left or to punish liberals who resisted. Thus, Ralph Nader's followers punished Al Gore in the 2000 presidential election. In liberal parts of the country, Democrats could never ignore radicals, even though radicals had only modest support. In addition, radicals frightened ordinary voters, who were quick to embrace a "law and order" message from Richard Nixon in 1968.[87]

Meanwhile, the white working class began to move away from the Democrats. Many southern Democrats, enraged by the party's strong support for black rights, bolted in 1968 to vote for the independent George Wallace for president. The Alabama governor's appeal went beyond race. Becoming the first candidate in American history to drape the speaking platform with American flags, Wallace exuded patriotism, stressed strong support for the Vietnam War, and made it clear that protesters should "love it or leave it." In a good bit of the North and parts of the South, Wallace's support came from war supporters who felt that Democrats and Republicans looked equally soft on the war and on antiwar protesters. Almost all these voters were white working-class Democrats, and their defection in November 1968 from Humphrey tipped several northern states into the Republican column. Nixon carried Illinois, Ohio, Missouri, and Wisconsin—and won the election.[88]

George McGovern Steals the Democratic Party, 1972

Party leaders at the 1968 Democratic National Convention had been desperate to find some basis for party unity to heal wounds for the fall campaign. Although they reached little agreement on the nominee or the war, George McGovern suggested a way forward. The antiwar delegates were bitter that Humphrey had won the nomination without competing in the primaries and that the platform did not reflect the strong antiwar sentiment primary voters had expressed. McGovern suggested that the party set up a reform commission to propose changes in how delegates were selected. Both the McGovern and McCarthy delegates eagerly embraced the idea, and a number of Humphrey delegates joined the effort to try to gain McGovern and McCarthy support for November. So the convention, by 1,305 to 1,206 votes, ordered a reform of the nominating system.[89]

George McGovern arranged to be named as cochair of the commission, along with the liberal Representative Donald Fraser of Minnesota, who had favored Humphrey for president. The chairs were theoretically coequal, but McGovern, as a senator and former presidential candidate, so dominated the proceedings that it became known as the McGovern Commission. Ultimately, though, the commission fell under the control of its staff, including Eli Segal and Rick Stearns. Both Segal and Stearns believed in the new left-liberal politics and had been active in the antiwar movement before being drawn into electoral politics during the 1968 primary campaign. On the staff, Stearns became expert at rules in nonprimary states and played a major role in designing the new caucus system.[90]

Following John F. Kennedy's dictum that a nominee should be popular with the party rank and file, the McGovern Commission staff might have tried to create a national nominating primary. But there was a major impediment to this idea: the states, not the federal government, legally controlled the nomination system, and only a minority of states in 1968 mandated presidential primaries. Nor did reformers necessarily want primaries. Activists wanted to replace boss control with their own elite control, not democratic control. Also, many party leaders disliked primaries because they inflicted wounds that were hard to heal, they soaked up money needed for the fall campaign, and they could lead to the nomination of a candidate who, while popular with the party base, either was unsalable to the general electorate or had embarrassing flaws—for example, alcoholism or corruption—that were known to party leaders but not to the general public.[91]

The McGovern Commission could not mandate primaries, but it could force changes on both the primary and the nonprimary states. For the primary states, the commission insisted on ending meaningless popularity contests. Primary winners had to be awarded voting delegates, and the number of delegates won had to be proportionate to the candidate's share of the primary vote. This rule endorsed the "one man, one vote" principle. The commission urged that primaries be closed so that non-Democrats did not pick the party nominee. It banned the unit rule, by which a majority of a state delegation could cast the entire delegation's vote for a single candidate. It banned the winner-take-all primary, though it gave an exception for 1972. Fred Dutton, a McGovern adviser, was pleased because he hoped to use California to make certain that the party nominated an antiwar liberal in 1972.[92]

In all states, the commission demanded that delegates be selected so that racial minorities, women, and youths would be represented at the national convention in proportion to their numbers among the Democratic electorate in that state. No longer would delegates be picked largely from among the party's wealthy donors. No elected officials were allowed to be automatic delegates. Labor's influence would decline. When some party leaders objected to these quotas, the commission declared that it was not imposing quotas. In reality, it did impose quotas. Numerical proportional representation gave African Americans and women increased representation and promoted identity politics, which the commission staff intended. Indeed, the antiwar staff, including Segal and Stearns, knowing that women were more likely to oppose the war than men, calculated that the requirement that women be half the delegates to the 1972 convention all but ensured an antiwar majority.[93]

The commission demanded that party leaders no longer appoint delegates in nonprimary states. In those states, delegates had to be picked through open precinct caucuses, where any registered Democrat could help choose the state's eventual national delegates. Lacking secret ballots, caucus voting favored the activist elite's manipulative skills. Delegates picked through the precinct caucus system had to be pledged to a particular candidate to prevent boss control. The precinct caucuses were reminiscent of the civil rights movement's and New Left's participatory democracy, and the commission's faith in the grass roots implied a distrust of top-down authority also typical of rights and radical organizations. Many state leaders disliked these requirements, and as a result most states switched to primaries. In contrast with activist elites, who wanted caucuses, ordinary voters preferred primaries.[94]

While many party leaders failed to grasp the radical significance of the McGovern Commission's reforms, George McGovern organized his own 1972 campaign around the new rules. To woo progressives, he stressed opposition to the war and proposed a thousand-dollar annual cash grant to each American. Ridiculed as "McGiveaway," he retracted this proposal. Taking advantage of the new quotas, he cultivated blacks with a strong civil rights position, and he backed a feminist agenda. In

1972 women were 39 percent of the delegates, triple their percentage in 1968. (A few states defied party rules on female representation, and in states where voters elected delegates directly, gender balance could not be controlled.) McGovern won only 25 percent of the total Democratic Party primary vote, finishing slightly behind Hubert Humphrey, but because of the way in which delegates were allotted, he got 65 percent of the primary state delegates. His modest victory in the winner-take-all primary in California, beating Humphrey 44 to 39 percent, provided 271 delegates and put him close to the nomination. Half of McGovern's convention votes came from six winner-take-all primary states, including California, New York, and New Jersey.[95]

The key to George McGovern's nomination, however, was his strength in the caucus states, where his zealous, young antiwar supporters turned out in record numbers to elect delegates. Many states where he had the highest percentage of support among delegates were Republican states that he could not win in November.

Other problems surfaced at the 1972 convention. Mayor Richard Daley's Illinois delegation was not seated on grounds that it contained too many elderly white men. Daley, of course, was a symbol of the old politics that McGovern and his delegates despised. Humiliating Daley may have been payback for Daley's handling of the 1968 convention in Chicago. It also guaranteed that McGovern would run exceptionally poorly in Illinois in November 1972.[96]

Labor took a hike. George Meany, the AFL-CIO president, described the McGovern convention thus: "We heard from the people who looked like Jacks, acted like Jills, and had the odor of Johns about them."

McGovern's disastrous electoral loss in 1972—the worst loss by a Democrat since the 1920s—might have given the party reason to revisit the rules under which he had been nominated. But the party organization was complacent, and few changes were made. In 1974 the Democrats elected many new members of Congress, especially from traditionally Republican suburban districts outraged by Nixon's Watergate scandal. But the so-called Watergate babies never seemed to grasp how politics worked, and many were swept out in Ronald Reagan's victory of 1980. By then the once-cocky majority Democratic Party was a shambles.[97]

In 1976 a southern moderate, Governor Jimmy Carter of Georgia, took advantage of the new nominating rules. A racial moderate and lay Baptist preacher, he won African American support by cultivating black Baptist clergy. Crusading as a populist who believed in bottom-up, grassroots control of government, he won the left-liberal activists who dominated the Iowa caucuses. He also gained support with a promise of a softer foreign policy, which he could do with credibility as a retired naval submarine commander. His victory in Iowa electrified the country because he was the first southerner to be taken seriously as a national presidential candidate in a hundred years. (Johnson had reached the presidency only by ascending through the vice presidency.) In November, Carter swept the South and carried a few key northern states, including Ohio, to beat the lackluster president Gerald Ford.

As president, Carter proved inept. The party's liberal base was disgusted, and the Georgian barely survived a challenge from Ted Kennedy for renomination in 1980. Carter went on to lose reelection by a huge margin. One-third of the voters who had supported Carter in 1976 switched to Reagan in 1980. Oddly, Carter failed to make any changes to the nomination system that tended to work against moderates. Perhaps Carter had no reason to reject the system he had used successfully. Carter was never fully trusted by party liberals and might have feared riling them. Nor was he popular enough among Democrats to be certain of success with any reforms.[98]

In the 1980s liberals, many of them New Progressives, controlled the Democratic Party. The party no longer had a conservative wing, and moderates were weaker than liberals. Although moderates may have outnumbered liberals and arguably had a better chance of winning a presidential election by having greater appeal to independents, liberals dominated the party by contributing more money and doing more party work. Liberals continued to make vigorous use of the precinct caucus system, which they effectively controlled, to push liberal presidential candidates like Walter Mondale and Michael Dukakis.

The rottenness of the caucus system can be seen in 2008 in Texas, which held both a primary and a caucus. In the primary, Hillary Clinton defeated Barack Obama 1,462,734 to 1,362,476, or 52 percent to 48 percent. Accordingly, Clinton won 65 delegates to Obama's 61 delegates. The party caucuses were held at the precincts after the polls closed. To participate in the caucus, a person had to show proof of having voted in the primary. The caucuses drew 1.1 million attendees, fewer than half of those who voted in the primary. Obama won this vote over Clinton, 56 percent to 44 percent. As a result, he won 38 delegates to Clinton's 29. Combining primary and caucus delegates, Obama got 99 delegates in Texas to Clinton's 94. Obama's stronger showing in the caucuses came primarily from greater support among party activists. The Texas caucuses had neither good security nor secret ballots. In one precinct an Obama supporter from New York "lost" all the Hillary tally sheets. So much for "reform" politics.[99]

The unfair caucus system; the quarrelsome nature of identity politics, which had a tendency to become a spoils system; the rise of radical pressure and influence on the party, which caused Democrats in liberal areas to watch in terror over their left shoulders; the decline of southern Democrats—all left the Democratic Party a far weaker party in 1980 than it had been during the forties, fifties, and sixties. A party that had once confidently represented a majority of Americans in their hopes and aspirations increasingly became a cantankerous collection of New Progressive ideologues, identity group politicians, special interests, and oddballs. A party devoted to elite control of governmental power in pursuit of social justice had little popular appeal.

The Democratic Party jealously guarded group rights at the expense of both the individual and the public good. It was also increasingly a party of nervous peaceniks that, at least until the Cold War ended, general election voters distrusted with national security. It was a party that, to the disgust of the public, frequently cavorted with and pandered to radicals. By 1980 it became harder and harder for millions of Americans to take the Democrats seriously. Democrats lost five of the seven presidential elections from 1980 to 2004, and the one Democrat who won, Bill Clinton, presented himself as a southern moderate, not a liberal. First elected in a three-way contest, Clinton failed to get 50 percent of the vote in either of his presidential elections.

Hard Left Turn

The 1960s were disastrous for the Democratic Party. In 1960 the party had breadth, coherence, and self-confidence. John Kennedy and Lyndon Johnson combined domestic liberalism with a strong anticommunist foreign policy. The civil rights movement changed the political system, inspired young radicals, and promoted identity politics. The Vietnam War enraged many liberals. Some antiwar liberals tried to transform the Democratic Party; others, having been radicalized, opted for third parties; and still others, even more radicalized, favored revolution. The 1968 election split the Democrats, and the party's new rules for 1972 gave left-liberals a large voice. In 1972, George McGovern ran as a progressive. Despite his disastrous defeat, the party kept the rules. The party continued to turn left, becoming increasingly unpopular in a center-right nation.

Electoral setbacks notwithstanding, left-liberals abandoned neither beliefs nor policies. Instead, they entered law, academe, think tanks, and the media. Congregating in powerful elite institutions in large numbers, New Progressives began to remake the country along the lines they intended. As will be shown in the following chapters, the invention of public interest law opened possibilities for advancing a progressive agenda. Other activists embraced radical environmentalism. The rights movement expanded to demand the "right to choose" an abortion and the "right to die"—that is, assisted suicide. Progressives also pushed for universal health insurance. In each of these arenas, the dynamic was the same: the progressive elite sought to use governmental power to impose its own version of social justice on everyone else.

2

From the Streets into the Courtroom
and the Neighborhoods

Young, charismatic, telegenic, hard-working, and exceedingly bright," "keen knowledge of everything," "defender of the little guy"—this was how the mainstream press described John Edwards after he won a U.S. Senate seat from North Carolina in 1998.[1] Progressives appeared to have found the savior of the Democratic Party. He was a southerner, a liberal, and the genuine article. Joshua Green, editor of the *Washington Monthly*, put it most succinctly (and hopefully) when he observed that Edwards proudly wore the "L" label. In fact, it was a double L, Green noted: Edwards was a liberal and a lawyer.

It did not bother Green, or those journalists working at the *Washington Post* and *New York Times* who lauded Edwards in these years, that he was not just a lawyer but a trial lawyer. Trial lawyers were commonly perceived (however unfairly) as a little reptilian, and the new senator had become a multimillionaire suing corporations and doctors for faulty products and malpractice. But Green declared that Edwards's career as a trial lawyer was a political asset. It showed he was idealistic and a protector of the little guy in America. Green noted that ever since Edwards was knee high to a grasshopper he had wanted to be a lawyer. His heroes were Thurgood Marshall, "who used law to bring down the system of legal segregation in the South," and Ralph Nader, "whose lawsuits forced an arrogant auto industry to install seatbelts and airbags . . . saving thousands of lives." Green enthusiastically quoted Edwards: "My idealistic view of lawyers was that they could help people who couldn't help themselves and couldn't fight for themselves."[2]

Following his 1998 senatorial win, Edwards's star rose quickly in progressive circles. By 2004 he was running for the Democratic presidential nomination on a theme of ending the "Two Americas—the rich and the poor." His good looks, apparent passion for the little guy, and skills as a fund-raiser, especially among trial lawyers, helped put him on the Democratic ticket as John Kerry's running mate. When the Kerry-Edwards ticket lost to Bush-Cheney, many looked to Edwards as a front-runner at least equal to Hillary Clinton for the next election.

Yet, as fast as he rose in politics, his crash came just as quickly when the tabloid press caught him in an extramarital affair with a New Age spiritualist who kept stroking Edwards's ego by telling him he was "king." Edwards's supporters might have overlooked his infidelity under different circumstances. They had watched Gary Hart and Bill Clinton fall from the public's graces under similar circumstances, and they were tired of this kind of personal morality interjecting itself into politics. After all, in Europe these things did not matter. But in this case, Edwards's wife had been diagnosed with a particularly virulent form of breast cancer. By 2008 progressives had deserted Edwards for Barack Obama. They forgot just how infatuated they had been with the North Carolina senator.

In hindsight, any number of things should have given the Left pause about Edwards. From the beginning he seemed too good to be true—and can any politician, any mortal man, be all that good? And should not his background as a trial lawyer have alerted them to the possibility he was a wolf in sheep's clothing? Few trial lawyers enjoy reputations as the "Honest Abes" of the world, at least in the eyes of average Americans. But progressives saw trial lawyers a bit differently. Trial lawyers rank as the largest financial contributors to the Democratic Party, which perhaps suggested to many progressives that their hearts were in the right place. After all, they were fighting evil corporations, which put them on the side of goodness, light, and social justice.

But the blind eye that progressives turned to Edwards may have reflected more than just the financial influence of trial lawyers within the Democratic Party. John Edwards's rise to the top ranks of the Democratic Party represented the perfect marriage of activist legal progressives and the liberal establishment. The field of activist public interest law was, in fact, central to the radical transformation of liberalism and progressive efforts to take over American society. Following the failure of radicalism in the 1960s, progressives learned that social struggle could be waged in the courts around specific, often local concerns. Whereas protesters had taken to the streets and college campuses to overthrow the system, public interest lawyers began suing tobacco, pharmaceutical, and medical device companies; manufacturers of consumer products; physicians; school districts; community organizations; civic organizations from the Boy Scouts to organizers of St. Patrick's Day parades; small townships; state and federal governmental agencies—all in the name of social justice. Trial lawyers shared progressive self-righteousness by proclaiming they represented the little people against powerful corporate interests. They learned that they could serve social justice and make money too.

Progressive lawyers emerged as leaders, strategists, and key advisers to militant environmentalists and consumer advocates, public interest organizations, progressive unions, feminists, pro-choice activists, and advocates for single-payer health care in America—to name just a few of the causes embraced. The emergence of public interest law in the late 1960s is thus crucial to understanding the transformation of liberalism. The story begins with the father of public interest activism, Ralph Nader.

Ralph Nader and the Anticorporate Crusade

Before Ralph Nader helped cost Albert Gore Jr. the presidential election in 2000 by drawing enough votes away from the Democratic Party to the Green Party, thereby giving the White House to Republican George W. Bush, Nader was the darling of the progressive Left. Eccentric, hard to get along with, and demanding of his coworkers to the point of exploitation, Nader nonetheless stood as an icon for young, public-minded progressive lawyers, activists, and foundation officers. They saw in Nader a crusader who shared their values of making a better world by injecting democracy into the corporate board room, bringing to heel the corporate special interests in government, and exposing the dangers of asbestos, nuclear energy, and unsafe cars.

Activist lawyers found inspiration for their causes in Nader, a self-proclaimed consumer advocate. For them, he was a modern-day secular saint. Obsessive, self-righteous, brilliant, Nader never married, wore rumpled suits, and did not drive, smoke, or eat junk food. He was quick to claim martyrdom in the struggle for social justice and just as quick to renounce materialism and to condemn his enemies as the agents of darkness. This vision was shared by the young radicals who sprang from the cinders of 1960s New Left radicalism. Like many New Progressives, Nader was educated at elite universities, earning a bachelor's degree from Princeton and a law degree from Harvard. He abhorred what he saw as the injustices of a capitalist society, but he understood that the street protests of the 1960s had failed to bring about necessary change. The struggle needed to be in the courts, in the halls of legislatures, and in public hearings. As Nader put it, New Left activists simply "cannot get it through their heads that they're on the sidewalk, but I'm catching it at a more basic level. What is more intimately involved with civil rights than the invisible violence of the corporations? Who do they think gets cheated, diseased, crippled, and generally screwed if not the minorities and the poor?"[3]

For Nader the evils of the corporation were omnipresent. He believed that corporations caused economic dislocation, racism, and income inequality. Corporate production caused respiratory diseases, circulatory ailments, and mental afflictions. He believed corporate power subverted democracy, making talk of political pluralism a farce. He warned of a mass social and political crisis when corporations extended their influence in government. As a prescription he called for public control of corporations and for anticorporate activists to undertake what he called a "New American Revolution."[4]

He never looked at the historic benefits of corporate capitalism for the average American. American consumption allowed better and longer lives for most Americans. Financial wealth, economic opportunity, property ownership, and the rule of law allowed American democracy to flourish. It was not a perfect system, but Nader was not the type of person to put things into context. His world was one of good and evil. There were no grays and little complexity. You were either for him or against him—a mind-set typical of the New Progressive.

Born in 1934 to Lebanese parents who had settled in the small river town of Winsted, Connecticut, Nader provided a transition in the Left from the older radicalism of the New Deal to the anticonsumption radicalism of the late 1960s. Nader's father, Nathra, owner of a small diner, was notorious for his adamant political opinions. He railed to customers about injustice in America, most often traced back to big business. Ralph's mother, Rose, doted on her clever son, who taught himself to read a clock at the age of three. Although raised as a Lebanese Catholic,

Rose took her family to the local Methodist church, which emphasized "good works" as the path to heaven.[5]

Ralph's hard work earned him admission to Princeton University, where he graduated with honors. Although his scores on the law school admissions test were low, his undergraduate grades were high enough to win admission to Harvard Law School. At Harvard, Nader joined the staff and later became president of the *Harvard Law School Record*. He wrote pieces denouncing capital punishment and the treatment of Native Americans in the West. Editorial disagreements about his insistence that the entire *Record* be devoted to muckraking articles led Nader to resign his position as president, but he stayed on as a staff member. While at Harvard, he read Harold A. Katz's article in the *Harvard Law Review*, "Liability of Automobile Manufacturers for Unsafe Design of Passenger Cars." Katz argued that car companies could be sued for failing to design safe automobiles. The article so impressed Nader that he phoned Katz to talk about it. Nader then decided to devote himself to the cause of auto safety. A crusader was born.

After a brief stint in the Army, Nader went to work for a small law office in Hartford, Connecticut, but he spent most of his time traveling, earning income as a freelance journalist. In April 1959 he traveled to Cuba to interview the country's new leader—Fidel Castro. Two years later, in the summer of 1961, he traveled to Scandinavia to see social democracy at work. He went to the Soviet Union, where he was disappointed by the lack of spontaneity among the people (although Nader was hardly the spontaneous type himself). He traveled to Latin America, where he wrote articles for the *Atlantic Monthly* and the *Christian Science Monitor*.

During these years, Nader continued to work on auto safety. In 1959, Nader's article "The Safe Car You Can't Buy" was published in the left-wing magazine *The Nation*. This article brought Nader to the attention of Daniel Patrick Moynihan, who became assistant secretary of labor to Arthur Goldberg in the Kennedy administration. One of Moynihan's tasks was to work on auto safety. In 1964, Moynihan asked Nader to join the staff to write a report on auto safety.

While working for Moynihan, Nader signed a book contract with the tiny publishing house of Richard Grossman Publishers. As the deadline loomed and Nader still had not completed the manuscript, Grossman traveled to Washington, rented a hotel room, and holed up with

Nader. They finished the book in sixty days. At Grossman's insistence, it was called *Unsafe at Any Speed*. Appearing in November 1965, the book argued that accidents were the fault not of drivers but of knowingly negligent automobile manufacturers who built unsafe cars. Nader targeted the "sporty Corvair" as a case in point, employing graphic language about severed limbs. He pointed to the tendency of Corvair's rear suspension system to cause instant vehicle rollover. Nader called the Corvair design "one of the greatest acts of industrial irresponsibility in the present century."[6]

Statistics later revealed a different story. Although from 1960 to 1963 the Corvair was involved in more single-car crashes than any other compact car, General Motors (GM) appeared to have corrected the problem by 1964, the year before Nader's book was published. In 1964 accidents for Corvairs were lower than for Volkswagens, Ford Falcons, or Plymouth Valiants.[7] Nonetheless, *Unsafe at Any Speed* had become a bestseller, and the American public refused to buy Corvairs.

Fearing potential financial losses, GM made one of the greatest public relations blunders in corporate history. Before the book's publication, GM hired a private investigator to look into Nader's qualifications and determine whether he had a financial interest in Corvair litigation. When the investigation turned up little, GM's legal staff ordered a more thorough investigation, asking former FBI agent Vincent Gillen to find out what made Nader "tick." Nader's acquaintances were questioned about his sex life, whether he was anti-Semitic, and about his politics. When word of this investigation got back to Nader, he turned it into national news by giving the story to the *New Republic* and the *Washington Post*.

Democrats in the Senate also seized on the story. Nader had gone to work for the Senate Subcommittee on Executive Reorganization, chaired by Abraham Ribicoff (D-Connecticut) and Robert Kennedy (D–New York), who were preparing to hold hearings on the federal role in highway safety. When Ribicoff heard about GM's investigation of Nader, he ordered GM president James M. Roche to testify under oath before the subcommittee. Acting on the advice of his legal counsel and former John F. Kennedy speechwriter Theodore Sorensen, Roche decided on a single course of action in his testimony: apologize. The Democrats at the hearing—Ribicoff, Robert Kennedy, Fred Harris (Oklahoma), and Henry M. Jackson (Washington)—had a field day. Ribicoff accused Roche of conducting an investigation that suggested witness harassment and violation of the U.S. Criminal Code. Kennedy warned Roche that "there is too much snooping going on in this country." The New York senator declared, "This must be happening all over America with many other Ralph Naders."[8]

These hearings made Nader famous. In late 1966 he sued GM for invasion of privacy, and in an out-of-court settlement he won $425,000 in damages. Nader used the money to expand his activities. He tried to organize a stockholders' takeover of GM. It failed. He called for the antitrust laws to enforce the breakup of GM. This attack, too, did not go anywhere. His demand to stop production of the VW microbus, which he alleged was unsafe, drew an adamant response from the company: "We don't have any evidence that the Volkswagen gets into any more accidents than any other car."[9] All Nader could do was to refuse to ride ever again in a Volkswagen.

As the war in Vietnam heated up and racial riots erupted in major cities, Nader pursued a different path toward a takeover of corporate society: consumer protection. This proved to be a better avenue for winning over the white middle class. Over time, Nader became involved in a mind-boggling number of causes. Recruiting young lawyers fresh out of law school, he launched investigations into nursing home abuses, land-use policies that favored mining and oil companies, alleged corporate ties inside the Federal Trade Commission, and the dangers of nuclear energy. Drawing on an extensive network, Nader demonstrated a genius for fund-raising.[10]

Nader was aided in his efforts by a new generation of investigative reporters who entered the elite media. These young reporters brought with them a changed conception of journalism. No longer devoted to reporting the news, they wanted to make the news through investigative journalism. By challenging existing government policies, revealing corruption in public institutions, discovering corporate abuse and greed, and exposing unsafe consumer products, journalists could set the agenda. They were no longer reporters but "journalists." Like the public interest lawyers, these young investigative reporters shared a suspicion of corporations, established politicians, and the free market. The two groups found themselves working hand in glove in the war against the established order.[11]

Nader's core team remained young, mostly Ivy League business school and law school graduates. Many came from established families.

Among Nader's Raiders was Edward Finch Cox, who came from a prominent eastern family. One forebear, Robert Livingston, had helped draft the Declaration of Independence. In 1971, Cox married President Nixon's daughter, Tricia. Others included Peter Bradford, Yale '64, and Judy Areen, another Yalie, daughter of a Chrysler executive, and later dean of the Georgetown University Law Center.

Also joining the group was William Howard Taft IV, the great-grandson of the former president. Taft, a Harvard Law School graduate, had worked for Eugene McCarthy's presidential campaign in 1968 and would go on to serve as a permanent representative to NATO and legal adviser to Secretary of State Colin Powell in George W. Bush's administration. These young Ivy League Naderites prided themselves on short hair, business suits, and ties. As Robert Fellmeth, another Nader's Raider from Harvard Law School, declared, "None of us was a hippie. No one was running around with flowers and beads, and there was no pot smoking. . . . We were all serious." They were out to transform the system, root and branch. "We were radicals," Fellmeth said, "but we weren't irresponsible radicals. We were hardworking radicals."[12]

Nader's troops found stations in an array of organizations he established. He set up the Center for the Study of Responsive Law, Public Citizen, the Health Research Group, and the Litigation Group. By the early 1970s he had established the Corporate Accountability Research Group, Center for Auto Safety, Tax Reform Group, Retired Professionals Action Group, and Center for Women's Policy Studies. These groups—along with others such as the Trial Lawyers for Public Justice—often had interlocking directorships and legal ties to one another. By the early 1980s nearly fifty organizations had ties to the Nader network.[13] This frenetic activism paid off. Between 1966 and 1973, Congress passed more than twenty-five pieces of consumer legislation. Nader was involved in many of them.[14]

Behind all these organizations lay a single goal: dismantle the power of the corporation. As one longtime associate of Nader, Michael Mariotte, executive director of the Nuclear Information Resource Service, observed, "One thing has held true throughout Nader's career. He has always been more interested in corporate power than the vague concepts like environmentalism, sexism, and racism." Joe Tom Easley, who worked on the anti-nuclear-power issue, concurred: "You have to step back and look at Nader's worldview. He is, shall we say, preoccupied with the issue of corporate power in this country and the lack of democracy. He is consumed by the fact that large corporations tend to have enormous power to distort the democratic process in every way."[15]

Already feeling the pain of inflation in the 1970s, American business increased lobbying activities in Washington to oppose what it saw as the overregulated economy. Industry had become so burdened by government bureaucrats on every level—federal, state, and local—that it was being smothered. Murray Weidenbaum, a respected economist at the American Enterprise Institute, estimated that in 1976 alone federal regulation cost the economy $66 billion in lost business opportunities, while bloating payrolls at bureaucratic regulatory agencies, increasing administrative costs to business, and adding legal expenses.[16]

Nader and Community Organizing

In the 1970s, Nader undertook to bring social change to America, not by a purely legislative strategy, but by organizing the grass roots from below. By pursuing grassroots activism, Nader sought to transform the structure of power and the distribution of wealth in America.[17] This turn to grassroots activism came as many former 1960s radicals called for a "new populism" to challenge the corporate order. Throughout the 1970s citizen action groups proliferated. Best known among them was the Association of Community Organizations for Reform Now (ACORN), organized in 1970 by former civil rights activist Wade Rathke. By 1980, ACORN had more than twenty-five thousand active members and branches in nineteen states. This was only one of dozens of citizen action groups. Harry Boyte, in his study of citizen action, *The Backyard Revolution: Understanding the New Citizen Movement* (1980), lists twenty-one national support networks for community organizing, ten national citizen organizations and coalitions, thirteen training schools across the country, twelve working-women affiliates, twenty-five occupational safety and health groups, and a sampling of forty-two major state and city community organizations.[18]

At the vanguard of Nader's community-organizing campaign was the establishment of the Public Interest Research Group (PIRG), which provided the foundation for a nationwide network of student activists and lobbyists. The state-based, self-supporting PIRGs worked on local problems including the environment, consumerism, utility prices, public transportation, and housing. Through PIRGs, Nader envisioned, as the organizer Donald Ross declared, "a legal revolution."[19]

The entire PIRG project was overseen by Gary Sellers, a son of a wealthy surgeon, former college varsity swimmer, and graduate of University of Michigan Law School. A true believer in the Nader cause, he invited Nader to be the best man at his wedding.[20] Within the first year, PIRG had petitioned the Food and Drug Administration (FDA) to demand better packaging on birth-control pills, initiated a case against pharmaceutical company Bristol-Myers for misrepresenting its product Excedrin in advertising, and pursued dozens of other cases.

Nader envisioned a network of state and local PIRGs that would be staffed by lawyers, mostly, but that would also provide opportunities for student activists. Nader struck on an ingenious source of funding: university activity fees. On most campuses a PIRG could assess an additional fee by a majority vote of the students.

The results were spectacular. At the University of Minnesota, thirty thousand students out of fifty thousand voted to pay $1 per quarter in additional fees to start a PIRG. The Minnesota PIRG had a first-year budget of $200,000, enough to hire four full-time attorneys and an administrator. Petition drives at the University of Oregon and other colleges in the state established a PIRG with an annual budget of $150,000. While Nader visited college campuses across the country, Naderite lawyers Donald Ross and James Welch also set up local and state PIRGs. They raised $75,000 in Ohio and helped the Connecticut Earth Action groups raise approximately $40,000.

PIRGs engaged in a variety of causes. The Missouri PIRG investigated conditions in local jails. In Vermont, college students examined dental health for elementary school children. The price of prescription drugs was analyzed by PIRGs in North Carolina, Illinois, and Texas. In Massachusetts, the state PIRG attacked what it considered unconscionably high utility rate increases.[21] By 1974, PIRGs were found in twenty-two states involving five hundred thousand students.[22] The reaction against the checkoff fee eventually forced PIRGs to get most of their funding by door-to-door canvassing, but in the meantime Nader had trained tens of thousands of young activists.

Among the activists who came out of the Nader ranks was a young Columbia University student, Barack Obama, who got his first community-organizing experience working for the New York Public

Interest Research Group (NYPIRG) from February through late May in 1985. The NYPIRG that Obama joined had proved to be an especially effective organization. The Brooklyn office of the NYPIRG only a few years earlier had pressured local banks into lowering credit standards for mortgages (subprime loans) in high-risk neighborhoods.

The progressive turn to community organizing was not an accident. It was a well-conceived strategy undertaken by former New Leftists who had become disillusioned with the revolutionary politics of the 1960s. Harry C. Boyte, Steve Max, and Paul and Heather Booth, among others, sought to transform society from within by organizing local community groups around specific local issues. They drew inspiration from Chicago's longtime community organizer Saul Alinsky, but unlike him they did not reject electoral politics. Indeed, they sought to remake the Democratic Party into an instrument for transformation and social justice. Community organizing was not new to America. Nor were these "stealth socialists" the hidden hand behind the upsurge in citizen activism in the 1970s and 1980s. But the importance of former New Leftists within many of these organizations should not be easily dismissed.

Harry Boyte became a major theoretician of community organizing through such books as *The Backyard Revolution* (1980) and *Citizen Action and the New American Populism* (1986). Boyte became an adviser to the Obama presidential campaign in 2008. Paul and Heather Booth, former leaders in Students for a Democratic Society (SDS), were instrumental in establishing the Midwest Academy, which became a major training school for community organizers and a critical force in Chicago and Illinois electoral politics, helping to elect Harold Washington as mayor in Chicago in 1983 and socialist Illinois state senator Alice Palmer, who chose Obama as her political successor in 1995.[23]

Nader in Washington

While encouraging citizen activism, Nader did not turn his back on lobbying the Washington establishment. From 1969 to 1976, Nader's influence in Washington was enormous, and the media's interest appeared insatiable. Typical was his crusade against nuclear power plants. In 1974 he joined science activist Barry Commoner, Nobel Prize winner George Wald, and actor Robert Redford in organizing "Critical Mass," a conference on nuclear power. The conference drew local anti-nuclear-plant activists, including members of the New England Coalition on Nuclear Pollution, Wisconsin activists in Northern Thunder, and New Hampshire activists in the Seacoast Anti-Pollution League. Each attendee received a 161-page booklet written by longtime Nader associate Joan Claybrook, *A Nuclear Catastrophe Is Too Big a Price to Pay for Our Electric Bill.*

Adding to the dangerous excitement of the conference was the death of Karen Silkwood, a union activist from Oklahoma, who had died mysteriously only a few days earlier in a car accident. An autopsy found sedatives in her blood, which gave rise to conspiracy theories that she had been murdered. She had been on her way to meet with a *New York Times* reporter to share documents supposedly showing serious safety violations at the Kerr-McGee Corporation's Cimarron River plant in Oklahoma, which produced plutonium fuel rods for nuclear reactors. A 1983 film starring Meryl Streep and Cher perpetuated the Silkwood conspiracy. Silkwood became a martyr in the Nader crusade against nuclear energy.

In 1975, Nader organized Congress Watch, headed by Claybrook, to further the antinuclear crusade. Congress Watch sought to alert the public to the dangers of plutonium in breeder reactors. The campaign targeted the Atomic Energy Commission (AEC) as a friend of the nuclear energy industry. The campaign proved highly successful, leading to the division of the AEC into two separate agencies, one charged with regulation and the other with the promotion of civilian nuclear energy use. Further success against the nuclear power industry came in 1975 after the Three Mile Island plant near Harrisburg, Pennsylvania, suffered internal control failures and released radiation. Nuclear power came under attack in Oregon, Vermont, Massachusetts, and other states. In 1983, Congress stopped funding breeder reactors. The last nuclear power plant in the United States opened in 1988.[24]

Nader was at the height of his power by the mid-1970s, so much so that presidential candidate Jimmy Carter promised during his campaign to consult Nader on consumer and environmental legislation. Carter went out of his way to cultivate Nader, meeting with him several times and requesting reading material. Nader told associates, "Jimmy Carter is something special. You need to watch this guy. Something's going to happen. I've never met a politician quite like Carter, and I know a lot of them."[25]

The honeymoon did not last once Carter won the presidency in 1976. Even before the inauguration, Nader was attacking Carter for not consulting him on cabinet-level appointments. Still, Carter appointed Joan Claybrook as head of the National Highway and Transportation Administration. He appointed Nader's Raider James Fallows as his chief speechwriter (launching him on his later career as editor of the *Atlantic Monthly*). Peter Petakas, another Naderite, went to the Office of Management and Budget (OMB). There were others as well.[26] It was not enough to satisfy Nader. He attacked Carter for betraying his promises to protect the consumer. He even turned on Claybrook, whom he accused of leaving a "trail of broken promises."[27]

The election of conservative Ronald Reagan in 1980 marked the nadir of Nader's influence in government. Reagan stepped into the White House with a philosophy completely opposite of Nader's. Embracing principles of classical liberty, he viewed American enterprise and the free market as embodying the virtues of a freedom-loving people. Reagan understood, as the framers of the Constitution had, that power loves more power. Whereas Nader sought more government regulation, regulation seemingly without end, Reagan sought to free business from intrusive regulation. Reagan's goal was to restart an economy suffering from runaway inflation and high unemployment.

By the time Democrats returned to the White House in 1992 under Bill Clinton, Nader was out of favor. The Clinton administration ignored Nader, and the one thing Nader disliked most was being ignored. He responded typically, declaring Clinton to be no better than Reagan or Bush. He referred to Clinton as "George Ronald Clinton."[28] Even Vice President Al Gore, who had made a reputation in the Senate for being pro-environment and anti–tort reform, turned a deaf ear to Nader's pleas to meet. In Congress, Nader did not find a better reception. When Representative Bernard Sanders of Vermont, a self-declared socialist aligned with Democrats in the House, invited Nader to address the Progressive Caucus in 1997, only five of the fifty caucus members came to Nader's talk.[29]

Radicalizing Law

Although Nader's own influence waned, his legacy endured through the generation of activists he had inspired and trained. Many of those activists had turned to public interest law to bring what they considered social justice to America. By focusing on the specific complaints of average people, they could reveal the naked power of corporations within American democracy. As Nader put it, raising environmental, consumer, and public issues "lets you talk about 'market power' and 'concentration of power' in concrete terms."[30]

These activist lawyers and their allies, community organizers, sought to redistribute wealth, remake the corporate order, and reduce and alter energy use. Americans, they proclaimed, should live in smaller houses, use less energy, replace fossil fuels with "sustainable" energy sources, including wind and solar (but not nuclear), and drive smaller cars fueled by electricity and hydrogen. Basically, activists of this generation believed Americans consumed too much, and they did not like it.

Activists dismissed the American success story. Nevertheless, American corporations had contributed to the most vibrant economy in the world. In the 1960s alone the national income had increased from $420.9 billion to $832.6 billion in 2012 dollars. The poverty rate had been cut in half, from an estimated 20 percent to 10 percent of the population. Economists attributed most of this decline to a growing economy. Inflation-adjusted per capita disposable income increased by 36 percent during the decade. Unemployment fell from 5.5 percent in 1960 to 3.5 percent in 1969. Although women's wages continued to lag, women in the workforce had increased from 38 percent to 43 percent. Homeownership had steadily increased from 62.1 percent of households owning homes in 1960 to 64.2 percent in 1970.[31]

To remedy this perceived crisis of consumption, postindustrial radicals called for a public morality in which individual rights were subsumed to the collective interests of the community—as defined by radical activists. If the morality of social justice did not persuade the public and the corporations, then coercion would be necessary. Not all anticonsumption progressives had faith that the Democratic Party could be reshaped to conform to the activist vision. New Deal liberals represented the past and therefore were enemies of a better future. Still, they could be used as temporary allies in the struggle for social justice. They shared many of the same concerns, having been rattled by the Vietnam War, urban riots, and campus protests. And like the younger activists, they were often ashamed of social, racial, and gender inequality in America and were eager to reform the system.

The new progressive activists were lawyers with causes: environmental justice, reproductive rights, prison reform, immigration rights, welfare rights, electoral representation, product safety, consumer rights. As Gary Bellow, a Brooklyn-born lawyer known for his work with union organizer Cesar Chavez and migrant farm workers in California, declared in 1969, "The problem of unjust laws is almost invariably a problem of distribution of political and economic power."[32] To make just laws, Bellow charged, power must be redistributed to the poor. After working in California, Bellow was called to Harvard Law School, where he founded the Legal Services Center, a counseling center for the poor and a training ground for the next generation of activist attorneys.

Power distributed from whom? The recurring theme found in public interest law as it emerged in the late 1960s was the conviction that the basic evil in American society was "concentrated corporate power." Like Satan's image of God in Milton's *Paradise Lost*, the corporation was omnipotent and ubiquitous. Former American Civil Liberties Union attorney Philip Moore asserted, "Corporations make all the decisions in this country." This was an amazing statement expressing a faith widely shared among activist lawyers: corporations were the cause of what was wrong in America—pollution, unsafe products, energy waste, inequality, you name it. Corporate power, it seemed, exerted an insidious, usually hidden influence on public officials at every level of government. The issue was not that specific businesses might be unscrupulous or negligent; the problem was systemic.[33]

Despite this hostility to the established order, America's elites financed and supported the radical public interest legal movement. The federal government under Lyndon B. Johnson actually provided the seed money to finance public interest law. To increase legal aid to the poor, the Great Society rapidly expanded the federal Legal Services Program. In 1965 all legal-aid societies in the United States had budgets totaling $5.4 million and a combined staff of about four hundred full-time lawyers. By 1968 the Legal Services Program had more than two thousand lawyers and an annual budget of $40 million. Funded directly by the federal government, the Legal Services Program became, in effect, a strategic litigant. Between 1966 and 1974, it submitted 169 cases to the Supreme Court.[34]

Meanwhile, the Ford Foundation, under McGeorge Bundy, who had resigned as Johnson's national security adviser in 1966 to become the foundation's president, undertook a more ambitious and far-reaching project to support a public interest law movement. Ford proved critical in promoting this movement in law schools and the legal profession. Through Ford Foundation grants, public interest law and legal clinics were introduced to America's leading law schools. A combination of Ford Foundation and government grants established centers in welfare law (Columbia University), housing (UC Berkeley), consumer law (Boston University), juvenile law (Saint Louis University), education law (Harvard), health law (UCLA), and geriatric law (University of Southern California).[35] In the process, poverty law, consumer credit law, family law, criminal law, and prison law were introduced into the curriculum.

Law schools became centers for training social activists and political advocates. At Yale Law School, Professor Robert Bork, one of the few conservatives on the faculty, recalled that even as liberal as the school was, it was "unprepared for the shock when student radicals first appeared in our midst."[36] The rise in radicalism coincided with a massive increase in the law school professoriate. From 1962 to 1977 full-time professors of law in the United State more than doubled, from 1,628 to 3,875. The legal professoriate was already liberal in the early 1970s; only about 20 percent of law school professors voted for Nixon in 1972. But by the 1990s law professors had become overwhelmingly left wing.[37]

Elite law schools became hotbeds of radical legal scholarship. Legal historian Laura Kalman observes in her history of Yale Law School that legal scholarship became "profoundly anti-liberal" in the 1970s. Yale law professor Charles Reich, for example, assailed the New Deal tradition in a stream of major articles. The scholarship of Critical Legal Studies held that bourgeois law reflected power, not principle, so the job of the radical lawyer was to unveil inequities in the law. As Kalman explains, Critical Legal Studies claimed that "rights are indeterminate, rights limit our imaginations, and rights inhibit political and social change." Individual rights, it was assumed, should be subsumed into the collective rights of groups and the larger community.[38] No fascist or Marxist could have said it better, but then more and more Marx was being absorbed into students' consciousness.

While imbibing the new scholarship, radical law students challenged admission standards, grading, faculty governance, and the curriculum itself. Demands for more admission of blacks and women into law schools led to student protests. At Yale Law School students demanded that first-year courses be graded only with pass/fail marks. Under pressure from the Black Law Student Union, Yale applied for and received Ford Foundation money to develop the Danbury Project, which sent law students to Danbury Prison to provide legal services to inmates. A Legal Services Clinic was set up in the city of New Haven to provide students with experience in representing the poor.

The radicalization of Yale Law School won the support of the university's president, Kingman Brewster. When Black Panther radical Bobby Seale was put on trial in New Haven for murder, Brewer declared, "I personally want to say that I am appalled and ashamed that things should have to come to such a pass that I am skeptical of the ability of black revolutionaries to achieve a fair trial anywhere in the United States."[39] Contrary to Brewster's prediction, a jury found Seale not guilty.

Legal Crusade

Across the country, activist young lawyers, fresh out of America's elite law schools, streamed into the radical movements of the day, becoming litigators, strategists, and leaders. Typical was David Schoenbrod, who brought his Yale Law School pedigree to, as he put it, "a group of ardent young attorneys who, in the afterglow of the first Earth Day," launched the Natural Resources Defense Council (NRDC). The NRDC had grown out of a Ford Foundation grant to Yale's Charles Reich and several students to support a law firm in fighting to halt the construction of a power plant on New York's Storm King Mountain.

The NRDC achieved early success, playing a critical role in the enactment of the Clean Air Act in 1970. Schoenbrod and the NRDC soon began campaigning against leaded gasoline. They became self-appointed watchdogs to make sure that the Environmental Protection Agency (EPA) oversaw the removal of lead from gasoline. By filing suits in federal court, the NRDC put pressure on the EPA to "Get the Lead Out," as its slogan went—something the Clean Air Act had not specifically addressed. Schoenbrod later recalled, "Here was government the way an elitist like me thought it ought to be. Experts were empowered to achieve an ideal, and I was empowered to make sure they did."[40] The New Progressive agenda was in place: social justice (no lead), elite control (NRDC), and governmental power (EPA).

It seemed that activist lawyers were found wherever the cause of social justice was proclaimed. They fought against nuclear power and population growth and for animal rights, food packaging, mass transportation, and low-income housing for the poor. Attorneys also became active on behalf of feminist causes, including reproductive rights, pay equity, and female athletics in high school and college. Progressive lawyers represented and advised welfare-rights campaigners, prison-reform advocates, militant civil libertarians, and local community organizers—all marching under the noble banner of social justice. The exact meaning of "social justice" remained unclear, appealing to the heart, good intentions, and the self-righteousness of the saint living in a world of sin.

The public interest law movement remained diffuse and fluid. Its goals were ambiguous and its strategies for social change varied. Causes of the day appeared, disappeared, and then reappeared. One day the leading issue might be opposition to nuclear development; the next it might be suburbanization, unsafe drinking water, food additives, McDonald's styrofoam containers, a nuclear-weapons freeze, the destruction of rain forests, or national health care. As causes such as the anti–Vietnam War movement began to lose momentum in the 1970s, progressive lawyers discovered civil liberties, from protecting high school lockers from drug searches to removing prayer and religious symbols from public places.

Many of these causes, especially those involving product safety, appealed to average Americans. Who did not want to protect children from lead in the air emitted by gas-guzzling automobiles? What American did not want to remove a toxic dump near a school? Should not girls be given the right to play high school sports with equal funding of the boys' football team? Job discrimination against women was inexcusable, was it not? Was it not a simple matter of justice to punish corporations that knowingly fouled the air or water supply with toxins?

Such questions appealed to Americans' sense of justice and desire for a better life for themselves and their children. By tapping issues such as a toxic dump in a neighborhood or the safety of a child's toy, activists could rally the public. Whether the marketplace might have addressed some of these problems better was beside the point. The larger goal of the politically conscious activists was to challenge corporate capitalism. They sought to transform society, not simply to remedy a particular problem.

Trial Lawyers, Politics, and Money

Like war itself, the struggle to use law for social change attracted both idealists seeking a better world and crass materialists looking for personal gain. Legal activism imparted an ever-expanding meaning to rights—privacy rights for high school students; the construction of a high wall separating church and state to protect the rights of a secular society; the equal right of boys and girls to play team sports; reproductive rights for women; equal rights for gays, lesbians, and transgender people. The drive for legal equality took unforeseen and varied paths—from equal opportunity in employment to affirmative action for racial minorities and women; from nondiscrimination against homosexuals to same-sex marriage.

Public interest lawyers, however enraptured they were with power, represented the idealism of the post-1960s generation. Professing no less of a concern for social justice were tort lawyers, who gained prominence beginning in the 1970s. Echoing the cries for social justice by public interest lawyers, tort lawyers sold themselves as helping the little guy. At one convention of trial lawyers, a lawyer offered this invocation: "You created us, Lord, not to accumulate treasure for ourselves, but to do your work." After the prayer, the conventioneers broke up to learn new ways to sue over hip implants, misdiagnosed breast cancer, recalled drugs, and other corporate malfeasance.[41]

Public interest law began as a movement to empower the people. In the late 1960s and early 1970s, activist lawyers embraced tort law as an anticorporate tool.[42] Here, too, Ralph Nader's influence was evident. In 1976, Nader edited a collection of essays entitled *Verdict on Lawyers*. In one essay, "Class Actions: Let the People In," longtime Nader associate Beverly C. Moore Jr. and former U.S. senator Fred Harris made the case for using trial law to bring corporate abuses to heel and serve the public interest.[43] Moore and Harris laid out a list of twenty-five potential class-action suits. They urged activist lawyers to consider suing the sugar industry for tooth decay. They declared that the tobacco and liquor industries could be sued for the ill effects of their products. Similarly, food manufacturers could be brought into court for inducing such maladies as heart disease, cancer related to fat intake, and diabetes. The automobile industry could be saddled, they wrote, "with an annual damage liability of perhaps $100 billion for accidents, air pollution, noise, congestion, and highway and traffic-control costs." Moore and Harris predicted that the pharmaceutical industry could be sued for liability for adverse reactions, overdoses, and side effects.

The Harris-Moore essay struck at the right time in the changing nature of liability law. From 1920 through the early 1960s, manufacturers generally bore liability for defective products only if a defect could be traced back to specific negligence on the manufacturer's part or if an express or implied warranty was breached. Liability rules were intended to promote safety by raising the price of negligence, product defects, and accidents.[44] Still, litigation remained a costly last resort. This began to change in the 1960s, when liability rules broadened. A defective product might involve a manufacturing flaw in a single product, a poor design in an entire line of products, an inadequate warning or poor instructions accompanying a product, or even consumer misuse of a product unforeseen by a manufacturer. The doctrine of strict liability was expanded. Neither negligence nor a contractual relationship was required on the part of the manufacturer to establish liability. The manufacturer, anyone in a chain of distribution of a product, the wholesaler, the retailer, the advertiser, and perhaps even the financier or the transporter could become liable.

Liberalized procedural rules invited attorneys to sue first, undertake fishing expeditions of discovery, rummage through corporate archives, and shop for courts and juries sympathetic to their cases. Certain courts run by judges linked to trial lawyers became notorious for providing pro-plaintiff decisions, including Holmes County, Mississippi, and Madison County, Illinois. At the same time, rules for class-action suits in the 1960s and 1970s changed to allow litigants to bring such suits by including as litigants all possible persons unless they specifically asked to opt out. This allowed trial lawyers to acquire a lengthy list of nominal "clients." As a consequence, court dockets were filled by what conservative legal scholar Walter K. Olson described as "mass torts" in which lawyers brought thousands of claims from every part of the country alleging injury.[45]

As trial lawyers gained influence, Nader threw his support behind them. He helped form Trial Lawyers for Public Justice, a networking organization. He became a major opponent of tort reform, which called for caps on punitive damages, the paying of legal costs by plaintiffs in lost suits, and various other reforms. Here, too, Nader was an absolutist. He maintained, "The prospect of tort liability deters those manufacturers, builders, doctors, and other tort-misfeasors from repeating their negligent behavior; it provides them with a proper economic incentive to curb their damaging practices and to make their endeavors safer."[46] One Florida trial lawyer, Frederic Levin, declared, "We are supporters of Nader. We contribute to him and he fundraises through us."[47]

Trial lawyers had plenty to contribute. By 1990, estimates of gross U.S. liability expenditures stood at $117 billion. More than half the total compensation dollars went to attorneys. One study in the 1990s showed that transaction costs consumed 30 percent of the cost of workers compensation and 15 percent of health insurance. Did this system serve justice? Were common people being protected? Here is one way of measuring whether consumers were better protected: the annual number of tort suits and liability insurance premiums rose sharply during the 1980s, but injury rates for consumers and workers, death rates from medical procedures, and aviation accident rates declined no faster than they had in the 1970s.[48]

The use of the courts to pursue a radical agenda fit perfectly with New Progressive ideals: social justice (tort-generated redistribution), elite control (trial lawyers and courts in a cozy relationship), and governmental power (use of the courts).

Political Collusion: The Case of Dickie Scruggs

Like public interest lawyers, trial lawyers joined ranks with the Democratic Party as they gained power. By the 1990s the American Trial Lawyers Association had become the largest political action committee (PAC) contributor to the Democratic Party.[49] In a twenty-year period, trial lawyers and their law firms contributed nearly nine times as much to Democratic candidates as to Republican candidates.[50]

The alliance of trial lawyers and Democrats reflected how widespread anticorporatism had become within the progressive establishment. It also showed the importance of political connections to pursuing social justice through the courts. The significance of those connections seemed to outweigh idealism: when Nader broke from the Democratic Party to run for president on the Green Party ticket in 1996 and 2000, the trial lawyers did not follow him, despite the role he had played in their rise. Then, in 2007, a high-profile case in Mississippi highlighted just how closely linked trial lawyers had become to the political establishment—and the risks of abuse and corruption those links entailed.[51]

Known as the King of Torts, Richard "Dickie" Scruggs of Mississippi gained a reputation as a political mover and shaker. Scruggs and his partner Paul Minor became important players in state politics, heading up such groups as the Institute for Consumers and the Environmental Political Action Committee. Another contributor to the group was best-selling author John Grisham, a former Democratic state senator. Scruggs's brother-in-law was former Senate majority leader Trent Lott, a Republican, and Scruggs made campaign contributions to some Republicans, such as Senators John McCain (Arizona) and Susan Collins (Maine). But his major allegiance was to the Democratic Party. Politicians who came to Mississippi in quest of campaign contributions included Senator Joseph Biden (D-Delaware), Senator Tom Daschle (D-South Dakota), Senator John Kerry (D-Massachusetts), and Senator Harry Reid (D-Nevada). Scruggs gave $300,000 to Howard Dean's left-leaning Democracy for America and $100,000 to the Democratic Party congressional reelection fund. Before his indictment, he was about to host a major fundraiser at his house for presidential candidate Hillary Clinton. The star at the reception was to be former president Bill Clinton. Scruggs's career is revealing of how easily litigation crosses over into politics.

Mississippi proved to be particularly good hunting grounds for trial lawyers such as Scruggs. The state had an elected judiciary, which encouraged litigation lawyers to contribute heavily to pro-plaintiff judges. In the 1980s, Scruggs took on the asbestos industry. In 1986 the state supreme court ruled that products that involved a Mississippi distributor or company were subject to state court jurisdiction. Scruggs made a fortune in asbestos cases, netting his firm in excess of $10 million.[52]

Scruggs's next step was to take on Big Tobacco. He did so by joining forces with Mississippi attorney general Mike Moore, a former law school classmate. Scruggs brought civil suits against the tobacco companies, while Moore sued for the repayment of state Medicare costs that the state of Mississippi had incurred in treating tobacco-related sickness.[53] Under pressure, Philip Morris and R. J. Reynolds agreed in 1997 to a $3.4 billion settlement. The consortium of private lawyers working with the state received $1.43 billion to split. Scruggs had become a dragon slayer. His reputation was further enhanced when Hollywood made a film about the case, *The Insider*, starring Al Pacino and Russell Crowe.

After Hurricane Katrina hit the Gulf Coast in late August 2005, the slim, smooth-talking Scruggs formed the Scruggs Katrina Group to sue State Farm Insurance for not paying full damages. The group included Scruggs's partner, his son Zach, and William Winter, a Democrat who had served in numerous elected positions in Mississippi. Although State Farm paid out billions of dollars to policyholders for wind damages, it refused to pay for flood damages. The company noted that flood insurance was available through the federal government and that its own policies did not cover floods. Scruggs saw the suit against State Farm as a political battle.[54]

Given the massive devastation and grief caused by the hurricane, Scruggs found it easy to rally the public to his side. He told the *New York Times*, "This is about my family, my friends, the people I grew up with. I wake up at 3:30 every morning thinking of ways to get at this thing."[55] Among his friends and family was his brother-in-law Lott, who had a personal claim against State Farm for payments on his multimillion-dollar waterfront home, which had washed away. Scruggs prevailed upon a political ally, the new Mississippi attorney general, Jim Hood, to file criminal charges against State Farm. Scruggs was Hood's largest political contributor. Caught in a scissors action with civil and criminal suits, State Farm agreed to a civil settlement worth at least $130 million.

The question for Scruggs was how to settle the $26.5 million in fees with his coattorneys. One firm filed suit, protesting that it was not getting its fair share. At this point, Scruggs slipped up. He ordered his legal associate Timothy Balducci to offer a $40,000 bribe to the circuit judge overseeing the case, Henry Lackey. The bribe was undertaken with the knowledge of Scruggs's other law partners, including his son Zach. Judge Lackey reported the attempted bribe to federal officials. Balducci was quickly "flipped" and caught Scruggs on tape confessing his involvement in the attempted bribery. Before confessing his guilt, Scruggs rallied longtime political supporters to his cause. John Grisham, a liberal Democrat, told the press that Scruggs was incapable of committing such a "boneheaded bribery scam." He was wrong. Scruggs was sentenced to five years in prison and a $250,000 fine. Joining him were his partners, Balducci, his son Zack, and former Mississippi auditor Steve Patterson.

Yet the story does not end there. Shortly before the sentencing, additional bribery charges against Scruggs were brought in a case involving another Mississippi circuit judge, Robert DeLaughter. DeLaughter, who had gained fame for trying Byron De La Beckwith, the murderer of civil rights leader Medgar Evers, was caught taking a bribe from Scruggs. Matters worsened when Paul Minor, a longtime financial contributor to the state and national Democratic Party, was found guilty of providing uncollected "loans" to other Mississippi judges. When Minor was sent to prison, liberals across the country protested that he was a victim of a "Bush-Cheney" plot to bring down Democrats in the state and to ensure that Mississippi went Republican in 2008.[56] Minor became a modest cause célèbre in left-wing Democratic circles.

From Court Theater to Public Fool: The Tale of John Edwards

By the time of Ralph Nader's estrangement from the Democratic Party, many progressives had already found a candidate they believed represented their highest ideas of social justice—John Edwards.

The step from trial lawyer to politician proved easy for Edwards. He came from a lower-middle-class family, a point he made repeatedly in the courtroom—and later on the campaign stump and on television. After graduating from the University of North Carolina's law school, he rose rapidly as a trial lawyer, winning his first multimillion-dollar verdict in 1984, at the age of thirty-one. In 1993 he started his own firm to specialize in medical malpractice suits. That same year he won a record $26 million settlement on behalf of a family whose five-year-old daughter had been partially disemboweled by a faulty pool drain.

Edwards became a hero to other trial lawyers. Young attorneys made it a point to hear his closing arguments. In court, Edwards was a consummate actor. He showed little emotional restraint in appealing to juries. On one occasion involving an obstetrician sued for not performing an immediate Caesarean section, Edwards stood before the jury and "channeled" the thoughts of the fetus in the womb.[57]

He was not without critics. He brought at least twenty cases involving fetal heart monitors and cerebral palsy births. One result of his successful medical malpractice suits involving fetal monitors was that Caesarean deliveries increased dramatically—from 6 percent in 1970 to 32 percent by 2010. Critics noted that even though Caesarean operations drove up medical costs and carried the risks of major surgery, cerebral palsy births did *not* decline. This result suggested that Edwards's complaint against fetal monitoring machines was based on "junk science."[58]

Whatever his methods, Edwards was undeniably successful. He became a multimillionaire, amassing a personal fortune of between $13.7 million and $38.6 million by the time he ran for the U.S. Senate. In 1998 the forty-four-year-old Edwards entered the Senate race against the two-term Republican incumbent, seventy-year-old Lauch Faircloth. Edwards brought to the campaign what political consultant Gary Pearce described as "raw political talent. . . . He knew how to connect with people. And he could look in a camera, master a script and deliver it better than anybody I've ever seen."[59] Edwards spent $6 million of his own money during the campaign, while drawing huge financial support from trial lawyers. In fact, 86 percent of his contributions came from personal-injury lawyers, and nineteen of his top twenty donors were plaintiffs' lawyers.[60] (It was not surprising that in the Senate he opposed class-action reform, medical-malpractice reform, and limitations on personal-injury lawsuits involving a terrorist attack.)[61] In the good old American style of campaigning, he downplayed his wealth. He drove an old beat-up Buick Park Avenue, leaving his Lexus and BMW in his garage.

At first, Edwards was not terribly specific as to where he stood on issues other than to declare, "We are a country that speaks out for those without a voice. . . . When we stand up for people without health care, for people who live in poverty, when we stand up for veterans, America rises."[62] Once he hit his stride he called for a balanced budget and reform of health maintenance organizations (HMOs). He called for restoring integrity to Washington, and he supported the death penalty. He promised not to support tax increases in the Senate. (Once in the Senate and after he got the presidential bug, he switched his position on many issues. He told the press that this was a sign of his growth and deepened understanding of the issues.)[63] Catching Faircloth off guard, Edwards won. He told his supporters, "The people of North Carolina voted their hopes, instead of their fears."[64]

Progressives immediately began to see him as the hope for the party. *Capitol Style* magazine put him on its February cover with the headline "Building the Perfect Senator." He was a rising star. By 2004, Edwards had put together a team of leading political operatives for a presidential campaign. Fashioning the message were David Axelrod and David Ginsberg, and the day-to-day campaign was handled by Nick Baldick.

In 2008 some of these advisers shifted to the Barack Obama campaign, employing many of the techniques developed in Edwards's campaign, including use of the Internet, a message of "hope and change," and calls for redistribution of wealth in the name of social justice.

When he decided to run for president in 2004, Edwards dropped his "moderate populism" in favor of a full-blown populism. He declared himself a candidate for the "other America," that of the neglected poor. At the suggestion of Axelrod, he promoted the theme of "Two Americas," one in which everyday people played by the rules and the other in which a wealthy minority wielded disproportionate influence. At the urging of Axelrod, Edwards developed a theme of hope for the future and resisted personal attacks on opponents.[65] He called for eliminating poverty in America; high taxes on the wealthy would be used to create a universal health-care plan, to provide one million housing vouchers to place poor people in middle-class neighborhoods, and to enlarge the Earned Income Tax Credit. He called for increases in capital-gains taxes, expanded federal programs for college students, and a public-works program. He supported full citizenship for illegal immigrants. On social policy, he was also a progressive, opposing a constitutional amendment banning same-sex marriage and favoring repeal of the Defense of Marriage Act. He was pro-abortion. He declared that he was environmentally green. He drew support from the political activist group ACORN and the public employees union Service Employees International Union (SEIU), often appearing at their events.

Edwards's rhetoric of two Americas, soak-the-rich taxation, and more economic regulations was explicitly anticorporate and antielitist. But Edwards understood that the key to a successful presidential campaign lay in fund-raising. He tapped into longtime political liberals such as R. J. Reynolds heir Smith Bagley and his wife, Elizabeth, as well as Rachel Lambert "Bunny" Mellon, the granddaughter of banker Andrew Mellon. His campaign was disproportionately financed by lawyers. His financial base included trial lawyers, such as his former partner David Kirby, Biloxi lawyer Paul Minor (who was to be indicted four years later), and Fred M. Baron of Texas, who had become superrich suing asbestos manufacturers. The Center for Responsive Politics calculated that about half of the $15 million Edwards had raised by January 2004 came from lawyers. One Dallas law firm involved in asbestos litigation contributed $77,250 to Edwards's campaign.[66]

Behind the populism was also a calculating lawyer who carefully watched over his own massive wealth.[67] Like many of America's wealthy, Edwards was happy to invest in corporations, even if doing so belied talk of two Americas. After the 2004 presidential run, he became a major investor in a company whose subsidiary made subprime loans to home buyers with poor credit histories. When his investment became public, he divested his funds and set up an ACORN-administered fund in Louisiana to help provide loans and grants to families who had been foreclosed by the company.[68] It was a good political show.

In the Iowa caucuses, Edwards came in a solid second with 32 percent of the vote, but unfortunately for him John Kerry came in first and went on to win the nomination. Kerry and Edwards did not especially like each other, but Edwards's ability to raise money and his southern roots made him an ideal choice for the vice presidential slot in 2004. In the end, the combination was not enough to beat the incumbent, Republican George W. Bush, but Edwards was set for his own presidential run in 2008.

He turned to a new group of political consultants and blamed David Axelrod for the timid Kerry-Edwards campaign. Edwards got a part-time job with a hedge fund called Fortress, which offered a salary of about $500,000 a year. He put close to $16 million of his own money into Fortress, which used various schemes to deliver high rates of return.[69] He transferred money into incorporated offshore accounts to avoid taxes. He began building a huge house in North Carolina. Meanwhile, he took to the road giving speeches about poverty in America at $55,000 a pop.

In 2008, Edwards faced Hillary Clinton and newcomer Barack Obama. The Edwards campaign never caught fire, and when Obama won Iowa, Edwards's campaign funds dried up. The campaign took a further blow when the Obama camp revealed that Edwards had been getting $400 haircuts that were charged to the campaign.

At this point a national tabloid newspaper discovered his ongoing extramarital affair. Things went from terrible to disaster when the tabloid press reported that the mistress was pregnant. During the Iowa contest, the campaign announced that Edwards's wife, Elizabeth, was fighting a virulent form of breast cancer. A few supporters such as Bunny Mellon and some former trial lawyer associates stuck with him at first, but Edwards had been revealed to be an emperor with no clothes. In 2012, Edwards was brought to trial for misuse of campaign funds by allegedly paying an aide to direct funds to his mistress, Rielle Hunter. He was acquitted by a jury of criminal charges, but long before this, progressives had found a better standard-bearer, the former community organizer Barack Obama. His political timing proved even more fortuitous than Edwards's in 1998—so good, in fact, that it carried him to the White House.

The path from Nader to Edwards was not a direct one, and surely Ralph Nader, rightfully so, would not claim Edwards as a successor to his crusade. What Nader and trial lawyers such as Scruggs and Edwards shared was an anticorporate populism. Nader was genuine in his anticorporate crusade. Trial lawyers such as Edwards used anticorporate rhetoric before juries to win large self-aggrandizing settlements. What Nader, radical public interest lawyers, and trial lawyers shared, though, was an anticorporate ethos that found eventual articulation in the left wing of the Democratic Party. However pristine Nader's views were, and however self-serving trial lawyers' goals were, these views became embodied by the New Progressives as they successfully transformed the old liberalism of Franklin Roosevelt's Democratic Party.

Building the Base of Power

The rhetoric of John Edwards's presidential campaign in 2004 and Barack Obama's campaign in 2008 was not the language of Wilsonian or New Deal liberalism. Instead, it echoed language the new wave of progressives developed in the 1960s and 1970s. This rhetoric projected a view of corporations as evil, ruthlessly driven by profits, and protected by lobbyists and self-serving politicians. Whereas socialists in the 1930s had called for public ownership of basic industries, the New Progressives were generally interested not in "controlling the means of production" but in constraining corporations, redistributing resources from the corporate sector. Ultimately they sought to control American consumption—the kinds of products Americans used—from the cars they drove to what they ate, drank, and smoked. All this was to be accomplished in the name of social justice, product safety, protecting the poor, civil liberties, and social equality.

Mostly, the New Progressives saw themselves as the proper elite necessary to improve society by bringing social justice to fruition. Earlier activists had stood outside the established two-party system, taking their protests to the streets. The New Progressives recognized that they needed governmental power to achieve their goal. The key to their long-term success, they saw, was in politics.

A left-wing base had been built from the ground up. Only when the Left came to power in 2008 would the full force of this progressive agenda be revealed.

3

Brave Green World:
Radical Environmentalism and the
New Social Justice

W riting in 2008 on the eve of Barack Obama's election, former vice president and presidential candidate Albert Gore Jr., a Nobel Prize winner, declared, "We can find the wisdom and the spirit we need to disenthrall ourselves and fulfill what is perhaps our ultimate manifest destiny: to save our planet."[1]

How were Americans to "save our planet"? Stop consuming such a disproportionate share of the earth's resources. Gore and his fellow environmentalists held that Americans overconsumed energy, natural resources, food, and goods.[2] The result was an ecological crisis of such cataclysmic proportions that it could be compared only to the Cretaceous period sixty-one million years ago, when dinosaurs became extinct. In his 2006 book, *An Inconvenient Truth*, Gore warned that global warming was causing polar ice caps to melt, which would eventually lead coastal cities to disappear under water, while drought conditions in interior regions would induce worldwide famine.

But environmentalists projected a deep pessimism about people's ability to control their appetites. Seattle environmentalist Alan Durning captured this sentiment when he observed, "If human desires are in fact infinitely expandable, consumption is ultimately incapable of providing fulfillment—the logical consequence ignored by economic theory. . . . High-consumption societies, just as high-living individuals, consume ever more without achieving satisfaction. The allure to the consumer society is powerful, even irresistible, but it is shallow nonetheless."[3] Environmentalists urged the federal government and international organizations to take the steps—draconian, if necessary—to do what its citizens might be unwilling to do voluntarily. Gore, for example, proposed federal mandates, regulations, and taxes to control consumption and international treaties to reduce carbon emissions.

Needed, environmentalists declared, was a total transformation of the American corporate economy and the global economy. Barack Obama made the promise of transformative change a theme of his presidential campaign. He reiterated this theme in his inaugural address when he promised to bend "the arc of history. . . . Now, there are some who question the scale of our ambitions, who suggest that our system cannot tolerate too many big plans. . . . What the cynics fail to understand is that the ground has shifted beneath them, that the stale political arguments that have consumed us for so long no longer apply." The change he promised went beyond the United States, or any single nation, to embrace global change. "And to those nations like ours that enjoy relative plenty," Obama stated, "we say we can no longer afford indifference to the sufferings outside our borders, nor can we consume the world's resources without regard to effect. For the world has changed, and we must change with it."[4] Upon clinching the Democratic nomination in June 2008, Obama declared that future generations would look back and realize that "this was the moment when the rise of the oceans began to slow and our planet began to heal."[5]

Environmentalists viewed economic growth as the cause of and not the solution to the ecological crisis they described.[6] The anticorporate, anticonsumption theme had begun with the progressive environmental activists of the 1970s, who saw themselves as ecologists who placed the needs and rights of nature on the same plane as those of humans. Ecological activists perceived a postindustrial order dominated by multinational corporate greed, toxic waste, and unsafe consumer products; they saw a planet being destroyed for the profit of the few—a nation of overconsumption. These postindustrial radicals aimed to redistribute wealth, remake the corporate order, and reduce and alter energy use. They sought to enforce standards of public morality when it came to consumption. Americans, they proclaimed, should live in smaller houses, use less energy, replace fossil fuels with "sustainable" energy sources including wind and solar (but not nuclear), and drive smaller cars fueled by electricity and hydrogen.[7]

By the time of Obama's election, environmental activists had been warning about impending ecological doom for nearly thirty years. They had managed to convince powerful politicians such as Obama and Gore as well as many government bureaucrats. They had not, however, persuaded American voters to put environmental issues high on their list of priorities. Even prior to the October 2008 financial meltdown, surveys showed that environmental concerns took a backseat to economic issues. In 2005, Duke University's Nicholas Institute found that only 22 percent of voters said environmental issues played a major role in how they voted.[8] Even more surprising, when Duke pollsters asked, "What is the most important issue to you personally?" the environment came in last, with only 10 percent of the respondents citing it as the top issue. First on the list were economy/jobs with 34 percent, followed by health care with 25 percent, Iraq with 22 percent, and Social Security with 21 percent. A June 2006 Pew Research Center survey found similar results. Voters ranked jobs and the economy first on their list of concerns, the environment twelfth, and global warming sixteenth.

American voters not only saw jobs and the economy as more important but also held increasingly negative views about environmental issues and environmentalists in general. The Environics social-values survey found that support for the statement "To preserve people's jobs in this country, we must accept higher levels of pollution in the future" increased from 17 percent in 1996 to 27 percent in 2004. Those viewing environmental activists as "extremists, not reasonable people" increased from 32 percent in 1996 to 43 percent in 2004.

Such disappointing results occurred despite oft-repeated promises that "green" technologies would bring job growth. Displaced auto workers in the old manufacturing sector would find new work in making electric cars; coal miners would find employment installing solar panels; and construction workers who used to build McMansions could erect urban light-rail systems. Obama's "New Energy for America" proposal, issued shortly after the 2008 election, promised to create five million new "green jobs" through a comprehensive plan to invest in alternative and renewable energy. He promised to "end our addiction to foreign oil" and address "the global climate crisis" by putting one million "plug-in-hybrid cars" on the road by 2015. His economy-wide "cap-and-trade program" called for reducing greenhouse gas emissions 80 percent by 2050.[9]

The failure to convert the population to the environmental cause after decades of activism helped explain the green movement's lack of faith in Americans to embrace transformative change. Even the threat of global warming, rising seas, drought, increased skin cancer, and mass starvation did not seem to scare average Americans into doing what environmentalists knew was the right thing. Green political theorists began to dismiss "liberal democracy" as a failure in the face of a global environmental crisis.

The politics of environmental scarcity and economic limits led to the politics of coercion, often with startling overtures to authoritarian government. How is it that the environmental movement, which sprang up in the 1970s using the rhetoric of "small is beautiful" and "citizens' involvement," became so severe in its distrust of American democratic values? Any answer to this question must begin with an exploration of how the environmental movement evolved in the postwar period, the battles fought by activists such as the scientist Barry Commoner and the New Left radical turned Democratic Party politician Tom Hayden, and their disappointment in the average American's willingness to do the right thing: limit growth and enter the gates of the brave green world.

The Anticonsumption Ethos of Postwar Liberalism

The environmental movement in the United States dates back to the nineteenth century, when protests against pollution, calls to conserve natural resources, and a campaign to save the wilderness began to be heard. The progressive Republican Teddy Roosevelt was proud to be America's first conservation president. After the Second World War, the first indications of linking environmentalism to anticonsumption sentiments were evident in the writings of two Harvard University professors, the historian Arthur M. Schlesinger Jr. and the economist John Kenneth Galbraith. Both were liberal intellectuals well positioned in the Democratic Party.[10] They saw material abundance—not economic scarcity—as the problem facing postwar America.

In a series of magazine articles, Schlesinger argued that the major issue confronting postwar liberalism was "abundance." Whereas New Deal liberals had focused on "economic security," postwar liberals needed to address "quality of life" issues such as the environment.[11] In *The Affluent Society*, which became a bestseller in 1958, Galbraith opened an attack on overconsumption that resonated with liberals. He wrote, "The family which takes its mauve and cerise, air-conditioned, powersteered, and power-braked automobile out for a tour passes through cities that are badly paved, made hideous by litter, blighted buildings, billboards and posts for wire that should long since have been put underground. . . . They picnic on an exquisitely packaged food from a portable icebox by a polluted stream and go on to spend the night at a park which is a menace to public health and morals." He concluded by asking derisively, "Is this, indeed, the American genius?"[12]

Two years after the publication of Galbraith's book, the *New York Times* ran a series of articles discussing the imbalance of private wealth and public squalor. The liberal *Times*, prefiguring themes in John Kennedy's presidential campaign, reported that many in Washington had concluded that the issue was "what share of America's total resources should be devoted to public as distinct from private purposes." The *Times* noted that "education is underfinanced. Streams are polluted. There remains a shortage of hospital beds. Slums proliferate, and there is a gap in middle-income housing. We could use more and better ports, streets, detention facilities, water supply."[13] In short, the marketplace was not going to address these ills—at least in the eyes of the *New York Times*.

The attack on American consumption was furthered by social critic Vance Packard in *The Waste Makers* (1960). Packard had already made a name for himself, and a good deal of money, with his attacks on American advertising and corporate life in *The Hidden Persuaders* and *The Status Seekers*. In *The Waste Makers*, Packard wrote, "A person can't go down to the store and order a new park. A park requires unified effort, and that gets you into voting and spending and maybe soak-the-rich taxes."[14]

Barry Commoner: From Environmental Activism to Political Radicalism

Liberals such as Schlesinger, Galbraith, and Packard focused on improving the "quality of life" of average Americans who lived in a material culture of overabundance. They called for urban parks, public transit systems, preservation of wilderness areas, less packaging, and fewer advertisements. As intellectuals who lived apart from, and frankly above, the masses, they were critics of American consumer culture. Their tone was anticorporate but not overtly anticapitalist. Their views were represented in the mainstream environmental movement. At the same time, however, the seeds of a more radical environmentalism were being sown.

Radical environmentalists saw the world on the eve of destruction. They called for social and economic transformation. Radical environmentalism did not spring forth fully grown. Instead, it took root in the 1950s, gained theoretical grounding in the 1960s, and emerged as a social movement in the 1970s as the New Left anti–Vietnam War movement dissipated into factionalism, terrorism, and self-indulgence.

Personifying this shift to radical environmentalism was Barry Commoner, who, though nearly forgotten today, stood next to bestselling author Rachel Carson as the leading environmentalist of his day. Carson's *Silent Spring* (1962) marked a turn to the left; her death in 1964 created a vacuum for the more radical Commoner. In February 1970, Commoner's picture appeared on the cover of *Time* over the headline "The Emerging Science of Survival." Described by the magazine as the "Paul Revere of Ecology," he presented an image of reasonable political activism combined with an abiding faith in scientific expertise.

Commoner entered the environmental movement in the 1950s as an opponent of atmospheric tests for nuclear bombs. He brought to activism an odd combination of populist rhetoric of citizen participation and an elitist belief in scientific knowledge. Holding a doctorate in plant physiology from Harvard University, he believed that public intellectuals such as himself embodied "a self-appointed moral conscience of their society."[15] He claimed that the purpose of the activist scientist was to challenge corporate-sponsored established technical information by means of true scientific knowledge. Yet behind Commoner's claim was more than a belief that the public needed to be informed: through his advocacy of environmental protest, he sought a radical overhaul of American democratic capitalism. Convinced that government was controlled by corporate interests, Commoner called for social control of technology.

The radical message became explicit in the 1970s. Commoner's enemy became free-market capitalism. In *The Closing Circle* (1971), he warned that "human beings have broken out of the circle of life, driven not by biological need, but by the social organization [capitalism] which they have devised to 'conquer' nature." Commoner called for a new "eco-socialism" to replace the "older forms of both capitalism and socialism, with their emphases respectively on profit and productivity."[16] In *The Politics of Energy* (1979), he demanded the complete transformation of the economy away from carbon-based energy and toward renewable energy systems. He called for trains to replace automobiles, for ethanol to supplant gasoline, for solar power to overtake coal and oil, and for Americans to lead simple lifestyles. He warned that vested interests in the traditional free-market system, as well as American habits and preferences, presented a massive roadblock to this transition. In 1980, Commoner ran for president on the socialist Citizens Party ticket. His vice presidential running mate was Donna Harris, wife of former U.S. senator Fred Harris, the longtime associate of Ralph Nader.

Commoner's anticonsumer and anticorporatist outlook became a theme in the radical environmental movement. He also found common cause with other struggles for social justice, including the antiwar movement, civil rights, feminism, and gay and lesbian rights. As he told an interviewer, "Since the age of seventeen, I was concerned with racial discrimination, labor problems, unemployment, so I didn't have to make a leap from environmentalism to the Peace Movement."[17] Writing in 1987, Commoner declared, "Environmentalism reaches a common ground with all the other movements."[18] Environmentalism became a wedge to challenge the existing political and economic system.

Born in 1917, the son of Russian emigrants, Commoner saw himself as a "Child of Depression." No doubt, the economic depression of the 1930s formed his socialist politics, but his environmental activism was shaped by the Cold War. Born with the last name Comenar, he changed the spelling to the less Jewish "Commoner" at the urging of his uncle, Avrahm Yarmolinsky, a radical who headed the Slavic division of the New York City Public Library. (Yarmolinsky's son and Barry's cousin was Adam, who later was appointed to the Arms Control and Disarmament Agency in the Kennedy and Johnson administrations.) As an undergraduate at Columbia University in 1933, Commoner attended numerous socialist and communist meetings and rallies to support Spanish loyalists, the labor movement, and the antilynching campaign. He recalled that he was a careful reader of Friedrich Engels and Karl Marx, as well as J. D. Bernal, a leading British Communist Party intellectual.

When he entered graduate school in biology at Harvard in 1937, he saw himself as a radical. Studying under biologist Kenneth V. Thimann, a progressive who sought to organize socially oriented fellow scientists, he joined the American Association of Scientific Workers, which called for the scientific community to use science's full potential to realize a socialist society.[19] An uneasy alliance of liberals, socialists, and communists, members shared the view that scientists should be directly involved in political and social issues. Many looked to the Soviet Union, with its five-year economic plans and espousal of "scientific socialism," as a model for advancing science. As with many popular front–type groups, however, the Nazi-Soviet Nonaggression Pact of 1939 caused a rupture in the organization; the Communist Party faction tried to push through a peace resolution calling for America to keep out of the war.

Where Commoner stood on this division remains unclear, but after receiving his doctorate from Harvard, he joined the U.S. Navy to fight in the Second World War. At war's end, Commoner joined the faculty at Washington University in St. Louis. There he renewed his commitment to being an activist scientist. As the Cold War heated up, he was certain that "something needed to be done right away to reverse the trend of inaction among scientists—and to start developing the means of speaking out on the issues which are bedeviling us."[20] Joining forces with Warren Weaver of the Rockefeller Foundation, Commoner in 1953 codrafted a statement brought before the American Association for the Advancement of Science (AAAS) to keep the integrity of scientific research from being twisted by external control from government, the military, or corporations. Commoner called for younger "scientific workers" to become involved in the broader issues of the day.

Their lobbying paid off in 1955, when the AAAS created a subcommittee to bring about the "integration of science into the general sociological structure." The new committee's chairman, University of Alabama biochemist Ward Pigman, resigned in less than two years when he found himself unable to control a radical faction on the committee that included Commoner, Margaret Mead, and Weaver. With Pigman out of the way, the reformed Committee on the Social Aspects of Science turned to the dangers of radioactive fallout from atmospheric testing.

By 1957 the United States and the Soviet Union were in a full-scale nuclear arms race. Both sides conducted widespread atmospheric testing of their weapons. From 1946 to 1963 the United States exploded 106 nuclear weapons in various parts of the Pacific and conducted 77 nuclear tests in Nevada. As scientists began to report nuclear fallout entering the food supply, including milk, public anxiety about atmospheric testing reached all-time levels.

The debate over the ill effects of radioactive fallout and the need to maintain American nuclear superiority spilled over into the pages of the *New York Times* and leading magazines such as *Saturday Review*. When the AAAS refused to release a public statement from the Committee on the Social Aspects of Science condemning atmospheric testing, Commoner published the statement in his own name. He wrote the AAAS board, "My original intention was to turn the AAAS into an effective agency in educating the public about politically sensitive, technological issues, as part of its mission." He later recalled in an interview, "It was urgent that it happen and I decided to do it on my own."[21]

In 1958, Commoner helped organize the Committee for Nuclear Information, a St. Louis–based grassroots organization opposed to atmospheric testing. The expressed purpose of the organization was to bring "objective" science about nuclear fallout to the public. The real agenda of the group, however, was to bring about a unilateral ban on nuclear testing. Commoner warned ominously that "we [the United States] are likely to put massive technological processes into operation before we understand their eventual biological consequences."[22] The committee had been formed by St. Louis progressives such as Edna Gellhorn, an upper-class social reformer devoted to women's rights, school reform, and civic causes; members of the local International Garment Workers Union; pacifists; and the Reverend Ralph Abele, the leader of the progressive St. Louis Metropolitan Church Federation and a member of the St. Louis Consumer Federation. Divisions later arose when Commoner urged that the committee take a public stance to ban nuclear testing.[23]

Five years later, when President John F. Kennedy signed the Nuclear Test Ban Treaty with the Soviet Union ending atmospheric nuclear tests, Commoner claimed much of the credit. He saw the treaty as an example of how citizen activism could change public policy. In reality, it was more a story of how statesmen could pursue arms control, often in the face of public and political opposition. The United States, the United Kingdom, Canada, France, and the Soviet Union began negotiations to end atmospheric testing in 1955. The negotiations bogged down when the Soviet Union refused to allow on-site inspectors to verify compliance. Nonetheless, President Dwight D. Eisenhower voluntarily placed a moratorium on testing. In 1961 the Soviet Union flagrantly resumed atmospheric testing, prompting President Kennedy to announce that the United States was restarting its testing program. Gallup polls showed that Americans supported testing by a margin of two to one. Negotiations on a testing ban reopened after the Cuban missile crisis pushed the two nations to the brink of nuclear holocaust.

The movement against atmospheric nuclear testing fed into the larger environmental movement that emerged with the publication of Rachel Carson's *Silent Spring* (1962). Prior to Carson's book, the environmental movement had been primarily concerned with preservation and conservation of natural resources. *Silent Spring* horrified the American public by describing how widespread use of the pesticide DDT released toxins into the environment. Carson warned that the unregulated industrial economy that had produced and indiscriminately used DDT had poisoned the natural food chain.

In her jeremiad, Carson began with a "Fable for Tomorrow," in which a bucolic American town lived in harmony with its surroundings until cattle died, children died, and the birds stopped singing: "It was silent spring."[24] Her literary technique represented a long tradition in American environmental writing going back to the Transcendentalist philosopher Henry David Thoreau before the Civil War, but its appeal struck a deep chord with her readers by depicting nature as something peaceful and balanced, only to be thrown into disequilibrium by human intervention.

Nature, as described by Carson and later environmentalists, is essentially harmonious and separate from humans. This view of man's fall from nature, with its deep theological roots in Western culture, ignored the profound disharmony of natural fires, volcanic eruptions, cyclones, tornados, hurricanes, flooding, and great extinctions of species long before the arrival of humans. Nor were indigenous peoples living in harmony with nature as they set fires to clear forests, hunted game, and pursued agriculture, cannibalism, and torture.[25] Carson reinforced a sentiment that would prevail in the modern environmental movement: humans, with their destructive technologies, profit-driven corporations, and uncontrolled need to dominate nature, had brought environmental catastrophe.[26]

Silent Spring became the most popular environmental book of the 1960s. It triggered a plethora of scientific and popular articles about the environment and alerted the general public to problems of industrial and environmental pollution.[27] Most important, it translated environmentalism into a broader challenge to living standards. Established environmental groups such as the Sierra Club, the Wilderness Society, and the Conservation Foundation built on public sympathies in their campaigns to protect the land, stop pollution, and champion the wilderness.[28] They called attention to massive increases in the production of chemical pesticides in the United States (from 124 million pounds in 1947 to more than

637 million pounds in 1960) and worsening air pollution (1960 saw more than 24.9 million tons of soot emitted).[29]

As awareness of these problems grew, officials began to redress pollution as a threat to public health. Both Democrats and Republicans responded by pushing new environmental legislation. Leading the charge were Senators Gaylord Nelson (D-Wisconsin) and Edmund Muskie (D-Maine), who earned the nickname "Mr. Pollution." Liberals demanded new environmental legislation, which meant working through the established legislative process. Many Republicans, drawing from a conservationist tradition that went back to Theodore Roosevelt, joined in supporting environmentalism.

President Kennedy responded to growing environmental concerns by appointing an activist secretary of the interior, Stewart L. Udall, an Arizonan who energetically promoted environmental protection. In 1962, Kennedy held a White House Conference on Conservation, and after the publication of *Silent Spring*, he asked his science advisers to look into the use of pesticides.[30] Following Kennedy's assassination, Lyndon Johnson pursued an aggressive environmental agenda by signing nearly three hundred conservation and beautification measures, as well as important legislation addressing air and water pollution, solid-waste disposal, wilderness preservation, and endangered species.[31]

The New Left Falls, Radical Environmentalism Rises

Although progress was being made, radical environmentalists warned that the crisis was at hand. Integral to this argument was a projection of global overpopulation, which portended widespread destruction of the environment, the exhaustion of natural resources, and famine. Paul Ehrlich's jeremiad *The Population Bomb* (1968) articulated this doomsayer vision, but the neo-Malthusian fears of an overpopulated world in turmoil were evident long before the publication of his book. Not all environmentalists agreed with Ehrlich's assessment. Commoner, for one, claimed that the environmental crisis was a result not of overpopulation but of capitalism's profit-first mentality, which led to the use of cheap, but polluting, technologies.[32]

The broader critique of capitalism had begun to appear in the early 1960s. Especially influential were social theorists Murray Bookchin, an

anarchist, and Herbert Marcuse, a Marxist. Writing under the pseud-
onym Lewis Herber, Bookchin published *Our Synthetic Environment* in
1962. This book linked a host of social and health problems to "human
ecology." Bookchin traced public health concerns, including heart disease
and cancer, to the "synthetic environment" created by corporate agriculture, food preservatives, nuclear testing, water pollution, and waste disposal. He declared that the "pernicious laws of the market place" had
been given precedence over the most compelling law of biology: survival.
He followed this book with *Crisis in Our Cities* (1962), in which he traced
urban blight and environmental deterioration to inequities in the social
system.

Marcuse, a Marxist philosopher who fled Nazi Germany before the
Second World War, provided a dense critique of how capitalism reduced
nature and genuine human feelings, including natural sexual urges, to
utilitarian ends. Marcuse's *One Dimensional Man* (1964) attracted much
attention on college campuses when it appeared, although it is doubtful
that many of those students who purchased the book had the intellectual
tenacity to wade through its heavy Freudian and Marxian analysis. Marcuse's general point, that capitalism's urge to dominate nature had led to
social alienation, seeped into the consciousness of many alienated youth
in the 1960s. The emergent counterculture held that modern man (and
woman) had become alienated from nature.

While radical environmentalists drew theoretical strength from
Bookchin, Marcuse, and Commoner, the counterculture of the 1960s
exerted an equally powerful influence on the environmental movement.
Young radicals and hippies rejected what they saw as a soul-deadening
consumer culture in favor of nature as a source of "authenticity."[33] Reports
of the defoliation of Vietnamese jungles by the United States projected
the horrors of out-of-control technology. For environmentalists, Vietnam
and the environmental crisis at home represented the same problem: a
technological and managerial ethos gone awry.

For many New Left activists, however, environmentalism presented
a distraction from the pressing liberation struggle of an oppressed black
minority at home and Third World peoples abroad. For certain political
radicals, environmentalists suggested granola-crunching, pot-smoking,
let's-all-live-together-in-peace-on-communes hippies. In the eyes of leftist activists, hippies were not revolutionaries. The struggle against racism
and imperialism lay in the streets, not in nature. At best, the environmen-

tal issue was seen as a way to educate people about the larger problems of capitalism, which leftists believed was built on racism and imperialism.

The election of Richard Nixon, a Republican, to the presidency in 1968 took much of the steam out of the student protest movement. The movement's last gasp came in 1970, with the protests following the Kent State shootings and the killing of two black students at Jackson State College in Mississippi.

Tom Hayden, one of the founders of Students for a Democratic Society (SDS), later captured the radical Left's descent into chaos when he observed that by 1969 "the radical movement became engulfed in bitterness, committing themselves to believing that reform was a fantasy and revolutionary rhetoric was somehow real."[34] Groups such as the Weatherman, a fanatical SDS faction led by Bernardine Dohrn and Bill Ayers, retreated underground to conduct a campaign of terror against government officials, the military, and local police. The final shock of the breakup of SDS came, Hayden writes, when Weatherman Terry Robbins, "working with manic urgency to begin armed struggle against human targets," crossed two wires and blew up himself and three others in a New York townhouse. Two others in the house, Cathy Wilkerson, a daughter of a wealthy business executive, and Kathy Boudin, the daughter of a radical attorney, stumbled out of the townhouse and went underground. The dynamiting of a University of Wisconsin building a few months later, killing a researcher, cast a "pall over what remained of the movement."[35]

Hayden, worried about a nascent police state, traveled to Berkeley, California, where he organized a commune, the Red Family. This group devoted itself to "consciousness-raising" sessions about male-female relations and studied Mao's *Little Red Book*, a collection of aphorisms by the leader of the Chinese communist revolution. Mao told readers, "People of the world, unite and defeat the U.S. aggressors and all their running dogs! People of the world, be courageous, dare to fight, defy the difficulties and advance wave upon wave. Then the whole world will belong to the people. Monsters of all kinds shall be destroyed."

By 1969 the reading of Mao was becoming rather passé in avant-garde revolutionary circles. Hayden's Red Family commune found, as Hayden put it, "a new object of idol worship"—North Korea's Kim Il-sung, whose "obscure theory of *juche* (self-reliance) called for struggle from the bottom up." Later, Hayden found it hard to believe that a group of "literate,

middle-class people" became "shrouded in this exotica," but this real-
ization came only after he was thrown out of the collective because he
was "into manipulating people" and a "politician." Hayden left Berkeley
and drove to Santa Monica, where he joined the Democratic Party and
became a politician in practice.[36]

As the New Left began to fall apart, Hayden realized the full potential of the environmental movement as an issue that concerned middle-
class white America. For radicals, problems of war, race, and the environment were part of a larger problem: corporate capitalism. As the New
Left magazine *Ramparts* argued in 1970, "Like the race crisis and the
Vietnam War, the ecological impasse is not merely the result of bad or
mistaken policies. . . . It is, rather, the expression of a basic malfunction
of the social order itself, and consequently cannot be dealt with on a
piecemeal, patchwork basis."[37] For New Leftists, ecological politics was
integral to general liberation politics and social transformation.

A massive oil spill off the coast of Santa Barbara in 1969 accelerated
the growth of the environmental movement by revealing the potential
for organizing the grass roots. Typical was the grassroots group Get Oil
Out (GOO), which sought to end offshore drilling. Activists mobilized
across the country to stop construction of power plants in "scenic" areas.[38]
In 1970, as the number of campus- and community-based eco-groups
proliferated, Senator Gaylord Nelson hired Denis Hayes, a twenty-five-
year-old former student body president of Stanford University and Harvard Law School activist, to organize a national environmental protest,
Earth Day.

Modeled after the Vietnam Moratorium in 1969, Earth Day was
intended to recognize the problems of pollution. Hayes, who had grown
up in a timber mill town in Washington State, took the stance of a radical critic of existing government and industrial policies. In a press release
shortly before the demonstration, he declared, "Ecology is concerned with
the total system—not just the way it disposes of its garbage." On Earth
Day, he spoke for social change when he told the crowd that gathered
in Washington, D.C., "We are challenging corporate irresponsibility.
. . . We are challenging the ethics of a society that, with only 6 percent of
the world's population, accounts for more than half of the world's annual
consumption of raw materials. . . . The major symbol of this death culture
is the institutionalized violence perpetrated upon people and the land by
corporations such as General Electric."[39]

One consequence of Earth Day was that the Republican administration of Richard Nixon sought to preempt the environmental issue by endorsing new clean air and water standards and establishing the Environmental Protection Agency (EPA). The Nixon program, however, failed to head off the emergent radical environmental movement. New consumer and public interest groups spearheaded by Ralph Nader and other activist lawyers, scientists, and environmental experts developed a more intense and anticorporate environmental legislative agenda. In the late 1970s key leaders from the Environmental Policy Center, the Environmental Defense Fund, and the Natural Resources Defense Council found positions in the Carter administration. So did Denis Hayes. Grassroots environmental groups led protests on the local level over toxic waste, river and lake pollution, nuclear energy, real estate development, and land use.

The environmental movement was not of one mind over strategy and issues. Some organizations sought incremental legislative reform or recourse through the courts. For example, the Environmental Defense Fund, incorporated shortly after Earth Day, pursued a policy of "sue the bastards" by taking polluters and developers to court. The Ford Foundation seeded money for another legal defense fund, the Natural Resources Defense Council, started by several recent Yale Law School graduates. (In the slow economy of the early 1970s, young lawyers had to invent new jobs for themselves.) In 1972 the Friends of the Earth was established to mobilize environmentally minded voters.

More radical environmentalists were not content with working within the legal and electoral system. They called for direct action, an idea borrowed from the civil rights movement. Calling themselves "eco-warriors," radicals adopted a "no-compromise" attitude toward environmental issues.[40] They were influenced by the Norwegian philosopher Arne Naess, who promoted what he called "deep ecology." Deep ecology rejected "biocentrism" for the view that everything in nature possesses intrinsic value. Man should not stand above nature but should accept "biospecies equality." Every living thing—deer, snail darter, tree, or human—should be seen as having equal worth.[41] Whether the concept extended to botulism bacteria or the polio virus is uncertain. Deep ecologists would be joined later by eco-feminists, who called for the end of "male" values that projected dominion over nature.

Over the next decade, direct-action environmental groups proliferated, including Greenpeace, which waged war to stop whale hunting. Earth First was formed in the early 1970s when five environmental buddies on their way back from a camping trip in northern Mexico decided that the only way to protect the environment was to throw "monkey wrenches" (sabotage) into development and timbering projects. Emerging at the same time was the animal liberation movement, which broke into animal testing laboratories, mink farms, and universities to release animals. Most famous were the Animal Liberation Front and People for the Ethical Treatment of Animals (PETA), but other animal-rights activist groups abounded, including Band of Mercy, True Friends, Last Chance for Animals, and Animal Liberators. In this same period, civil rights groups such as the National Association for the Advancement of Colored People (NAACP) began calling for environmental equity for racial minorities by claiming that African American communities were bearing the brunt of toxic waste dumps and pollution.[42]

In the late 1970s, Tom Hayden entered this emerging radical environmental movement.

Tom Hayden and the Big Green Campaign

Hayden personified the drift into environmental activism by former antiwar and civil rights activists. After he was expelled from his revolutionary collective in Berkeley, the distraught Hayden settled in Santa Monica in southern California, where he began to reevaluate his life. He understood that an American revolution was not in the works. The New Left had failed. As he recalled in his memoir, written when he was forty-nine, New Left revolutionaries had become "isolated, self-enclosed in a universe of political rather than human life." "In this sealed universe," he wrote, "social relationships were contained within organizations, language turned to jargon, disputes were elevated to doctrinal heights, paranoia replaced openness, and the struggle to change each other became a substitute for changing the world."[43] Hayden decided that the system needed to be changed from within.

He committed himself to working for Democratic presidential candidate George McGovern in 1972 and then became an enthusiastic supporter of the liberal Democrat Jerry Brown in his successful race for California governor in 1974. Hayden was attracted to Brown's "new generation" theme of a postliberal politics based on building local and state organizations around environmental, feminist, and disability rights, and anticorporate issues. Brown's election encouraged Hayden to challenge U.S. senator John Tunney in the 1976 Democratic primary.

Hayden began his quixotic challenge to Tunney by publishing a 278-page campaign document, *Make the Future Ours*. Hayden argued, "The radicalism of the sixties has become the new common sense of the seventies." The document called for "Government of the People" to replace "Government of the Corporations." It proposed an "economic democracy" in which a grassroots citizens' movement would provide a decentralized, nonbureaucratic alternative to "big government" or "corporate solutions." The themes echoed those of Brown's campaign. There was a good deal of rhetoric and a surprising lack of specifics in Hayden's call, but his campaign tapped into a generation of '60s activists who wanted to remain involved in politics.

Garnering more than 36 percent of the votes in the closed Democratic primary, Hayden did surprisingly well against an incumbent. The result left Tunney fatally wounded, leading to the election of conservative Republican S. I. Hayakawa, the president of San Francisco State University, who had gained national attention for breaking a yearlong, violent student strike at his university. Hayakawa's moment of glory came when, on television, he personally ripped out the wires to the protesters' loudspeaker system.

Hayden, the consummate organizer, transformed his Hayden for Senate network into the Campaign for Economic Democracy (CED). The CED sponsored successful rent-control initiatives in Santa Monica ("the People's Republic of Santa Monica") and helped elect more than fifty local candidates throughout the state. Its proposal for a solar-energy program was accepted by Governor Brown. Hayden became a member of Brown's inner circle and chair of the state's solar program. Brown also appointed Hayden as his representative on the U.S.-Mexican border. In Hayden's words, he became "the symbolic bridge for Jerry Brown to the sixties generation."[44]

By the late 1970s, life was treating Hayden well. He was married to actress Jane Fonda, whose Hollywood career was flourishing, with major roles in *Coming Home, Julia*, and *The China Syndrome*. The success enabled the couple to purchase a 160-acre ranch high in the mountains above Santa Barbara, while still keeping their residence in Santa Monica.

Their political efforts had built an extensive political network that laid the foundation for Hayden to run for the California state legislature in 1982. Although the district was 57 percent Democratic and quite liberal, the Democratic establishment opposed Hayden. In an especially vicious primary battle, each side spent more than $1 million, with Fonda spending over $300,000 on her husband's behalf. Hayden won the primary and went on to win the general election, 53–44.

In the State Assembly, Hayden worked on higher education and labor, but his greatest effort came on the environmental front. In 1986 he played a critical role in organizing Proposition 65, the Safe Drinking Water and Toxic Enforcement Act, which banned toxic chemicals in workplaces with more than ten people. The initiative was backed by a coalition calling itself Campaign California, which included the Natural Resources Defense Council, the Environmental Defense Fund, and the Sierra Club. It drew the support of key Democratic politicians including California attorney general John Van de Kamp, the heir to a food processing company. The campaign attracted the support of organized labor and Ralph Nader's Public Interest Research Group. Hayden and Fonda contributed more than $800,000 to the campaign, and through Fonda's contacts, Hollywood celebrities gave time and money to the initiative. The initiative won by a two-to-one margin in the general election. Inspired by this success, environmental groups took similar measures to New York, Massachusetts, Texas, Oregon, Tennessee, and Hawaii.

Jubilant about the success, Hayden and Van de Kamp decided to push the envelope further on the environment. In 1990, after months of planning with environmental groups and their lawyers, they came up with the most ambitious environmental legislation ever proposed up to that point. The initiative, Proposition 128, became known as "Big Green."[45] One of the most hotly contested measures in California history, Big Green called for phasing out all food pesticides determined to cause cancer or birth defects, the elimination of chlorofluorocarbons (CFC), and the reduction of carbon emissions by 40 percent by 2010. In addition, the measure would ban offshore drilling in the state and stop cutting in old-growth redwood forests. Perhaps the most radical provision was the creation of an elected environmental "czar" who would have the power to supersede all state environmental agencies and overrule the governor. Hayden was so personally invested in Big Green that early in the campaign he said publicly that running for the post of environmental czar was an option. Later, when opponents began to draw blood on this issue, he publicly denied any desire to become the czar.[46]

Van de Kamp saw Big Green as a way to reach the governor's mansion. The popular incumbent Republican governor, George Deukmejian, had announced that he would not seek a third term in 1990, opening the field to a Democrat. Initially, Van de Kamp's support for Big Green paid off, and he took an eighteen-point lead in the polls over his major rival for the Democratic nomination, San Francisco mayor Dianne Feinstein. But his own campaign staff split into warring factions, and his call for cleaning up politics in California alienated the Democratic political establishment. He lost the nomination to Feinstein, who would be defeated in the general election by moderate Republican Pete Wilson. Still, Van de Kamp established a formidable alliance of major environmental groups, including the California League of Conservation Voters, Campaign California, the Natural Resources Defense Council, and the California Sierra Club. Even after losing the primary, he contributed heavily to the Big Green initiative.

Van de Kamp also drew upon his close connections with Hollywood to promote Big Green.[47] Jane Fonda, who had divorced Hayden the year before, personally gave $100,000 to the campaign while generating more than $500,000 in campaign contributions from Hollywood. Robin Williams, Chevy Chase, Whoopi Goldberg, and Cher went all out for the initiative. Meryl Streep helped stage a fund-raiser that brought together celebrities and doctors in support of the antipesticide component of Big Green. On the evening of the Academy Awards, the Big Green entertainment committee, including Chase, Streep, Fonda, and Ted Danson, hosted a briefing on the initiative. Fund-raisers were held featuring popular rock groups such as the all-female band the Go-Gos. Wealthy Hollywood trial attorney Browne Greene hosted a fund-raiser at $5,000 per ticket for trial lawyers and stars. Cocktail parties were given by Kris Kristofferson, Burgess Meredith, Chevy Chase, Susan and Jeff Bridges, John Candy, Tom Hanks, Steve Martin, Nancy and Martin Short, and many others. Actor Ed Begley Jr. hosted a roller-skating party, and singers Bette Midler and Bonnie Raitt donated fund-raising concerts. As the campaign heated up, major stars produced and narrated a thirty-minute commercial backing Big Green.[48] The spot cost $100,000, and the executive producer was Tom Hayden. The commercial aired seventy-four times on local and cable stations in Los Angeles, San Diego, and the San Francisco Bay area.

The California effort received a big boost as the national media played up environmental issues. The organizer of Earth Day, Denis Hayes, planned a huge international campaign to commemorate the twentieth anniversary of the original event. The Turner Broadcasting System (TBS), the leading cable network at the time, made "saving the environment" into a major theme in its programs and public announcements. It produced an animated cartoon series, *Captain Planet*, in which the hero fought oil spills, plugged the hole in the ozone, and fought "smog monsters." TBS also introduced the weekly program *Earthbeat* to show how communities could help save the planet. In addition, Ted Turner hired environmentalist Barbara Pyle to produce documentaries for his network. Turner himself produced or acquired more than forty documentaries on the environment. He was a genuine environmentalist, but it was not a coincidence that he had begun dating Jane Fonda and would later marry her. The way to Jane's heart was through Mother Earth.

Turner was not the only industry mogul supporting the environmental cause. CBS began airing sixty-second spots, entitled "Earth Quest," that highlighted environmental problems. Network executives announced five one-hour specials on the environment. The title character on CBS's popular series *Murphy Brown*, played by Hollywood activist Candice Bergen, pledged to make her "lifestyle" more environmentally friendly. Not to be outdone, ABC's sitcom *Head of the Class* produced six episodes on the environment. Actress-singer Barbra Streisand and actor Kevin Costner hosted a two-hour special called *A Practical Guide to How You Can Save the Planet*.

Backed by the entertainment industry, the Big Green campaign made huge promises to the public for what the bill could accomplish if passed. Van de Kamp claimed that passage of Big Green would be a "bill of rights" for all Californians. He proclaimed, "This is a moment in history when we are waking up to the reality that we are killing ourselves." For his part, Hayden claimed that this was the most significant environmental proposal ever placed before the American public. This initiative would "end a decade of environmental neglect and begin a decade of environmental action." Other environmentalists told voters that through support of this initiative they would be making "a personal commitment to the planet."[49] Yet proponents realized they were asking a lot from California voters. As the Sierra Club *Yodeler* observed, Big Green asked the "voters to take some short-term economic risks in the name of preserving the planet and future generations."[50]

The thrust of the campaign was all or nothing. For instance, the antipesticide component of the bill took a zero-risk approach, declaring that any substance that might cause cancer or birth defects in humans should be banned, no matter how small the dose. Much of the data the campaign employed came from researchers at the Natural Resources Defense Council, which, in the words of social scientist Ronald Libby, had a "reputation for being careless with scientific data and exaggerating the danger of chemicals in food production."[51]

Sure enough, Big Green supporters made absurd claims in promoting the bill. The pediatrician Harvey Karp maintained that the pesticide Alar presented a mortal danger of cancer to anyone eating apples, especially the young. He warned, "When a two-year-old eats an apple, it's a little like an adult eating five apples—pound for pound. Over the lifetime of the child there is a cause for concern."[52] Echoing the sentiment in a TV ad, film director Oliver Stone declared, "I want my son to bite into an apple without worrying about cancer—today and fifty years from now."[53] Such fantastic claims belied scientific evidence: for humans to absorb the same amount of Alar that produced cancer in rats in laboratory testing, a human would have to eat 861 pounds of unwashed apples a day. Moreover, to blame increased rates of cancer on pesticides flew in the face of medical science, which said that the exact cause of cancer was unknown. Furthermore, medical research showed that cancer-causing agents were found in much of nature, including sunlight. Natural toxins and cancer-causing agents were found in tobacco, but also in beans, tomatoes, potatoes, lettuce, carrots, and corn.[54] Nonetheless, the campaign for Big Green played to public fears of cancer.

Initially, the intensity of the pro–Big Green campaign caught California business and farmers off guard. Business opponents divided into three groups: the Western Agricultural Chemical Association, the agricultural community, and the oil, aerospace, automobile, and utility companies. Opponents of the initiative were dismayed by the low rate of corporate giving. As field director for Prop 128 wondered, "Maybe the large corporations don't want to be perceived as not caring about the environment."[55]

But California industry and agriculture both feared that Big Green would drive business and agriculture out of California. Nonpartisan estimates suggested that there were considerable costs to the legislation. The California Legislative Analyst office in Sacramento estimated that the direct cost of Big Green would exceed $2.6 billion over twenty years. In addition, the bill's ban on offshore oil drilling might cost the state as much as $3 billion in lost revenue.

With early polling showing that voters favored Big Green, industry opponents organized a political action committee, the California Coordinating Council. Funding came from the California Manufacturers' Association, the Western Agricultural Chemical Association, and other business groups. Polls showed that they could have success personalizing the Big Green campaign. In meetings, they floated the idea of labeling Hayden the "environmental Ayatollah"; they did not use that term, but they did tag Big Green as the "Hayden initiative." In the end, the California Coordinating Committee's strategy centered on the economic costs of the initiative, which was estimated by them at $12 billion in direct losses plus a 40 percent increase in food costs if Big Green passed. The committee raised approximately $17 million to defeat the initiative.

California industry and agriculture, however, was not of one mind on how to defeat the proposition. California growers and the timber industry decided to propose their own counterinitiative, called CAREFUL, which called for strictly monitoring pesticides, not banning them. They hoped that CAREFUL would receive more votes than Big Green, neutralizing the banning provisions. Although CAREFUL drew upon previous state legislation that provided the most restrictive pesticide-control and food-safety regulatory programs in the country, environmentalists attacked it as a fraud to protect the pesticide industry.

In the last ten days of the campaign, each side spent more than $1 million on high-profile TV and radio ads. TV spots promoting Big Green featured television actors Kyle MacLachlan and Michael Ontkean claiming that CAREFUL would not protect Californians from cancer-causing pesticides. They also claimed erroneously that even Republican gubernatorial candidate Pete Wilson opposed CAREFUL.

Opponents countered with their own ads. In one spot, former U.S. surgeon general C. Everett Koop declared that Big Green was based more on emotion than on science. He said that there was no scientific link between pesticides and health. Koop told the press, "Big Green is a scare tactic not based on science." Big Green responded by saying that Koop was a shill for the pesticide industry and that CAREFUL was being financed by the chemical industry, even though financial records showed otherwise. Opponents of Big Green ran other, more sensationalist ads. One accused Proposition 128 of being "sponsored by Vietnam's representation to our Assembly, Tom Hayden."[56] Printed literature warned that Meryl Streep might become the environmental czar and that "Jane Fonda and Ted Turner will keep us happy watching the boob tube all day while eating our rice bran–fortified imitation crab legs." The vilification became so intense that the Sacramento County Superior Court ordered both sides to withdraw ads that were clearly false.

On Election Day, California voters rejected both Big Green and CAREFUL. Fully 64 percent of voters said no to Big Green. Proponents of the initiative said that negative advertising had confused voters over its intent. But by the fall of 1990 the economy was in a downturn, and public priorities had shifted away from environmental issues to economic issues. At election time only 28 percent of California voters placed the environment at the top of their list, while economic issues and jobs headed their concerns.

Some environmentalists realized that they had overreached. Carl Pope, conservation director of the Sierra Club, told the press, "It is clear that the public sent the environmental community a message. They said that they want environmental reform presented in smaller chunks, and that is the lesson for us."[57]

Others drew different conclusions. To some, the lesson was that ecological reform had to be dissociated from political elites. Reform needed to be sold to the average Jane and Joe as something that would immediately benefit their lives. Big Green had been supported by political elites in the state legislature and the state Democratic Party, and it had drawn a wave of celebrity support, but when faced with a choice between the economy and the environment, voters would choose a better economy. Environmentalists such as Tom Hayden, who remained committed to working within the system, realized that environmental issues needed to be linked to job creation.

More radical environmentalists, however, concluded that the democratic system could not solve the environmental crisis facing the nation and the world. The defeat of Big Green, and later defeats with the Republican administrations of George H. W. Bush and his son George W. Bush, led some radicals to conclude that the political system itself needed to be changed. Faced with what they perceived to be a cataclysmic environmental disaster, these radical ecologists dismissed working within the system.

Enter the Brave Green World

Both views within the radical environmental movement—that the political system needed to be reformed and the more extreme position that the existing system needed to be replaced entirely—were based on an apocalyptic vision that the global environment was on the verge of destruction. The scientific discovery in the 1980s that a hole had been burned in the ozone layer encouraged further despair. Radicals agreed that it was too late for incremental environmental change. The United States and its free-market system, as Barry Commoner had so persistently argued, simply did too much damage.

Facts about environmental progress belied radical cries of gloom and doom. In the two decades since Big Green was proposed, sulfur dioxide and particle emissions have steadily decreased.[58] Automotive emissions of toxic pollutants have been cut. Moreover, science and technology have improved the lives of people all over the world. Air and water have gotten cleaner. Endangered species are being rescued. Forests have improved. Americans are being exposed to fewer toxic chemicals, have more and better food to eat, and are living longer and better lives.

What radical environmentalists lacked was historical perspective. From the twelfth century through the mid-twentieth century, most people living in European cities, and later American cities in the industrial age, experienced filth: raw sewage; air filled with soot, smoke, and smog; water unsafe to drink; and epidemics that felled huge populations. Life was, nasty, brutish, and short. Although the discovery of germ theory in the mid-nineteenth century led to improvements in sanitation and community cleanliness, the industrial revolution after 1850 and even more so after 1900 introduced new problems, such as the pollution of groundwater supplies, toxic auto emissions, and factory effluents including metals, ozone, sulfur, and nitrogen oxides. Workers were exposed to asbestos, bis(chloromethyl) ether, beta-Naphthylamine, vinyl chloride, nickel, beryllium, and radiation.

Few people remember how bad the air used to be in cities. In Los Angeles, smog was so bad that television antennae disintegrated, houses were repainted every year, and people were warned not to go outdoors. Yet by every measure, emissions of sulfur dioxide, nitrogen oxides, volatile organic compounds, and lead and carbon dioxide have declined dramatically, owing to the introduction in the past two decades of petroleum and coal containing less sulfur, the installation of scrubbers and cleaning devices in power plants, and the introduction of catalytic converters and other technologies in cars. For example, emissions of lead fell from close to 350,000 tons in 1970 to zero by 1995; carbon dioxide emissions fell from over 120,000 tons to a little under 100,000 tons in the same period.

Perhaps most notably, the world production of chlorofluorocarbons (CFCs) has fallen precipitously, from more than 1,000 tons in 1986 to 200 tons in 2000. Corporations such as DuPont voluntarily restricted their emissions, and international agreements such as the 1986 Montreal Protocol brought further cuts. The result: the depletion of the ozone layer has been halted and reversed. To be sure, CFCs remain a danger to the atmosphere because they have a half-life of about fifty years. But the good news—which radical environmentalists have generally ignored—is that the ozone layer as a whole is safe for now.[59]

There is good news on other fronts as well. The water that most Americans drink is cleaner and safer. Although many streams and rivers are still polluted with phosphates, the ban on phosphates in detergents and the institution of local regulations and manufacturing standards have greatly reduced phosphate pollution over the past decade and a half. The release of toxic chemicals such as dioxin has fallen sevenfold since 1995. There are now twice as many lakes, ponds, and reservoirs as there were in 1950. There are more acres of forest in the United States than existed a hundred years ago.

The Endangered Species Act, signed by President Richard Nixon in 1973, marked the beginning of a concerted effort to save listed threatened species in America. This was an extremely ambitious and complex task. Recovery for an endangered species averages thirty to fifty years, and for whales a hundred years. Yet the record of recovery has been impressive for animals, birds, and plants. For example, there were an estimated 500 bald eagles in America when the legislation was passed; today there are more than 8,000. In Ohio, river otters increased from about 500 in 1995 to 5,400 in 2005; beavers from 12,000 to 30,000; and Lake Erie water snakes from 2,000 in 1999 to 7,700 in 2006. In the West, desert bighorn sheep increased from 7,000 in the 1960s to 19,000 in 1993. In

North Carolina, wild turkeys grew from 2,000 in 1970 to 17,000 in 1988. Efforts by the United States, Russia, and Japan have saved the Aleutian Canadian goose from extinction.[60]

Recent decades have brought other great improvements in American environmental health and safety. Since 1970 the rate of worker-related deaths has decreased more than 80 percent in U.S. factories and workplaces. Food is better. In the United States the AIDS epidemic peaked in 1995 with 73,274 cases, dropping to 38,730 cases in 2004. These improvements suggest that human life in America and the world has improved for the most part. Why? New technologies were developed to improve auto and industrial emissions. Drugs have been introduced to the marketplace to cure and alleviate human illness. American environmental consciousness, reflected in voluntary community efforts and in local, state, and federal legislation, have protected endangered species, recycled trash, preserved forests, reduced toxic waste, and improved the quality of lives. American democracy, as Seymour Garte of the Center for Scientific Review observes, is "good for the health of the environment and of the people, and the lack of freedom usually translates into poor health, degraded environments, and human misery."[61]

Instead of progress, radical ecologists have chosen to see a planet on the verge of catastrophe. They have called for a radical transformation of political and economic systems. For some, such as the influential ecologist Bill McKibben, radical change means that Americans should live differently. McKibben maintains that "growth is no longer making most people wealthier, but instead generating inequality and insecurity." His conviction that "we do not have the energy needed to keep the magic going" rests at the core of the belief that Americans need to downsize their economy, their lifestyles, and their expectations of the good life. Instead of pursuing economic growth, he argues, we need to change "our daily habits and our worldview in face of energy shortages, of global warming, and of the vague but growing sense that we are not as alive and connected as we want to be."[62]

McKibben calls explicitly for Americans to pursue a European model. Europeans, he writes, live in homes less than half the size of American homes, drive smaller cars shorter distances on average, and take public transit or walk or bike far more often. In touting the European model, he points out that Europeans use half as much energy as Americans use. While Europeans pay more in taxes to support health care and university education and "other things," they have less to worry about than do Americans. McKibben acknowledges that Europe is not perfect but still presents it as a model for what Americans can become. He ignores that welfare states across western Europe are bankrupt, with governments spending more than the revenue coming in through the high tax structure. And he fails to recognize that America spends about 40 percent more on its entitlement programs than what is being brought in by tax revenues. As a consequence, the United States at this point is financing its welfare state with ever more borrowing. A declining and aging population throughout western Europe has worsened this crisis. The European financial crisis, which is a result of profligate spending by public officials to support the welfare state and public service employees should have called into question the affordability and wisdom of extending further the hyper-regulatory state and projecting Europe as a model for the United States. If anything, Europe should present a warning to Americans as to how the green-entitlement-welfare state can bankrupt a nation.

Radical environmentalists' relentless call for economic transformation has focused more and more on changing the political system itself. Authors David Shearman and Joseph Wayne Smith argue in *The Climate Change Challenge and the Failure of Democracy* (2007) that the only way to avoid environmental disaster is to impose a new form of authoritarian government by experts.[63] They assert that the "U.S. democracy that offered freedom with diminishing collective responsibility is not a model that can sustain the world." The only alternative is authoritarian government. Shearman and Smith believe powerful elites in finance, media, business, and the military control liberal democratic politics in the Western world already. This elite controls citizens through a "cult of consumerism," a false consciousness in which people become convinced that happiness can be found through buying more and better things than their neighbors. "Consumerism," they declare, "has become the engine of capitalist society, consuming the earth's limited resources and creating jobs to stroke it. The fundamental nature of democracy is unsustainable."

In their view, liberalism is a philosophy of government based on man's control over nature. Instead, government ought to be founded on the principle of deep ecology, which sees "human beings as only one valuable species among many, and humans . . . are not more important than nature." This new government should be led by a "team of technocratic elites." Shearman and Smith warn that "humanity does not have the luxury of waiting."[64]

This dismal view of the world is echoed by the green political theorist Robyn Eckersley, who warns in her book *The Green State: Rethinking Democracy and Sovereignty* (2004) that democracy has failed in the face of an environmental catastrophe. Eckersley, too, believes that the liberal democratic state is finished. Instead, a new system of governance must discipline "investors, producers, and consumers." Drawing on class and gender critiques of liberalism "waged by social democrats, democratic socialists, and feminists," she calls for an "eco-socialist" system. She observes that "green theorists" are much more willing to "countenance restrictions on a range of freedoms," particularly those related to "investment, production, consumption, mobility, and the use of property." To save the environment, big government needs to restrict freedom, Eckersley says. Freedom to invest in a business of one's choice, or to produce what one wants, or to consume, move, or use one's property however one wants, must be abandoned. Government must control everything in order to work for the perceived larger community. The enlightened elite running the eco-socialist state should serve as trustees of nature because they "know enough about nature to protect it."

Eckersley's vision projects a nightmarish world in which arrogant, self-proclaimed ecologically conscious leaders restrict the freedoms of citizens in the name of environmental protection. In the older Marxist state, leaders claimed to represent the interests of the working class; in her vision, nature replaces the working class as the foundation of the state.[65] The concept of an elite, privileged vanguard in power remains intact. She imagines green social justice imposed by elite control of governmental power. The stench of authoritarianism, and worse, threatens to pollute the green paradise.

Through the Looking Glass Greenly

In pursuit of environmental justice, Bill Clinton issued Executive Order 12898 in February 1994. This ambitious proclamation instructed federal agencies to integrate "environmental justice" into their missions and programs. Clinton's order was in direct response to EPA administrator Carol Browner's promise to combat environmental inequity, a view that low-income communities, mostly African American, were suffering disproportionately from pollution and discriminatory regulatory enforcement. Such claims came from racial advocacy groups seeking funding and political empowerment. Careful studies of these claims have proved them to be false,[66] but racial justice and environmental justice were not easily disentangled in the political world.

A clear example of how racial justice has combined with environmental justice can be found in the case of Anthony K. "Van" Jones. In 2007 he founded Green for All, a nonprofit organization based in Oakland, California, dedicated to building what it described as "an inclusive green culture." The group promised to create millions of quality jobs for the poor by building a new clean-energy economy. Green for All wanted to set up community organizations that leveraged public and private investment aimed at disadvantaged communities to narrow income and social disparities. Jones's book *The Green Collar Economy*, published in October 2008, shortly before Barack Obama's election, reached number twelve on the *New York Times* bestseller list.

Jones brought to the environmental justice crusade a long history of black social activism. After receiving his J.D. from Yale Law School in 1993, he traveled to California, where he became involved in a protest over Rodney King, an African American severely beaten by arresting police officers in Los Angeles. Jones had supported a Marxist organization, Standing Together to Organize a Revolutionary Movement (STORM), which supported revolutionary democracy, radical feminism, proletariat dictatorship, and Third World communism. In 2001 he started a small organization with the pretentious title of the Ella Baker Center for Human Rights.

Jones moved into the environmental justice movement following Hurricane Katrina in 2005, when the Baker Center launched a campaign to promote green jobs within Oakland's African American community. By 2007 he had become such a nationally known figure that he was invited to be a delegate to the Clinton Global Initiative, an event sponsored by Bill Clinton's center to promote a new green global economy. Jones had traveled the path from radical socialism to environmental activism with ease. The road had been lit by the glow of social justice. While Jones was forced to resign as environmental czar, the mantra of environmental justice continued to be chanted within the administration. In February 2012, EPA chief Lisa Jackson announced that the concept of environmental justice was required in EPA regulatory standards and grants. "If we aspire to build an economy and a society that works for every American," she declared, "we can't allow the heaviest burdens of pollution and health threats to fall on our poorest citizens. Bringing together our federal partners to tackle these challenges is a major step toward health, environmental and economic benefits in communities across the nation." Her sentiments were echoed in other quarters of the administration. "We know that all too often, low-income and minority families live in the shadows of some of the worst pollution, leading to higher rates of diseases and threatening the economic potential of their communities," said Nancy Sutley, chair of the White House Council on Environmental Quality. "With these environmental justice strategies, Federal agencies are following through on the Obama Administration's commitment to reduce public health threats."[67]

Other activists had followed similar paths from political radicalism to environmental justice. Rennie Davis, a founder of SDS and codefendant with Tom Hayden in the trial following the Democratic National Convention riots in Chicago in 1968, became a New Age mystic warning of an environmental holocaust in which only countercultural freaks would survive and take power. Twenty-four years later, Hayden, who had at first been repulsed by Davis's mysticism, published *The Lost Gospel of the Earth: A Call for Renewing Nature, Spirit, and Politics* (1996), an eco-spiritual call for the world's religious to reflect great environmental awareness, an imperative step if the planet was to be saved. Having begun their careers trying to save America from itself, the New Progressives now sought to save the people of Planet Earth from themselves.

4

Controlling Life and Death

On a crisp morning, December 13, 1971, Sarah Weddington, a twenty-six-year-old attorney from Austin, Texas, appeared before the U.S. Supreme Court to argue for the plaintiff in one of the most important constitutional cases in modern American history: *Roe v. Wade*. When the court ruled in favor of the constitutional right to abortion in early 1973, it was a remarkable victory for Weddington, who had appeared in court only once before in her career, while arguing the case in Texas. Although the Supreme Court sought to balance the interest of a pregnant woman with the state's interest in "protecting the potentiality of human life," the decision upheld the constitutional right of a woman to have an abortion. This constitutional right, as the court interpreted it, was founded on the right of privacy and the due process clause embodied in the Ninth and Fourteenth Amendments. As a consequence, the state had no compelling reason to prohibit abortion. The Texas law prohibiting a woman from seeking an abortion was unconstitutional.

This right to privacy was exactly the argument Weddington had used in her brief. The brief itself was the work of a team of attorneys associated with the small radical student political community and the incipient feminist movement in Austin, Texas, the home of the University of Texas. This rights argument had great appeal in an era of black civil rights. Indeed, a rights argument for abortion gained wide appeal not only among progressives and feminists but also among large numbers of Americans, including many on the right, who believed that the United States was founded on the principle of individual rights and liberty. So attractive was this appeal to rights that longtime activists for euthanasia would translate their demands for assisted suicide and mercy killing into a rights argument—the right to die with dignity.

Yet the rights argument cut both ways: opponents of abortion and euthanasia pushed to uphold the rights of the unborn and the rights of persons who were aged or critically ill. The argument thus opened deep fissures in American politics and society. Those who proclaimed themselves defenders of the rights of women and the rights of those suffering from incurable diseases to die with dignity stood against those upholding, as they saw it, the "right to life." This argument over rights reflected irreconcilable value systems.

When arguing for abortion and assisted suicide, progressives also appealed to deep humanitarian concerns of the general American public. What kind of person, they asked, could force a fifteen-year-old girl to bear a baby produced by rape or incest? Which of us has not seen a loved one, relative, or friend suffer horribly from an incurable disease, leaving his or her family emotionally, and financially, drained? Should a person suffering from an incurable disease be allowed to die with dignity and without pain? By raising such questions, progressives made emotional appeals to universal human sentiment while promoting abortion and assisted suicide as a matter of rights, based on elusive definitions of privacy.

The progressive defenses of abortion, assisted suicide, and euthanasia expressed more than just an extension of individual rights within the long-standing American liberal tradition; they were part of a larger leftist crusade for social justice. Progressives saw abortion and euthanasia as instruments to address other social concerns, including limiting population growth, controlling welfare and medical costs, and reducing prison populations and indigence in America.

When Weddington brought the *Roe* case before the court, many on the left feared that the world faced an impending crisis of famine, war, and political turmoil caused by rampant population growth. Her political associates had emerged from the Austin New Left, whose underground newspaper, the *Rag*, continued to warn of the coming population crisis. Paul Ehrlich's *The Population Bomb* (1968) had warned of mass human starvation unless population was limited. Shortly before the *Roe* decision, the U.S. Commission on Population Growth and America's Future, headed by philanthropist John D. Rockefeller III, a grandson of the oil tycoon, had called for population control through family planning, sex education in public schools, immigration restrictions, and abortion on demand.

Sarah Weddington's husband (they would divorce shortly after the *Roe* decision) was a population-control fanatic. During the debate over the release of the morning-after abortion drug, RU-486, in the 1990s, he wrote to Betsey Wright, Bill Clinton's director for public outreach, in support of the new pill. "You can start immediately to eliminate the barely educated, unhealthy, and poor segment of our country," he declared. "No," he continued, "I'm not advocating some sort of mass extinction of these unfortunate people. Crime, drugs, and disease are already doing that. The problem is that their numbers are not only replaced but increased by the birth of millions of babies to people who can't afford to have babies. There, I've said it. It's what we all know is true, but we only whisper it, because as liberals who believe in individual rights, we view any program which might treat the disadvantaged differently as discriminatory, mean-spirited, and . . . well . . . so Republican."[1]

Progressive involvement in family planning and euthanasia had deep roots in the American reform tradition extending back to at least the early twentieth century. Involvement in such causes often overlapped. Many of the financial backers of family-planning organizations were also supporters of euthanasia, abortion-reform, and population-control groups. Supporters of these causes were brought together by a common belief that by breaking long-standing customs, especially those based on religious tradition, individual human beings could realize their freedom. Yet freedom meant control: control over living and dying. Control was to be exerted by the enlightened in the name of humanity.[2]

Progressive reformers in the early twentieth century were often explicit in their demands for social control over the population. They were convinced that America was threatened by waves of ignorant new immigrants from southern and eastern Europe and by social degeneracy of the native lower classes, including criminals, imbeciles, and the mentally and physically handicapped—all of whom brought poverty, social chaos, and the subversion of republican values and institutions. Reformers called for immigration restriction, which Congress enacted in 1921 and 1924. They convinced state legislatures throughout the country to pass laws that allowed state officials to sterilize the mentally disabled, the mentally ill, the deaf, the blind, epileptics, and criminals convicted of sex crimes.

Eugenics—the science of improving the physical and mental qualities of a population—was taught in biology, economics, sociology, and social science textbooks used in primary, secondary, and college courses. In the famous 1925 Scopes "Monkey" trial in Tennessee contesting a state law banning the teaching of evolution—a law ridiculed by eastern elites—the textbook in question included a chapter on eugenics, a fact ignored by pundits at the time and later.

The New Progressives who came of age in the 1970s were no less concerned with control than were their predecessors. They brought to the cause the emphasis on individual rights and choice. They expanded the progressive agenda, especially with the rise of feminism. Feminists called for the expansion of maternal health care at home as well as the humanitarian intervention of international organizations abroad to promote women's rights, female education, and economic development through projects designed for women. They also pushed for the global redistribution of wealth from advanced nations to developing nations. The new generation of feminists transformed organizations focused on economic development, world population, and global health, including the United States Agency for International Development (USAID), various United Nations programs, and private philanthropic foundations such as the Population Council and the Ford Foundation. In the 1970s women were sent into developing countries to promote maternal health and women's economic development projects, often on the village level. Typical of these field workers was Barack Obama's mother, Stanley Ann Dunham, who worked as a consultant for USAID, the Ford Foundation in Jakarta, and the Asian Development Bank in Pakistan on developing cottage industries for women.

The New Progressives envisioned a world revolutionized through new transnational organizations that would eventually replace the antiquated nation-state. The old establishment would be overthrown in the name of equality, the redistribution of wealth, and women's rights.

Creating the Population-Control Establishment

Population control is not a new concept. Plato spoke of population control in his *Republic*, in which a Guardian class could be bred to rule and the unfit were left to die. Clergyman Thomas Malthus proclaimed the need for population control in the eighteenth century. The policy of taking active steps to control world population, however, is a modern phenomenon.[3] At the end of the Second World War, many in the American establishment concluded that future wars could be prevented by a simply remedy: population control. Those associated with the Population Council argued that the cause of the Second World War was rooted in population growing at a geometric rate that outdistanced food supplies, natural resources, and land. After all, was not Europe crowded, and had not Hitler demanded *Lebensraum*? When overpopulation occurred, the inevitable result was famine, war, and death. But how could global population be controlled? Philanthropists, military leaders, wealthy industrialists, and scientific experts joined together to undertake one of the most massive global efforts in postwar history.

Giving shape to this vision was John D. Rockefeller III, an heir to the Rockefeller oil fortune and the brother of both Nelson Rockefeller, who became governor of New York and vice president of the United States under Gerald Ford, and David Rockefeller, who became president of Chase Manhattan Bank. In 1952, Rockefeller formed the Population Council. The first draft of the council's charter spoke of the need to control overpopulation and called for creating conditions in which "parents who are above the average in intelligence, quality of personality and affect will tend to have larger than average families."[4] The eugenics aspect of the new organization was dropped in subsequent revision, but the grandiose vision of controlling the world's rate of population growth remained. The Population Council set up birth-control centers throughout the world—in Hong Kong, Japan, Korea, Pakistan, Taiwan, Thailand, Malaysia, Ceylon, Tunisia, and the United Arab Republic (Egypt).

The Population Council represented the establishment. Serving on the council's board were university presidents, high government officials, and key figures from the foundation world.[5] Other organizations entered the field as well and coordinated with the council. The Ford Foundation poured millions of dollars into population control.[6] Advising on India's developing program on fertility control, the foundation provided technical advisers and research programs that led to millions of forced sterilizations. In the early 1960s the United Nations got involved in the worldwide effort to reduce population growth. Also joining the cause were Planned Parenthood of America and the Population Crisis Committee, founded by industrialist Hugh Moore, the founder of Dixie Cup. Moore predicted worldwide famine unless rampant population growth was stopped and played a critical role in creating the International Planned Parenthood Federation (IPPF) to take on overpopulation. He and other leaders of IPPF were participants in the First International Conference on Voluntary Sterilization in 1964, sponsored by the Association for Voluntary Sterilization, which Moore had helped to revamp. Financial support for these efforts came from the Rockefeller Brothers Fund, the Milbank Memorial Fund, the Scaife Foundation, and the Avalon Foundation. Mrs. Philip Pillsbury, the scion of the Pillsbury fortune, helped found and fund IPPF.

Funds from these large philanthropic foundations poured into research projects to produce better contraception, including new intrauterine devices (IUDs). Research funds from the Population Council and associated foundations helped develop an oral contraceptive—the Pill—that hit the market in 1960. Later funding was provided to develop the morning-after pill.

In its early years the population-control movement focused on international family planning by working with host nations to set up programs. With the election of John F. Kennedy, the movement saw an opportunity to increase federal involvement. To put pressure on the Kennedy administration, Hugh Moore placed full-page advertisements in the *New York Times* and the *Wall Street Journal* in August 1961 imploring the federal government to address the "population explosion."[7] At the same time, population-control advocates such as Cass Canfield, an influential New York publisher who had published Kennedy's *Profiles in Courage*, and General William H. Draper began lobbying State Department officials to send experts to developing nations to assist in family-planning programs.[8] They remained cautious about urging federally run programs within the United States.

Following Kennedy's death, Lyndon Johnson rapidly expanded federal efforts to eliminate poverty in the United States. The population movement put on a full-court press to link family planning to the "war on poverty." Advocates promoted family planning as a means of solving social problems in the United States. The rationale was simple: if the federal government could prevail upon the poor to have fewer children, poverty in the United States could be reduced. To accomplish this meant making family planning accessible to an estimated 5.2 million poor women in the United States. A disproportionate number of these women were black. It meant establishing birth-control clinics in America's inner cities.

This lobbying was done quietly and without fanfare, so as not to alienate the Roman Catholic bishops in the United States. One of the first signs that the lobbying efforts of Canfield, Draper, and Rockefeller were paying off came when Bill Moyers, an aide to Johnson, inserted in President Johnson's 1965 State of the Union message a single sentence that read, "I will seek new ways to use our knowledge to deal with the explosion in world population and the growing scarcity of world resources."[9] This line marked the beginnings of government involvement in promoting family-planning programs at home and abroad. Elite control and governmental power were starting to bring about the elite's version of social justice.

Family planning became integral to Johnson's war on poverty. The Public Health Service began supporting community health services through project grants and grants-in-aid to states. Secretary of the Interior Stewart Udall directed the Public Health Service to make family-planning services available to Native Americans. The Defense Department issued a policy that allowed for family-planning services to military personnel. USAID was given the go-ahead to initiate family-planning projects on a global basis. The head of this agency was Reimert Ravenholt, who had his business card printed on condoms.

U.S. involvement in domestic and international family planning drew the support of Republicans and Democrats alike. The impetus for this movement came from within establishment circles. In 1965 eight family-planning bills were introduced in Congress. By 1966 more than thirty states provided family-planning services. The Office of Economic Opportunity, a key agency in the war against poverty, launched fifty-five projects, located in public housing projects, churches, and community centers, designed to provide family-planning information and services to indigent women. The Children's Bureau provided formula grants to states for family planning, while the Office of Education funded 645 programs for developing family planning.

Under Richard Nixon, these programs were rapidly expanded through the Family Planning Services and Population Research Act of 1970. This legislation provided $382 million for services, research, and training in family planning. After Medicaid, Title X of this legislation became a primary source of federal funding for contraception. Critical to the enactment of this legislation were John D. Rockefeller, Hugh Moore, and William Draper, who actively lobbied Congress. In this way, the American establishment joined forces with Republicans and Democrats in Congress and the White House.

The population-control establishment was at the height of its power. By the late 1960s and early 1970s, anxiety about overpopulation had reached a fervid pitch. Popular magazines were full of reports of overpopulation. Science fiction books and movies such as *Logan's Run* (1967) and *Soylent Green* (1973) depicted the disastrous effects of what would happen when a society did not control its population growth.

Paul Ehrlich's *The Population Bomb*, published in 1968, exerted wide influence. Distributed by the Sierra Club, the book was a main selection of the Book of the Month Club and became a bestseller, going through thirteen printings in a two-year period. The Stanford University biologist predicted that the world faced mass starvation, irreparable environmental damage, and world war unless immediate steps were taken to reduce the rate of population growth. Indeed, he called for zero population growth in America and in the world. Draconian measures were necessary to save the planet. He said that adding sterilants to the water might have to be considered in the future, but before taking this step, Congress should enact "coercive legislation" that discouraged Americans from having more than two children. He recommended that Americans delay marriage and have childless relationships. Also, sterilized men should be given government grants. He spoke with the authority of a professor who knew what he was talking about.[10]

The book heavily influenced the environmental movement. Hugh Moore, who had established the Population Crisis Committee in the early 1950s, arranged to have *The Population Bomb* produced and distributed throughout university campuses across the country. Moore had become dejected by student protests against the Vietnam War, because he believed that the major crisis facing the world was overpopulation, not war. He saw in the emerging environmental movement the opportunity to highlight population issues. He helped fund the first Earth Day rally in 1970.

Predicting a horrific environmental crisis caused by overpopulation, activists began demanding coercive measures to stem domestic and global population. Kingsley Davis, a well-known demographer at the University of California, opened the debate as early as 1967, when he published an attack on voluntary family planning in an article in *Science* magazine, "Population Policy: Will Current Progress Succeed?" Rebuking the population movement for its voluntary approach to family planning, he wrote, "By sanctifying the doctrine that each woman should have the number of children she wants, and by assuming that if she only has that number this will automatically curb population growth to the necessary degree," leaders were missing the essential point. To attain zero population, they must first impose indirect coercive measures such as tax incentives and then, if these failed, take more extreme measures. He did not list what these measures were but said that they might read like "a catalogue of horrors." He declared, "The measures that would be required . . . though not so revolutionary as a Brave New World or a Communist Utopia, nevertheless, would tend to offend most people."[11]

Davis was not alone in his attack on voluntary family planning. Richard Bowers, founding member of Zero Population Growth, which had been formed in 1969 to promote a radical reduction in the rate of population growth, declared, "Voluntarism is a farce." He asserted that even legalized abortion on demand in all fifty states would not stop rampant population growth. Bowers urged leaders to consider requiring prospective parents to have licenses before conceiving, sterilizing welfare recipients, and enacting new criminal laws to limit population, "if the earth was to survive."[12] He proposed a model penal code that called for compulsory sterilization of parents with five children.[13] Zero Population Growth found widespread support among the wealthy. Davis gained the backing of donors such as Cordelia Scaife May, heir to the Mellon banking fortune, although more moderate advocates of population control such as John D. Rockefeller III refused to meet with representatives of the group.

So powerful were the calls for population control that even federal family planning went beyond the distribution of contraception in this period. In 1973 a lawsuit revealed that a federally funded antipoverty program had sterilized two African American sisters, Minnie Lee Relf, age twelve, and Mary Alice Relf, age fourteen, whose parents supported them through welfare. Further investigation revealed that under Great Society poverty funding, more than twenty-two thousand female patients had been sterilized in 1972 alone. Of these women, 40 percent were African American and 30 percent received public assistance. This sterilization program heightened fears within the black community. Even before revelations about the Relf sisters appeared in newspapers, the Black Panthers and other activist groups had already denounced federal involvement in family planning as a conscious program to reduce the African American population. Brenda Hyson writing in the *Black Panther* in 1970 warned that abortion and family planning were being used by "the oppressive ruling class" to kill off blacks and other oppressed people. She proclaimed that black women should reject abortion just as they had rejected "the attempt to force family planning in the guise of pills and coils."[14]

Many on the left were caught in a dilemma: their fears of overpopulation conflicted with their concerns for the rights of African Americans at home and women in developing countries, who were the focus of family-planning efforts. The calls for tougher coercive measures produced a backlash from feminists. Female activists had begun to pay greater attention to issues related to maternal health care, higher educational attainment for women, and advancing women's economic and social status in developing nations. Women's health groups called into question implanting birth-control devices into women in developing nations—often poor village women—without proper health-care systems. Problems of inserting IUDs on a large scale without proper follow-up care had become evident as early as 1965, when a Population Council study in Taichung revealed that 28 percent of girls and women in the thirteen-to-twenty-four-year-old age group had experienced pain and excessive bleeding. Feminists also criticized the so-called voluntary nature of these programs, pointing out that village women were offered money, food baskets, and rice to undergo IUD implantation or sterilization. USAID, headed by Ravenholt, came under particular attack. He had promoted a self-pumped "menstrual regulation" kit designed by a California abortionist.[15] Feminists were further outraged when USAID purchased and distributed the Dalkon Shield IUD even after allegations arose that it caused severe pelvic infections.

Protests from host countries reaffirmed the sense that population control had become a nightmare of coercion, ill treatment of poor women, and draconian programs. India's family-planning program under Sanjay Gandhi, the son of Prime Minister Indira Gandhi, was particularly shocking. Encouraged by Western leaders, American foundations, and the United Nations, Gandhi had instituted a far-reaching sterilization program. Through an incentive program and state-sponsored sterilization camps, millions of Indians underwent vasectomies and tubectomies. In the state of Gujarat one official declared that a "new world record" had been set when in just a sixty-day period 224,060 people were sterilized.

A political backlash in India caused the sterilization camps to be closed down, but state-sponsored sterilizations did not stop. A United Nations grant of $40 million in 1974–75 funded more than 1.4 million sterilizations.[16] In the village of Uttar in Haryana, the police surrounded a village and rounded up every eligible male, who was then sterilized. Sterilization became a condition for land allotments, water, electricity, ration cards, medical care, and promotions. In a one-year period, the Indian government recorded 8 million sterilizations, 6.2 million vasectomies, and 2.05 million tubectomies. World Bank president Robert McNamara observed, "India is moving effectively to address its population problem."[17]

Feminists and other activists were far less sanguine in witnessing these programs. The backlash came to include field officers who were charged with executing family-planning programs. These people in the field had grown discontented; they questioned the effectiveness of the programs and sought a larger social agenda. Reports of the political backlash filtered into the foundation community in New York.

The clash of worldviews erupted into a fight at the World Population Conference of 1974 in Bucharest, Romania. It was a strange place for a meeting on population control, if only because Romania's communist government had instituted a policy of expanding its population. At the meeting, the American delegation, headed by Health, Education, and Welfare Secretary Caspar Weinberger and General Draper, recommended reducing the average size of families and setting national quotas for population growth. The proposal drew fierce fire from an odd coalition of Catholic and Muslim nations, as well as China (which did not disclose that it had instituted its own restrictive population policy).

Opponents of the U.S. proposal were described as the "Non-Malthusian" coalition. Crucial to this opposition were feminist leaders who had gathered at the conference to call for a new social program to aid poor women of the world. Although women made up only 20 percent of delegates, Western female leaders including British feminist Germaine Greer, American feminist Betty Friedan, and anthropologist Margaret Mead led the attack on the American proposal. They found only one paragraph on women in the American draft plan. They joined with other female delegates to call for gender equality in education, employment, and development planning.

They found encouragement from John D. Rockefeller III, of all people. Ever sensitive to criticism, Rockefeller had commissioned Joan Dunlop, a feminist who had worked in the foundation and New York political worlds, to assess the Population Council and its programs. She helped draft Rockefeller's keynote speech to the Bucharest conference. It shocked even representatives from the Population Council. In the speech, Rockefeller issued "an urgent call for a deep and probing reappraisal of all that has been done in the population field." No longer, he argued, could programs simply target fertility. Instead, family planning needed to become an "integral part of a development program with a moral purpose: meeting human needs." He added the clincher that any such program needed to give "new and urgent attention to the role of women" and recognize that women themselves needed to decide what their role would be. Elite social control was beginning to become the elite pursuit of social justice.[18]

Rockefeller's opposition to the American proposal was stunning. The next day the proposal was voted down. As one Population Council member stated, "It was a humbling experience for everyone."[19] More was to come. In the following years the Population Council, the Ford Foundation, and other philanthropic organizations shifted their focus to improving the status of women. Change came more slowly to the World Bank, USAID, and the United Nations, but it came. The focus on women's issues did, however, contribute to the slowing of population growth: as women attained more education, entered the workforce, and delayed marriage, families had fewer children.

With a new agenda, feminists pressed the call for reproductive rights. In the process they clashed with antiabortion activists. Meanwhile, Americans remained divided on the issue of abortion. Then the Supreme Court reached its decision in *Roe v. Wade* in 1973, which opened a fissure in American politics.

How Abortion Became Constitutional Law

The population-control movement set the backdrop for the movement to legalize abortion. On the surface, legalized abortion should have been a logical consequence for the advocates of population control, but initially differences over abortion were apparent among family-planning advocates. Actually, Margaret Sanger, the founder of family planning in the United States, opposed abortion, although her critics claimed that this was only a political ploy to disarm opponents. In 1971, Frank Notestein, former president of the Population Council, argued in a lengthy memorandum that abortion should be seen as a "personal and social failure. Moreover, its widespread proliferation would, I suspect, detract from the value put on the protection and nurturing of individual life."[20] Many black leaders opposed abortion, including Malcolm X and the Reverend Jesse Jackson, because they believed abortion targeted the black population.

But in the 1960s the movement to liberalize abortion gained momentum. A loose coalition of feminist groups, population movement organizations, and single-issue abortion advocates helped organize a grassroots movement to liberalize abortion laws. At the time, each state determined the legality of abortion. All states had laws making abortion illegal but allowing exceptions for therapeutic abortions performed to save the life of a mother. Recent scholarship suggests that in the first half of the twentieth century, therapeutic abortion was more widespread than previously thought. (In the 1930s, Dr. Frederick J. Taussig, a recognized expert, estimated that at least 681,000 abortions were performed per year in the United States.)[21] Beginning in the 1940s, however, local prosecutors and medical practitioners began to enforce stricter guidelines for therapeutic abortions. Such abortions were still legal but became harder to get. Those women who did secure safe, legal therapeutic abortions in hospitals were mostly white women with private health insurance. Illegal abortions appear to have increased, creating a level of secrecy.

Some well-publicized medical cases helped foster public support for reforming abortion laws. In 1961, for example, the cases of pregnant women who sought abortions after taking the drug thalidomide, which was discovered to cause fetal deformity, drew widespread attention. Then, in 1963, an outbreak of rubella measles, a disease that often caused fetal deformity when contracted by a pregnant woman, drew further attention to the abortion issue.

Progressive elites capitalized on this attention to organize and promote a movement for reforming abortion laws. As early as 1959 the American Law Institute, supported by Planned Parenthood, drafted a model abortion law to provide guidance for liberalizing existing state laws. In 1964 abortion activist Alan Guttmacher organized the Association for the Study of Abortion to advocate reform of abortion laws. Soon the legal and medical communities joined the campaign to reform or even repeal existing state abortion laws. Crucial to these efforts were the American Civil Liberties Union, the American Medical Association (AMA), the American Public Health Association, and Planned Parenthood.

The campaign proved highly successful. Between 1967 and 1969, fourteen states passed legislation allowing for therapeutic abortion in the case of rape, fetal deformity, incest, or maternal health, which in some states was broadly defined to include mental anguish. Women in all regions of the country found legal abortions available in their own states or in nearby states. In the 1960s abortion services under these liberalized laws were widely advertised in the underground press. The mainstream media and the phone directory still found the topic too controversial to be mentioned.

The growth of feminism in the 1960s advanced this movement. Feminists demanded the right to legalized abortion. "My Body Belongs to Me" buttons captured the militant sentiment of the day. Legal activists such as Harriet F. Pilpel, legal counsel to Planned Parenthood, brought their expertise to the movement. Feminists helped shift the abortion debate to a rights issue. The National Organization for Women (NOW), founded in 1966 to promote equal opportunity for women, endorsed the repeal of abortion laws at its second national convention in 1967. Some NOW members resigned their membership in the organization over the pro-abortion resolution, but this was a minority opinion. Militant feminist groups on the local level, many made up of New Left and antiwar activists, translated their support for abortion into a larger social agenda to transform gender relations in America.

In 1968, Lawrence Lader, a longtime population activist, helped form the National Association for the Repeal of Abortion Laws (NARAL). He enlisted population activist Garrett Hardin, a biologist at the University of California at Santa Barbara. Also joining was Richard Lamm, a Colorado Democratic legislator and later governor, who called for restricting population growth through abortion, family planning, and immigration restriction. Lamm later advocated euthanasia for the indigent elderly to save taxpayer money. Betty Friedan, a founder of NOW, joined the new organization as well.

NARAL proved especially effective in its campaign. In just two years four states, beginning with Hawaii, repealed their abortion laws, permitting hospital abortions for "nonviable" fetuses. In New York, Governor

Nelson Rockefeller, John D. Rockefeller III's brother, signed a law in 1970 that removed all restrictions on abortion performed in the first twenty-four weeks of pregnancy. The law had been drafted by a Rockefeller commission headed by Alan Guttmacher. Alaska and Washington enacted similar laws. In California, Governor Ronald Reagan in 1967 signed a liberal abortion law, although he later regretted his acceptance of the bill.

Despite NARAL's legislative successes, the American public remained deeply conflicted over abortion. Polls showed that Americans did not support abortion in any and all circumstances, and the level of support for abortion under certain conditions often depended on the wording of the poll. Only when abortion was performed to save the life of a mother did a clear majority of Americans support the procedure. In general, African Americans were far less supportive of legalized abortion than whites. The public's ambivalence was evident not only in polls but also when abortion appeared on the ballot. In 1970 pro-abortion measures were placed on the ballot in Michigan and North Dakota. Both went down to heavy defeat. NARAL's Larry Lader admitted that the "abortion movement has been increasingly pushed to the defensive."[22]

Activists contended that the best approach to achieve a pro-abortion agenda was to file rights cases in the federal courts. The most helpful sign was that the Supreme Court had decided to review restrictive state abortion laws in Texas and Georgia.

The Texas case, *Roe v. Wade*, involved Norma McCorvey, a young, working-class woman who wanted to terminate her pregnancy. She was single, nearly destitute, and confused. She had been discovered by Linda Coffee, a feminist lawyer in Austin, who had joined Sarah Weddington, an attorney just out of University of Texas Law School, to challenge a state law prohibiting a woman from seeking an abortion. After the case, McCorvey accused Weddington of having used her; she had sought out an attorney in hopes of getting abortion counseling, not becoming a court case. Relations between the two sides did not get any better when McCorvey, a former alcoholic, drug abuser, and lesbian, converted to Roman Catholicism, rejected her lifestyle, and became a spokesperson for the antiabortion movement. Whatever the legitimacy of these later claims, McCorvey became only a name on the court case—Jane Roe— and once the case was filed, Weddington and her colleagues did not have much to do with her, especially when she eventually gave birth to the baby that the case was all about. In 2008, McCorvey endorsed Ron Paul for president.

Weddington, unlike many feminists who became leaders in the pro-abortion reform movement, did not come from an upper-class background. The daughter of a socially activist Methodist minister, she had bounced around west Texas as her father took up different churches in the region—Wylie, Munday, Canyon, and Vernon, "places so small many Texans have never heard of them."[23] Weddington recalled in her memoir that, "as a preacher, Daddy was not the fire-and-brimstone variety." Instead, his focus was the gospel of Christian social concerns. He acted in the reform-minded progressive tradition in pursuit of social justice. She was the good minister's daughter, singing in the choir, playing the piano, leading church youth groups. She shared her father's social concerns to "try to help others." After graduating from a college in Abilene at the age of nineteen, she decided to go to law school, in part because a guidance counselor told her that women did not do such things. In 1965 she became one of about forty women among 1,600 students at the University of Texas Law School.

Here she encountered a new world. Already inclined toward social activism, she became a feminist and began hanging around Austin's alternative newspaper, the *Rag*. She met Ron Weddington, an older law student and army veteran. He considered himself a radical and took it upon himself to educate the small-town girl new to the big city of Austin. When she got pregnant, both decided that they were ready neither for marriage nor parenthood, so Ron arranged for them to travel to, as she later put it, "a dirty, dusty Mexican border town" to have an abortion.[24] The day after the operation, Sarah was back in classes. They married the next year, but they never had children. Theirs was a generation that was convinced that the world was overpopulated, standing on the edge of a cataclysm of famine, mass starvation, and horrendous war.

Such fears were regularly featured in the *Rag*. That newspaper had begun in the mid-1960s as the official voice of the Austin chapter of Students for a Democratic Society (SDS), offering vigorous defenses of black power, feminism, and antiwar and anticapitalist sentiment. Even when the national SDS began to fall apart, the *Rag* continued publishing for the next ten years, remaining at the vanguard of the Left in Austin. As an alternative newspaper, the *Rag* brought together New Left radicals and the hippie counterculture through its espousal of the sexual revolution and "free love."[25] Through the *Rag* and the group that formed around it, Sarah Weddington was introduced to feminism and radical politics.

After graduating from law school in 1965, Weddington failed to get a position with a law firm, even though she was in the top 25 percent of her class. She felt it was because she was a woman. (We do not know how the other women in her class did, so there is no way of verifying her claim.) She got a position at the law school working as a staff member for an American Bar Association special task force to reevaluate professional ethical standards. She began attending meetings of Austin Women's Liberation, a women's consciousness-raising group organized by Judy Smith, a doctoral student at UT.

Smith and her sister Linda, who was studying anthropology at UT, exerted a powerful intellectual and personal influence in Austin's women's liberation circle. They brought to the group a political sophistication of East Coast activism that set them apart from a provincial Texas girl such as Sarah Weddington. The Smith sisters were raised in affluent Oak Park, Illinois, where their father was the superintendent of schools. Judy went to Brandeis University, where she took philosophy classes from Marxist philosopher and New Left guru Herbert Marcuse. After kicking around in political and civil rights activist circles, she moved to Austin to begin graduate work. Linda followed. The consciousness-raising group they helped form began reading a prepublication mimeograph of the feminist tract *Our Bodies, Our Selves*. Many of the participants in the group were writers for the *Rag*. In a house near the university, feminists in the group started Everywoman's Center to provide "liberated space" for women.[26]

Austin Women's Liberation, an activist group organized in Austin and at the University of Texas, established the Women's Liberation Birth Control Information Center. Weddington began doing volunteer work there. The center made connections with the national pro-abortion movement through the Clergy Consultation Service on Abortion, a national network of clergymen that had been organized in 1967 by twenty-one liberal Protestant ministers and Reform Jewish rabbis. But the Austin women's group lived in perpetual fear that they were going to be busted for offering abortion counseling, which itself was against Texas state law. As a result, women at the center were circumspect in offering advice on how and where to get an abortion and on which clinics below the border were safe. They created a cumbersome system to provide counseling.

Women seeking abortion advice would call a hotline at the Women's Liberation Birth Control Information Center during a certain hour and get a volunteer counselor's home phone. From there the counselor would get the caller's number, go to a pay phone, and return the call. It seemed a little paranoid, but as Weddington later observed, "In those days, as the saying went, you weren't paranoid if they were after you."

As the center counseled more women, many of the counselors were becoming burned out and increasingly fearful of the law. The Austin group did not believe it could work through the political system. A 1969 attempt to liberalize Texas abortion law had failed in the legislature. The activists saw the legislature, dominated by men, as a bulwark against reform. Texas was, as Weddington put it, "hopeless." Anyway, the Austin women did not want to liberalize the abortion laws in Texas; they wanted to make abortion an unrestricted constitutional right. The best way, perhaps the only way, to accomplish this was through the courts.

This was a logical conclusion for progressives to draw in the early 1970s. Electoral politics did not seem to be going their way. Richard Nixon had been elected president, and average voters were not getting on the progressive bandwagon. Thus, while proclaiming the virtues of democracy and speaking on behalf of the masses, progressives distrusted the people. They concluded that the courts were better instruments to promote their ideal of social justice. In this way, they followed in the footsteps of Ralph Nader and the early pioneers of public interest law. Judy Smith and another activist, Bea Durden, urged Weddington to undertake research into overturning the Texas abortion law, which had been enacted in 1854. In doing research, Weddington discovered both *Griswold v. Connecticut*, a 1965 U.S. Supreme Court decision overturning a state law that outlawed the distribution of birth-control devices, and a California Supreme Court decision, *California v. Belous* (1969), which overturned the state's antiabortion law. Both decisions pointed to a "right of privacy" and "liberty" in matters related to marriage, family, and sex. While Weddington was busy researching, challenges to abortion laws in the District of Columbia, Illinois, New York, and Wisconsin were pending in the Supreme Court.[27] The Texas feminists decided to join the legal fight. In the words of Weddington: "Around the nation, the big advances seemed to be coming from the courtrooms, not legislative halls. Shouldn't we be following the example of those who were winning, and file a court challenge?"

The Texas activists quickly decided to take the case to the federal courts. Early in the legal planning session, Judy Smith remarked, "It will take forever to change the laws against abortion in a state-by-state legislative process. But if we could overturn the laws through the federal courts, that would apply nationwide. Is that a possibility?"[28]

Weddington decided that she needed an attorney familiar with federal lawsuits to help her on the case, so she turned to her former classmate Linda Coffee. Coffee had clerked for federal district judge Sarah T. Hughes, a Kennedy appointee named at the request of Hughes's close friend Lyndon Johnson. After Kennedy's death, Hughes had sworn in Johnson as president. Coffee and Weddington had hopes that the case might be assigned to the Hughes court. But first they needed a plaintiff. They found one in a married woman who was not pregnant but who had a neurochemical disorder that might threaten her life if she became pregnant. They filed suit on her behalf, knowing that it was not the strongest case. What they needed was a pregnant woman seeking an abortion.

They found such a person in Norma McCorvey, a young woman who had gone to a Dallas lawyer for advice on how to get an abortion. The lawyer referred her to Weddington and Coffee. Weddington and Coffee believed that they had "discovered" their perfect case. They arranged to meet McCorvey at a pizza parlor in Dallas. McCorvey explained that she was pregnant and did not want to go through with the pregnancy. She had given birth already to one child, a daughter who had been taken away from her. She was uneducated, had a drinking problem, and could be classed in what later would be called the working poor. McCorvey met with Weddington and Coffee because she thought they could help her get an abortion. It seems clear from the historical record in Weddington's memoir, *A Question of Choice*, and McCorvey's two memoirs, one written as a pro-abortion lesbian and the other as an antiabortion born-again Christian, that McCorvey did not understand the full legal ramifications of the case. McCorvey's goal was to secure an abortion, not to win a historic case on behalf of all women. Revealing was her query whether it would help her case if she said she had been raped. She believed mistakenly that a woman who became pregnant after a rape might be eligible for an abortion. Weddington told her that it would not help; in any case, both attorneys did not want the Texas law changed to include only abortion in cases of rape.

The lawyers told McCorvey that she could remain anonymous and would not have to answer written or oral questions from opposing lawyers.

She agreed to be a plaintiff. After that, Weddington and Coffee did not have much contact with her other than to tell her later they had won the case in the federal district court. McCorvey could have been anyone for Weddington and Coffee. As Weddington put it, the case stood for "all women, not just one." McCorvey represented an abstract universal cause, not a case of a poor, disoriented, and scared woman faced with the ugly reality of her own limitations as a parent and a person.[29]

The legal petition the attorneys filed on behalf of "Jane Roe" and against Henry Wade, the elected district attorney of Dallas County, was only three legal-sized papers. They got lucky. *Roe* landed in Sarah Hughes's court on May 22, 1970. When Sarah Weddington stood to argue the case, she was only twenty-five years old. As the nervous Weddington rose, Judge Hughes gave her a "reassuring smile and a slight wink," as if to say, "Don't be nervous, everything will be fine."[30]

The court ruled in favor of the plaintiff on June 17, 1970, making it national news when the Dallas district attorney decided to appeal the decision. The case ended up in the U.S. Supreme Court. Weddington and Coffee received phone calls from across the country from pro-abortion lawyers and activists. Among these callers was Margie Pitts Hames, the attorney in *Doe v. Bolton*, a Georgia case in which a married pregnant woman who had been a mental patient in a state hospital was seeking an abortion. This was to become a companion case to *Roe* in the Supreme Court. Another who called was Roy Lucas, a New York City attorney and president of the James Madison Constitutional Law Institute. Weddington accepted his offer to assist on the case. She traveled to New York to spend the summer of 1971 working with him to prepare for argument.

In his final year at New York Law School in 1965, the South Carolina–born Lucas had played a critical role in developing a privacy argument on behalf of married couples using contraception. This privacy argument became the basis of *Griswold v. Connecticut* (1965). Lucas developed a more finely tuned privacy argument for abortion based on the First, Fourth, Fifth, Ninth, and Fourteenth Amendments. Weddington drew on Lucas's refinement of the right to privacy in preparing for her argument.

At the heart of the brief Weddington prepared was a call for fundamental personal rights, including the right to marital and personal privacy. At issue was whether a fetus could be equated with a human being. Here, Weddington drew on the research of her husband, Ron, who argued that the unborn fetus was not legally a human being and the destruction of a fetus was not considered murder under the law. The logic of their argument was that abortion at any stage should be made a private decision of the woman. As Justice Potter Stewart suggested when Weddington argued before the Supreme Court, "If it were established that the fetus were a life, you would have a difficult case, wouldn't you?"

Although the right to privacy became the focus of the Supreme Court case, concerns about overpopulation provided much of the impetus for the pro-abortion side. Through Lucas, Weddington made contact with Harriet Pilpel of Planned Parenthood. Pilpel was a skilled lawyer who had served on the Kennedy Commission on the Status of Women and as a legal consultant to the Women's Bureau of the United States Department of Labor. She saw abortion as a woman's right and as a means of population control. In "The Right of Abortion," an article in the June 1969 *Atlantic Monthly*, she argued that although abortion should not be the first method of population control, "to cut down on population growth we should make abortion easy and safe while we continue to develop other and more satisfactory methods of family limitation." She noted that when Japan liberalized its abortion laws some years back, "it halved its rate of population growth in a decade."[31]

Pilpel was not the only addition to the legal team who saw legalized abortion as a necessary means of population control. Nick Danforth, the vice president of the James Madison Constitutional Law Institute, was an avid population-control advocate. A graduate of Phillips Academy Andover, Yale, and Columbia, he was a specialist on Africa and world population. He became director of the Population Law Center and after *Roe* went to work for USAID organizing population-control programs. Another member of the team, Yale law student David Tunderman, studied the links between environmental problems and world overpopulation.

For men such as Hugh Moore and John D. Rockefeller III, who saw overpopulation as the primary threat facing humanity, legalized abortion may have been more of a means than an end. But for Weddington and many women, legalized abortion was not simply about dealing with the approaching population crisis; it represented part of the larger struggle for women's liberation in modern America. Abortion and population control were conjoined causes, distinct but related entities.

On January 22, 1973, the U.S. Supreme Court issued its ruling in the case of *Roe v. Wade*. By a 7–2 vote, the court ruled in favor of McCorvey, determining that abortion was a fundamental right under the United States Constitution. Justice Harry Blackmun, who was both an attorney and a physician, wrote the majority opinion. The court noted that the abortion issue was "sensitive and emotional," complicated by issues of "population growth, pollution, poverty, and racial overtones." While the court granted that a woman had a constitutional right to abortion under the due process clause, it held that the state in the second trimester of a woman's pregnancy could regulate the abortion procedure "in ways that are reasonably related to maternal health, and in the third trimester, the state could restrict or proscribe abortion as it sees fit when the fetus is viable." As a consequence, the court did not accept the plaintiff's implicit argument for what later became known as abortion on demand.

The decision ignited a firestorm of grassroots protest that shaped American politics for the next generation. The court's peculiar trimester approach, Blackmun's singular gift to jurisprudence, ensured a never-ending series of legal battles as state legislatures sought to regulate abortion. Never had an inexperienced justice seeking to impose a "reasonable" compromise provoked so much rage.

One of the first signs of the political explosiveness of the abortion issue came in the summer of 1969 when President Nixon's Commission on Population Growth and America's Future, chaired by John D. Rockefeller III, formally recommended the liberalization of state abortion laws to provide for abortion on demand (or as the commission politely put it, "abortion on request"). Rockefeller's commission also called for abortion services to be provided for poor women. The commission's concern with overpopulation shaped its recommendations. The commission's final report noted, "We are impressed that induced abortion has a demographic effect wherever legalized." The commission was careful to note that abortion should be "only a back-up measure in cases of contraceptive failure." But the report added, "To the moral poignancy involved in [abortion's] use must be balanced the moral poignancy of a woman giving birth to an unwanted child and even more, the moral poignancy of the child's prospective life."[32]

The Rockefeller Commission's report immediately proved controversial. Two members of the commission, a Hispanic and an African American, were so disturbed by the report's call for abortion on demand and immigration restriction that they issued a minority report. When the Rockefeller report was released, it drew fire from Roman Catholic bishops, who opposed abortion. Eager to lure Catholics away from the Democratic Party, Richard Nixon rejected the Rockefeller Commission report in a press conference organized to draw publicity to his newfound commitment to "life."

John D. Rockefeller III was shocked by the president's rejection and the negative public response to his report. He believed that the commission had failed not just because of Nixon's political calculation to win the Catholic vote but also because of an intransigent and unenlightened public. Public attitudes needed to be changed.

Rockefeller became quite visible in his support of abortion. By 1976 he was writing in an op-ed in *Newsweek*, "We must uphold freedom of choice. Moreover, we must work to make free choice a reality by extending safe abortion services throughout the United States." Over the next decade he became a major donor to NARAL, Planned Parenthood, the American Civil Liberties Union Reproductive Freedom Project, the Center for Constitutional Rights, the Association for the Study of Abortion, the Alan Guttmacher Institute, Zero Population Growth, and an array of other activist groups. When NARAL began experiencing financial problems in 1974 after the victorious *Roe* decision seemed to have concluded the battle, Rockefeller stepped in to boost the organization's annual budget.

At the same time, he promoted sex education. Joining forces with the Ford Foundation, he became a major donor to the Sex Information and Education Council of the United States (SIECUS), headed by Dr. Mary Calderone, a longtime population-control and abortion advocate who had worked for Planned Parenthood. Rockefeller provided $50,000 to fund SIECUS programs in New York to make students aware of their sexual identities so as not to feel guilty about their natural self-exploration, masturbation, and desires "to explore the genitals of other children."[33] This interest in sex education led Rockefeller to support homosexual rights. In 1977 he became a major financial backer in the making of a public television documentary, *Who Are We?* Produced by pioneering filmmaker Peter Adair, the hour-long documentary focused on eight homosexuals from various walks of life to provide role models for young gays and lesbians. Rockefeller hosted a private showing for civil and religious leaders in his office at Rockefeller Center.

In the two decades that followed *Roe*, the battle over abortion rights continued to be fought in the courts. The Supreme Court issued twenty major decisions concerning abortion that basically upheld the core of *Roe*, even while the trimester approach came under challenge. In *Planned Parenthood of Southeastern Pennsylvania v. Casey* (1992), the court substituted the doctrine of undue burden as a new standard for state regulation of abortion, but *Roe* remained the law of the land—somewhat bruised, still under attack, but standing.

The rights argument developed by abortion advocates had a powerful effect on the American public. Proponents of assisted suicide and euthanasia turned to this rhetoric in promoting their own causes. Whereas eugenics and overpopulation had provided the impetus for the early proponents of euthanasia, now it was medical costs, easing human suffering, and the right to control one's life, even in death, that became the focus of the euthanasia debate.

Controlling Death

The Judeo-Christian tradition from the first century A.D. to the twentieth century condemned suicide and mercy killing as an outrage against the sanctity of human life.[34] Medical doctors, having taken the Hippocratic Oath to protect life, have accepted this tradition. Indeed, organized medicine's opposition to "active" euthanasia—that is, terminating a very sick patient's life so as to prevent pain (as opposed to removing life support from a dying patient)—became more adamant at the end of the nineteenth century as advances were made in modern medicine.

Yet the Progressive Era brought a new faith in scientific progress to address social ills. Anxious about the nation's growing social problems related to poverty, urban squalor, prostitution, alcoholism, and crime, many progressives embraced eugenics as central to reform. Interest in euthanasia and state sterilization laws coincided with this enthusiastic embrace of eugenics. Such reformers believed they were working from humane motives, but their efforts also embodied a progressive belief in elite leadership and an impulse for social control.

Progressives advocated selective infanticide for physically defective infants and mercy killing for epileptics, imbeciles, and incurable alcoholics. In 1906, Ohio became the first state to introduce a bill permitting assisted suicide through narcotics of consenting adults "suffering enormous pains that could not be relieved otherwise."[35] Although the bill was buried in committee, legislation of this kind gained momentum during the next two decades of the Progressive Era. America's entry into World War I put a temporary brake on the drive for eugenic sterilization and euthanasia legislation, but the movement was far from dead. Sterilization laws continued to be enacted throughout the 1920s. From 1905 to 1931, twenty-eight states passed such laws. In 1927 state sterilization laws survived constitutional challenge in *Buck v. Bell*.

The crusade for eugenics reform was carried on by activists such as Charles Francis Potter, a Unitarian minister who played a central role in the founding of the Euthanasia Society of America in 1938. Progressives such as Potter saw in eugenics a catholicon, a fulfillment of human freedom. In the 1930s he became America's leading advocate of mercy killing. He argued that if women deserved the freedom to control their fertility through contraception, then all humans deserved the right to decide when, where, and how they died. In language startlingly similar to that used in the Third Reich, he declared that mercy killing should be "legalized, safeguarded, and supervised by the state."[36] Potter's demand for mercy killing went beyond voluntary choice. He declared that handicapped infants, the incurably insane, and the mentally retarded should be "mercifully executed by [the] lethal chamber," noting, "It is simply our social cowardice that keeps [imbeciles and idiot 'monsters'] alive."[37]

Eugenics as a theory came under disfavor after World War II, when Nazi genocide in the name of "race betterment" was revealed to a shocked world, but the euthanasia movement had hit upon a strategy of voluntary euthanasia that became the focus of their crusade. Not every member of the Euthanasia Society agreed with this approach, and fierce factionalism divided the organization. In 1943 one society committee called for involuntary euthanasia for "idiots, imbeciles, and congenital monstrosities." Eugenics continued to lurk beneath the surface of the euthanasia movement.

In the aftermath of the Second World War, the movement to legalize euthanasia, voluntary and involuntary, continued to attract progressive support. The euthanasia movement gained traction with the American public in the mid-1950s and further momentum in the 1970s. In the latter decade, Americans became obsessed with death, or so it appeared. Movies such as *Brian's Song*, *I Never Sang for My Father*, and *They Shoot Horses, Don't They?* revealed that dying (not just death) had become a major theme in American culture. Colleges and medical schools taught courses about dying. In the summer of 1972, Senator Frank Church, a liberal Democrat from Idaho and a near-death cancer survivor at nineteen, held congressional hearings on "death with dignity." Elizabeth Kübler-Ross's *On Death and Dying* (1969) sold one million copies.

The Euthanasia Society welcomed this new awareness of dying, as it began allying itself with new reform groups and leading figures. Society speakers began sharing the podium with Alan Guttmacher, president of Planned Parenthood, and the society's board member John Rock, co-discoverer of the oral contraceptive pill, as well as representatives of pro-abortion groups. By 1975, after changing its name to the Society for the Right to Die, the organization claimed seventy thousand members and had an annual budget of $400,000.

The power of a rights argument gained momentum with books such as Olive Ruth Russell's *Freedom to Die: Moral and Legal Aspects of Euthanasia*, published in 1975. In this triumphant history of the right-to-die movement, Russell depicted euthanasia as an achievement of reason. She dismissed the "slippery slope" argument that assisted suicide might lapse into a Nazi practice of having the state eliminate unwanted or burdensome citizens. If assisted suicide was an open practice, as opposed to the cold-blooded, secretive practices of the Nazis, Americans need not worry about euthanasia. *Freedom to Die* conveniently skipped over the eugenic support for euthanasia that had characterized the early movement. Russell also did not mention that she was a strong supporter of mercy killing for disabled persons without their consent. In addition, she advocated euthanasia as one method for addressing the "surging rise of the number of physically and mentally crippled children" caused by the "population explosion."[38] Russell's book proved highly influential in the growing debate over euthanasia.

That debate reached state legislatures. In 1974, Democratic state representative Walter Sackett, a physician, introduced a euthanasia bill in the Florida state legislature and tried to get "the right to die with dignity" into the state's bill of rights. Between 1969 and 1976, thirty-five bills were introduced in twenty-two state legislatures.

The euthanasia movement's image was set back early in the 1990s by Dr. Jack Kevorkian's crusade to legalize physician-assisted suicide. Kevorkian had gained national attention when he appeared on the television talk show *Donahue* to promote his suicide machine, the "mercitron."

When he used his machine on a woman in Michigan diagnosed with Alzheimer's disease, he became a national figure. Over the next eight years he assisted in the suicides of ninety-three people. Kevorkian's dour image and categorical fanaticism repulsed the general public. Reports that involuntary euthanasia was occurring in the Netherlands, which had legalized physician-assisted suicide, also hurt the movement.

How Oregon Became the First State to Legalize Physician-Assisted Suicide

Despite those setbacks, the euthanasia movement achieved a political and cultural triumph in 1994 when Oregon became the first American state to legalize physician-assisted suicide. How this initiative was passed reveals just how far the euthanasia movement had come. It marked a New Progressive triumph in using governmental power to enact a leftist vision of social justice.

The architect of the measure was Derek Humphry, a British advocate of euthanasia. Humphry had developed his own "expertise" in the field. In 1975 he helped his first wife, Jean, who was suffering from terminal breast cancer, commit suicide by mixing a lethal dose of drugs. He recounted his involvement in her suicide in *Jean's Way* (1979), which became a bestseller. In 1991 he wrote *Final Exit: The Practicalities of Self-Deliverance and Assisted Suicide for the Dying*. It would sell more than one million copies and be named by *USA Today* one of the most influential twenty-five books of the past quarter century. Along the way he had written a number of books on race relations in America, including *Because They're Black* (1971) and *Police Power and Black People* (1972), an exposé of police brutality against blacks. A strong supporter of abortion, Humphry was a self-described investigative reporter on the left side of the political spectrum, as evidenced in his self-published memoir, *Good Life, Good Death: Memoir of an Investigative Reporter and Pro-Choice Advocate*.[39]

In 1980, Humphry formed the Hemlock Society to advocate for euthanasia at the grassroots level. Under his guidance, the Hemlock Society specialized in offering "how-to" advice to commit suicide, including describing ways of suffocation with a plastic bag, providing drug-dosage tables, and listing the merits of eighteen different barbiturates. Humphry left the society in 1992, because it had become too conservative for his taste. By then, however, the Hemlock Society boasted eighty-six chapters across the United States with fifty-seven thousand members. The society's activists played a major role in the battles for legalized assisted suicide.

Humphry had founded the Hemlock Society with his second wife, Ann Wickett. The marriage lasted only nine years, ending in divorce. Two years later, at the age of forty-nine, Ann committed suicide. She was battling breast cancer, which was in remission, as well as recurring depression. In her suicide note, she claimed that Humphry was a "killer" who had murdered his first wife, Jean. There was no evidence to support this charge, but the accusation cast a shadow over Humphry—a hero to euthanasia advocates, a figure darker than Dr. Kevorkian to his enemies. His opponents ignored Humphry's declaration that "suicide as such should be prevented wherever possible. I would campaign against suicide for the elderly, or the disabled, or the mentally ill."[40] Instead, they focused on Humphry's tough-minded, detailed description of how a terminally ill patient could use a plastic bag to kill himself.

Humphry moved to Oregon from California in 1988. He played a key role in pushing the Oregon assisted-suicide legislation that appeared on the ballot in 1994. His protégé Cheryl Smith authored the first draft of the measure at the Hemlock Society headquarters in Portland. Described by local newspapers as "a brilliant, if eccentric woman," Smith held a law degree from Iowa and had served as top aide to the Hemlock Society from 1989 to 1993, editing Humphry's *Final Exit*.

As the measure was drafted, tensions immediately rose among supporters over the means of assisted suicide: whether to legalize a prescribed oral drug or a lethal injection administered by a registered caregiver. Humphry was for lethal injection—much along the lines of the Dutch system. Smith sided with her mentor Humphry, and the first drafts of the legislation endorsed active euthanasia by allowing direct doctor involvement in assisted suicide.

In August 1993, Humphry commissioned a national poll to determine what words worked best for the legislation. Sixty-five percent of the respondents endorsed the phrase "to die with dignity." The initiative became known as the Oregon Death with Dignity Act. Smith and the authors of the initiative rejected lethal injection by physicians, owing to the public's concern about abuse, and the Oregon medical profession overwhelmingly opposed it, because it went against the Hippocratic Oath and raised liability issues.

The initiative was filed in December 1993 after this small group of activists organized a petition drive. It appeared as Measure 16 on the ballot. The measure came under immediate attack by the Roman Catholic Church, right-to-life groups, disability advocates, and the AMA. The AMA warned that fatal dosages of prescription medicines varied widely, and some patients could take days to die.[41] Among those endorsing the initiative were the Oregon Democratic Party and state chapters of the American Civil Liberties Union and NOW.

Both sides mobilized to win the public. Proponents warned that the Catholic Church and fundamentalist Christians were trying to impose their religious beliefs on the larger society. One Measure 16 petitioner declared, "They [Catholics] want to impose their own unique theological perspective on the entire state."[42] A television ad asked, "Are we going to let one church make the rules for all of us?"[43] In the most secular state in the union, where less than a third of the population had any religious affiliation, warnings about religious intolerance were especially powerful. Oregon's 297,000 Catholics were only about 10 percent of the state's population, and Catholic Church attendance in the state was the lowest in the country.[44]

The AMA's opposition to physician-assisted suicide also drew criticism. The AMA had come out against the legalization of assisted suicide, arguing that it was an unethical act inconsistent with the physician's professional role and that advanced techniques in pain management made assisted suicide unnecessary. Humphry attacked the AMA for being a reactionary organization that had opposed women doctors, Medicare, and legalized abortion.[45] Meanwhile, the Oregon chapter of the AMA deadlocked over the measure, finally voting not to take a position.

Much of the debate was ideological. It was also about money, although most advocates shied away from this argument. Barbara Coombs Lee, a nurse and vice president of a Portland-based managed-care company, was an exception. She was particularly critical of the American healthcare system for prolonging the life of the terminally ill. She maintained that the health system promoted "invasive care over conservative management, heroic measures over compassionate ones, and pursuit of futile intervention over peaceful and painless death." Doctors who enlisted technology to keep terminally ill people alive, she said, did so for ethical reasons and because "it also pays." She called physician-assisted suicide a call for rationalized care—and compassion.[46]

Proponents of Measure 16 adopted the rights-based argument that had proved so powerful for advocates of abortion. Calling physician-assisted suicide a right, supporters of the measure mounted an advertising campaign that appealed to autonomy, a deeply held value for Oregonians. Ads told emotional stories of people in horrible pain, wanting to die, if only they could. Measure 16 campaign coordinator Geoff Sugerman felt that it was simply a "choice and control issue."[47] The initiative was about individual choice and control over one's body. As Humphry put it, physician-assisted suicide was "the ultimate civil liberty."[48]

Religious opponents of Measure 16 feared that physician-assisted suicide was the first step toward generalized euthanasia for the infirm, aged, and poor. Dr. Thomas Manning, a Catholic physician who worked for the Indian Health Service, captured this sentiment when he told a reporter, "One of the biggest concerns I have is that we would see incredible pressure being placed on people, poor people, to reduce the financial burden on themselves and their families and society." He was joined by Dr. Thomas M. Pitre, a fifty-year-old urologist who pointed out that doctors don't always know whether someone is terminally ill. He recalled one of his first patients, a man who was brought into the emergency room, "comatose, paralyzed, anemic and in kidney failure and from all observations about to die" from prostate cancer. Six weeks later this man walked out of the hospital, returned to his business, and remarried five years later. Eventually, he did die, eight years after leaving the hospital, "peacefully at home with the love of his new family."[49]

On Election Day, Measure 16 prevailed, winning a surprising 52 percent of the vote. Analysts pointed to several keys to victory, including the Oregon Medical Association's neutral stance, an antireligious backlash in one of the country's most unchurched states, and, as the state's leading newspaper, the *Oregonian*, observed, "a scrappy campaign that framed the issue as one of choice."[50] Oregonians accepted physician-assisted suicide because it appeared to leave the final act of death in the hands of the individual, not of a doctor, as was the case in the Dutch euthanasia system. A majority of voters accepted the argument that allowing the individual to choose suicide guarded against the slippery slope to involuntary euthanasia.[51] But the architect of the Death with Dignity Act was not satisfied: Derek Humphry criticized the measure because it did not go far enough.[52]

In 2000, six years after the enactment of the Oregon Death with Dignity Act, the state Health Division issued two reports on the practice of assisted suicide. The state found that in 1999, thirty-three people received lethal medication through the act. These people were 96 percent white, evenly divided between men and women, single and married. Most were dying of cancer. Ninety-three percent had at least a high-school education. An overwhelming 81 percent stated that their reason for committing suicide was fear of "losing autonomy." Only 26 percent stated that they did not want to be a burden on their families. About the same number listed as one of their reasons "worsening pain." For most, death came within thirty minutes.

The Oregon Death with Dignity Act was a victory for the euthanasia movement. That victory was affirmed in 1997 when voters rejected a measure that would have repealed the Death with Dignity Act.[53] But Oregon did not set a trend for the rest of the nation to follow. It would be fourteen years before another state enacted a similar assisted-suicide act. In November 2008, the voters of neighboring Washington State, another secular stronghold, approved a measure legalizing physician-assisted suicide. The measure received 57.9 percent of the vote, outpolling Barack Obama by a point.

The Irony of Individual Autonomy

The New Progressives advanced an agenda through population control that projected arrogance and power in its rawest forms. Although driven at first by concerns of race betterment through eugenics and fears of global overpopulation, foundation elites and feminist activists discovered that the appeal to individual autonomy encouraged popular support for the abortion and assisted-suicide movements. As a consequence, the appeal to individual rights argument ultimately functioned, in effect, to advance elite goals of controlling demographic outcomes by pushing the aggregation of individual choices in the direction of long-term goals desired by these elites. Theirs was a postmodern vision full of paradox in which individuals are offered apparent choice, while elite-controlled government extends its powers to manage individual lives.

5

The Dream of National Health Insurance

When Barack Obama signed the Patient Protection and Affordable Care Act on March 23, 2010, he fulfilled the longtime dream of progressives to move the nation away from private insurance into a government-regulated and government-controlled national health-care system. The dream was not fully realized—it was not socialized medicine per se—but it was a major advance toward it. Obama and the Democratic-controlled Congress enacted a national health insurance system mandating that all Americans carry insurance obtained through their employers, state-run health insurance exchanges, or Medicaid. Underfunded, expensive, highly regulated, and hideously bureaucratic, Obamacare promised to transform the American health-care industry, at least one-sixth of the entire economy of the United States when it was enacted. In June 2012 the Supreme Court in a complicated 5–4 ruling determined that the individual insurance mandate, imposed in the legislation, was unconstitutional as an exercise of the commerce power but could be interpreted as a tax, a valid exercise of the taxing power of Congress. The court also held that Health and Human Services, which the act charged with the responsibility of expanding Medicaid, could not force states to expand this program by threatening them with the loss of Medicaid funds. Four dissenters to this decision wanted to throw the whole act out. This controversial decision ensured that the political fight over health care in the United States was far from over. At the heart of this battle is the story of how progressive forces came together to fulfill their dreams of controlling health care for all Americans.

Presidential candidate Obama told American voters that there would be no new taxes, that no one would be required to buy insurance, and that people would be able to keep their present health insurance plans if they wanted. The final bill betrayed each of these promises. The law imposed new taxes, the individual mandate forced coverage, and many people faced losing their plans under the legislation. These were serious problems, but Obamacare portended even worse. The cost of the plan, its mandated coverage of the uninsured, and its expansion of Medicaid threatened to bankrupt the country. The progressive dream was about to turn into a national nightmare.

Progressives did not get everything they wanted with Obamacare. Some were disappointed with the legislation because it did not go far enough. Left-liberals had called for a single-payer plan in which the federal government assumed complete control of health care. Before he ran for president, Obama had declared himself for a single-payer plan. The next best thing that could happen, according to the Left, was a "public option," in which the federal government offered its own plan to compete with private insurance companies. Progressives understood that the public option would drive private health insurers out of business because they would not be able to compete against a heavily subsidized government plan, especially when the federal government was regulating the entire market in the first place. In the early stages of the congressional debate over health care, Obama favored the public option, but under pressure from the insurance industry and a voter uprising, he backed away from this proposal. For this he would be flayed by his left-wing activist base.

Still, he accomplished what no other president had. Government was now in charge of the nation's health-care system. Liberal Democrats in Congress, led by House Speaker Nancy Pelosi and Senate Majority Leader Harry Reid, had thumbed their noses when the Congressional Budget Office and the Republican minority warned that the plan would break the bank. Pelosi and Reid turned their backs on a popular uprising against the government takeover of health care. With great disdain, they denounced the public outrage as faux protest. It was "AstroTurf," not genuine grassroots populism. To those Democratic caucus members who worried that voting for the plan meant electoral defeat in the 2010 midterms, Pelosi and Reid said not to worry. This was a chance to make history. Once Americans discovered all the benefits of the act, they would rally to the new health-care entitlement. Even Republicans would support it. Just look at how they had reversed their positions on Medicare, which they initially opposed when it was enacted in 1965.

No doubt, liberal politicians showed hubris in enacting the Patient Protection and Affordable Care Act, yet hubris alone does not explain their success. To understand how we arrived at this point, we must look at the decades-long struggle to bring national health insurance to America. The struggle can be traced to the Truman administration in the 1940s. It continued through the Johnson administration in the 1960s and turned into a bitter conflict in the Clinton administration in the 1990s. In each of these episodes, the Left learned from its mistakes, but the defeat of national health care in the Clinton administration taught the most important lesson: the need to mobilize progressive unions and health-reform activists.

Where old-style liberals such as Truman and Johnson had failed, the New Progressives succeeded.

Give-'em-Hell Harry Truman and National Health Insurance

Stepping into the White House in April 1945, following Franklin Roosevelt's death, President Harry Truman undertook to expand the New Deal welfare state. As a good liberal, Truman believed that the federal government could provide better for the indigent and the working poor than could the market. The New Deal welfare state aimed primarily at taking care of the unemployed, the poor, widows, children, and the elderly. New Dealers were less interested in creating what became known later as "middle-class entitlement" programs than in regulating capitalism and protecting those unable to work. In this respect, New Dealers differed from the New Progressives who emerged in the late 1960s, who sought to extend government control over nearly every aspect of Americans' lives.

Only three weeks after the end of the Second World War, Truman made a stunning announcement. He called for a "national health program to promote adequate medical care for all Americans and to protect them from financial loss and hardships resulting from illness and accident."[1] Liberals were ecstatic. Sam Rosenman, Roosevelt's liberal domestic policy adviser, wrote that Truman's call had set forth "a progressive political philosophy and liberal program of action."[2] Southern Democrats and Republicans were shocked. They thought the New Deal had ended with the Second World War.

Truman was well informed about earlier efforts to achieve national health insurance. He did not take much convincing that a compulsory health system should include everyone, not just the poor. Such an appeal resonated with liberals. In 1946 private health insurance was not well developed in America, and only a small minority had private coverage. Liberals in Congress accepted Truman's challenge and crafted the Murray-Wagner-Dingell bill to establish a compulsory health-care system. The crafty trio of sponsors avoided the financial details of how to fund this program so that it would have an easier time getting out of committee and winning votes in the House and the Senate. The bill called for building more hospitals, expanding maternal and child health services, funding medical education and research, disability insurance for workers, and national health insurance. The bill did not, however, refer to nationalized health insurance; the drafters adopted the euphemism "prepayment of medical costs" to avoid being accused of proposing "socialized medicine."

In early April 1946, Senator James Murray (D-Montana) opened hearings on his cosponsored bill by asking opponents of the legislation not to call it "socialistic" or "communistic." At this point, Senator Robert Taft, Ohio's "Mr. Republican," interrupted to say, "I think it is very socialistic." Indeed, he continued, it was the "most socialistic measure" that Congress had ever seriously considered. Murray lamely replied, "That's a slander and a falsehood." He threatened to have Taft removed from the room. Taft left, making it clear that he was going to boycott the hearings because he saw the committee only as a "propaganda machine."[3]

Legislation for compulsory health insurance went down in 1946 with hardly a whimper. The following year Republicans won both houses of Congress for the first time since the 1929 stock market crash. Opponents of a federally mandated national health insurance program began targeting those Democrats who supported nationalized health care, accusing them of pushing "socialized medicine"—exactly what the bill's drafters had hoped to avoid. The charge carried extra weight at a time when congressional investigators were revealing communist infiltration into dozens of government agencies in the 1930s. Linking national health insurance to communism and socialism was a powerful political weapon.

Still, Truman pressed on, declaring in his State of the Union address in 1948, "This great Nation cannot afford to allow its citizens to suffer needlessly from the lack of proper medical care."[4] He commissioned the former chair of the Democratic National Committee, Oscar Ewing, a staunch New Deal liberal, to produce a report on the nation's health. Released in September, *The Nation's Health—A Ten Year Program* showed the inadequacy of private health insurance. The report found that in forty-six states, fewer than half the people had health insurance; in twenty states, less than 10 percent of the population was insured.

On the campaign trail in 1948, Truman gave the Republicans hell, blasting them as the party of reaction and of Wall Street, as the people who had produced the Depression of 1929. It was class warfare at its worst. He called Republicans "gluttons of privilege" and seekers of "a return of the Wall Street economic dictatorship." He especially lashed out at Republicans for calling national health insurance "un-American." Truman asked, "Is it un-American to visit the sick, aid the afflicted, or comfort the dying? I thought that was simple Christianity. Does cancer care about political parties? Does infantile paralysis concern itself with income?" He told his audiences that more Americans were dying because they lacked proper medical care than were killed throughout World War II.[5] The Republican candidate, Thomas Dewey, the governor of New York, avoided taking a strong stand on any issues, and voters went for Truman. Democrats regained control of both chambers of Congress. Truman had successfully rallied his organized-labor base and African American voters.

Although Democrats had won the White House and Congress, the Truman administration encountered fierce opposition when it put forward national health insurance legislation again. Conservative Democrats and Republicans balked at the costs of the measure. Meanwhile, the American Medical Association (AMA) launched a massive negative public relations campaign against nationalized health care. Hiring the public relations firm Whitaker and Baxter, the AMA spent more than a million dollars—a huge sum in those days—to convince the American public of the ills of socialized medicine. It distributed more than seventy thousand copies of a brochure warning that Truman's proposal threatened to "bind up your family's health in red tape. It would result in heavy payroll taxes—and inferior medical care for you and your family. Don't let it happen here."[6] Later scholars and health-care activists seized on this extensive public relations effort to show how "special interests"—the medical lobby—prevented nationalized health care from being enacted. Blaming the "special interests" for the failure to nationalize health care— under Truman, and again under Nixon, then Ford, then Carter, then Clinton—became a mantra on the Left and in the academy.

But it was not just the "special interests" that opposed national health insurance. Whenever the debate arose, economic analysts warned about the costs of nationalized health care in a country with a huge and diverse population. The Brookings Institution responded to Truman's proposal by issuing a report, *The Issue of Compulsory Health*, warning that the program would be too political, too expensive, and ultimately detrimental to the nation's economic health. The report pointed out that for most people, medical expenses amounted to only 4 to 4.5 percent of their budget. Furthermore, the Brookings Institution maintained that most Americans had resources to carry health insurance but preferred not to spend their money on it. To support a compulsory national health insurance system, the report added, would require huge tax increases on the middle classes and "professional men" who held family responsibilities. More broadly, the Brookings Institution worried that compulsory health insurance would create a citizenry dependent on government. Using language that sounds especially antiquated to twenty-first-century ears, the report questioned the wisdom of "impairing the incentives of those whose native abilities, training, experience, and willingness to assume risks are so important to the success of any social and economic program." Rather than move ahead with a massive (and probably unnecessary) health insurance program, federal and state governments should, the Brookings Institution concluded, fund health research and education and provide for the systematic care of the indigent.[7] These arguments would be echoed in every subsequent debate over national health care, often boiling down to a simple question: "Can we afford it, and is it worth it?"

It was a question Americans asked in 1948 when confronted with compulsory health insurance. Truman did not help his case because, as the *New York Times* noted, he "gave no detail on the cost or the methods of financing the program."[8] By 1950 the issue was all but dead. The administration had become bogged down in Korea, the first of several postwar military interventions in which America proved unable to proclaim victory or admit defeat. Moreover, Truman was pushing an ambitious legislative agenda that called not only for health care but also for civil rights, fair housing, and reversing Republican labor reforms enacted in the Taft-Hartley legislation. Congress did not approve national-ized health insurance, but it passed a hospital-construction program and appropriated funds for medical education. Without compulsory government-run health insurance, private insurance expanded through a variety of programs to help working Americans with health-care costs. During the Second World War, employer-based health insurance pro-grams had expanded because government-imposed wage controls encour-aged employers to expand employee benefits, as these were not subject to caps. Under the employer-based system, employees received a tax break for their health insurance. This system, however, created incentives for large corporations and unions to provide ever more expensive and broader employee-benefit packages, often with little concern for long-term costs.

As the Truman health-care proposal failed, health activists laid the groundwork for an eventual counteroffensive. Critical in laying out this new strategy was Oscar Ewing, Truman's right-hand man on health care. He proposed creating a national health insurance program for peo-ple over sixty-five, an idea supported by officials in the Social Security Administration. Ewing, key advisers inside Social Security, and other health-reform activists saw—it turned out correctly—that a health insur-ance system for the elderly could be a wedge in creating a national health-care system. In April 1952, Senators James Murray (D-Montana) and Hubert Humphrey (D-Minnesota) joined Representatives John Dingell (D-Michigan) and Emanuel Celler (D–New York) in introducing legis-lation to provide hospital insurance for people over sixty-five years old.

It would take more than a decade, but the plan finally became law. The federal insurance program became known as Medicare.

Medicare: The Start of Nationalized Health Care

On July 30, 1965, a triumphant Harry Truman stood next to President Lyndon Johnson in Independence, Missouri, for the formal signing ceremony of the Medicare Act. The act provided for the largest entitle-ment program since Social Security had been enacted under Franklin Roosevelt in 1935. Medicare provided a health insurance program for a projected 19 million elderly. The act covered hospital costs in a mandatory plan (Part A) and physician fees through a voluntary program (Part B). Prescription drugs were so cheap in 1965 that they were not covered. In addition, the final bill included the Medicaid program to provide health insurance for the poor.

Johnson aides had recommended against signing the legislation in Truman's hometown of Independence. They warned that this might incite the AMA, which had fought Truman to a standstill over nationalized health care. Johnson rejected his aides' advice because he knew the AMA leadership had been won over through flattery, compromise, and incentives. The act promised physicians payment for treating the elderly, meaning that the medical profession could bill the federal government at high rates.

Without Johnson's leadership it is doubtful that Medicare-Medicaid would have been enacted. Taking up the Kennedy promise following the tragic events in Dallas on November 22, 1963, Johnson began his push for a health insurance bill for the elderly early in his administration. Health insurance for the elderly had languished in Congress for years, held up by conservative Democrats and Republicans who feared the cost of "socialized medicine." To craft a bill, Johnson skillfully worked with key members of the House, especially the chairman of the House Ways and Means Committee, Wilbur Mills, and Senate Democratic leaders. Johnson played to Mills's vanity, promising him that passage of the bill would determine his place in history. Mills was a well-known opponent of health insurance for the elderly because he feared any such program was financially infeasible. The nation could not afford it. Dinner meetings, late-night telephone calls, and Johnson's cajoling brought Mills around. When Johnson won a landslide victory in 1964, acceding to the presidency in his own right, the time appeared right to move the bill forward.

Johnson and Mills put together a "three-layered cake," a bill that included hospital insurance for the elderly (Medicare A), physician insurance for the elderly (Medicare B), and comprehensive insurance for the poor and newborn (Medicaid). Johnson and the White House twisted arms to win liberals who wanted a more generous bill, as well as recalcitrant conservative Democrats. As for Republicans, Johnson believed, "They're against any proposal I make," but, convinced of his own popularity, he pushed the bill through Congress.[9] He insisted that the bills go forward as soon as they came out of the appropriate committees, before the opposition could organize.

Johnson kept fiscal critics within Congress and his own White

House at bay. When Mills expressed concerns about the cost of adding Part B and Medicaid to the package, Johnson told him, "Four hundred million's not going to separate us friends when it's for health, when it's for sickness, because there's a greater demand . . . for this bill than all my other programs put together."[10] He instructed his own health experts not to run projections for more than one year out, because it would allow the budget sharks to devour his bill. By checking liberals in the Senate who wanted to include catastrophic insurance, pharmaceutical benefits, and more eligible age groups, Johnson projected an image of fiscal restraint.

Once the legislation passed, Johnson personally oversaw the program to make sure it was implemented efficiently and without disruption. The federal government set up records, printed identification cards, established a payment system, and took care of sundry other details in this massive program. As a political and public relations gesture, Harry Truman was sent the first Medicare card. Although some physicians at first threatened to boycott Medicare, the medical profession swung behind the program when it realized that Medicare rules for paying both doctors and hospitals were extremely generous, accepting whatever doctors charged, with little federal oversight or control.

Writing in 2007, scholar James Morone and health expert David Blumenthal praised Johnson's ability to keep his economists "muzzled" by telling them to de-emphasize the numbers and underplaying Medicare and Medicaid's long-term economic impact. Johnson's strategy was to expand coverage now and worry about affordability later. Morone and Blumenthal found in this a strategy for future health-care reform. They wrote, "It's the same old lesson: expansion never fits the budget. . . . For successful health reform: first expansion then cost control."[11] The problem is that cost control does not necessarily follow—indeed, from looking at federal entitlement programs, one might conclude that cost containments have never followed.

Harry Truman, Oscar Ewing, and other health reformers believed that once Americans saw the benefits of health care for the elderly, everyone would want to join the compulsory health-care system. It did not turn out that way, but activists did manage to use Medicare to make the case for a broader nationalized health insurance program. They did so, oddly enough, by playing off the financial catastrophe that Medicare became. As the twentieth century closed, Medicare was being crushed under the burden of rising medical costs. Even worse disaster loomed ahead: the baby boomers—the generation that was just beginning to enter the world in the Truman era and that had turned on Lyndon Johnson—would soon flood the Medicare rolls. Enrollments were projected to expand dramatically—from 45 million elderly in 2010 to 80 million by 2030, when the last baby boomer reached retirement age. The system was unsustainable. The average-wage, two-earner couple retiring in 2011 would have paid $114,000 in Medicare payroll taxes during their careers; they would take out $355,000 for medical services, from prescriptions to hospital care— more than three times what they had put in.

Medicare, President Johnson's gift to the aged, had become an albatross around the necks of all Americans. But to health-reform activists, this disaster was an opportunity. The only way to save this unsustainable system was to bring in the younger population. Going to a nationalized health-care system would mean younger workers were paying into the system. Only in this way, the activists advised, could Medicare be saved, the uninsured be covered, and health-care costs contained.

Hillarycare: The Dream Unfulfilled

Dreams do not die easily. Having achieved federal health coverage for the aged in the 1960s, progressives were not about to give up their dream of a nationalized health insurance system that covered all Americans. Progressives spoke the language of "access" and "justice," even while their plans required compulsion and punishment for the recalcitrant. If conservatives believed that the failure of nationalized health care under Nixon and Carter, both of whom proposed guaranteed public-funding programs to ensure all Americans had health insurance, had pushed the issue off the table, they sorely underestimated the tenacity of the Left and Bill Clinton's willingness to appease the left wing of his party. During his 1992 presidential campaign, Clinton had promised to reform a bloated health system. Once he entered the White House, he moved to fulfill his promise.

Clinton had long been interested in health-care policy. His mother was a nurse. In his unsuccessful run for Congress in 1974, he had come out for national health insurance. When he became governor of Arkansas in 1978, he won federal funds for state health care and opened four rural clinics in the state. Moreover, Clinton, an astute politician, understood that health care was an issue that appealed to the activist base of the Democratic Party and was also a concern for the American public. In a special election for the U.S. Senate in Pennsylvania in 1991, former Bryn Mawr College president Harris Wofford, a left-liberal Democrat with strong civil rights ties, won on a promise of universal health insurance.

Democratic politicians were not tone-deaf to these results, so in the 1992 presidential primaries all the contenders rushed forward with plans. Senator Robert Kerrey of Nebraska came out in favor of a single-payer plan. Paul Tsongas, the former senator from Massachusetts, running as a fiscally responsible candidate, called for "managed competition." Dark horse Bill Clinton proposed a scheme in which all employers would either pay for health insurance for their employees or contribute to a national fund that would purchase insurance for workers not covered by employer plans. This was a "pay or play" scheme reminiscent of the national health-care plan President Richard Nixon had proposed. Whatever their differences, the Democratic presidential contenders agreed that major health-care legislation needed to be enacted.

Clinton's initial proposal lacked details. His own camp was divided over whether to support pay or play, which meant raising taxes and regulating health care to generate enough funds to pay for universal health care, or managed competition, which allowed consumers to choose among multiple health plans. The beauty of managed competition, proponents argued, was that universal coverage could be achieved without raising taxes, because competing insurers would drive down wasteful costs.

The strongest supporters of managed competition on the Clinton team were Ira Magaziner, a tall, unkempt former Rhodes Scholar and close friend of Clinton's, and Atul Gawande, a young medical student. Together with Princeton University sociologist Paul Starr, a longtime proponent of national health insurance, they drafted a detailed plan in which private insurers would compete to provide universal health care in a marketplace the government regulated and controlled. Their proposal included an employer mandate. The plan combined a conservative solution, market-driven insurance, with the progressive dream of a universal system under federal government control.

They brought their proposal to Bill Clinton in the fall of 1992, just as the presidential campaign was heating up. Clinton was anxious to introduce a health-care proposal in his race for the White House. Clinton tended to glide over the details, which had not been fully worked out in any case, but he was adamant that his plan, as vague as it was, would contain costs and avoid raising taxes. Behind closed doors, however, many on Clinton's team believed that the federal government would have to raise taxes to cover the uninsured and that cost savings would not occur in the short run. Nonetheless, this approach to health care caught the Republicans off guard. Sixteen years later, when Obama proposed a similar scheme, it once again caught Republicans off guard.

Following the election, President-elect Clinton appointed a transition team focused on health care. Led by a political scientist specializing in health care, Judy Feder, and Gawande, the team quickly developed disagreements. Feder concluded that it would take years for managed care to replace the efficiency of the current system and that taxes would have to be raised by as much as $100 billion a year. Other advisers warned Clinton that, because of the costs of such a program and political opposition, it was politically impossible to bring about the radical changes managed-competition advocates proposed. Nevertheless, Clinton decided to go with the managed-care proposal. He appointed Magaziner and his wife, Hillary Clinton, to head health-care reform. The new president understood that Hillary knew something about health care, harbored a progressive passion to enact a universal scheme, and shared her husband's desire to build the Clinton legacy.

Charged with drafting the proposal, Magaziner and Hillary Clinton organized a task force. In the end, they brought in more than six hundred health-care experts and other advisers. The sprawling planning apparatus divided into subgroups, subgroups within subgroups, and advisory committees. After months of intensive labor and incessant meetings, the Clinton task force proposed a system that was inordinately complex, built on a myriad of new government regulatory agencies, local and state health exchanges, and insurance and physician cooperatives. Economic advisers in the Clinton administration warned that the plan just could not be financed.

But for political reasons, President Clinton decided to forge ahead. Senate Majority Leader George Mitchell (D-Maine) and House Majority Leader Richard Gephardt (D-Missouri) told Clinton that any health-care legislation needed to move quickly, before opposition had a chance to mobilize. The president, Hillary Clinton, and Magaziner decided in early 1993 that they might be able to sneak their health-care bill through by attaching it to budget-reconciliation legislation, which required only a majority vote in the Senate. With Democrats controlling fifty-six seats, it looked like the strategy might work. Then they ran into a roadblock in the form of Senator Robert Byrd (D–West Virginia), who objected to passing this historic legislation through the legislative gimmick of budget reconciliation.

In any case, the Clinton administration did not even have a bill ready to present to Congress. The clock was ticking, as the president was scheduled to give a major speech on health care before a joint session of Congress on September 23, 1993. Magaziner and his team worked day and night to turn their proposal into legislative language. It still was not ready when Clinton went on television to announce his plan before Congress, but this was not evident when the silver-tongued Clinton—the man of the people—gave the speech. He was glib and knew the basics of the legislation.

After the speech, polls showed that public opinion favoring national health care soared. Most Americans agreed with the principle that everyone in the world's wealthiest nation should have access to affordable health care. Then the opposition began to organize. Opponents looked at Clinton's plan and found that it was unaffordable and that the cost was going to fall on the taxpaying populace. Clinton had pledged not to raise taxes to support the plan, so inevitably the burden fell more heavily on the wealthy, smaller insurance companies, and richer states.

Small businesses and private health insurers launched a major media counteroffensive against the Clinton proposal. The Health Insurance Association of America (HIAA), a trade association of health insurance providers, was especially effective in its "Harry and Louise" television commercials, which showed a middle-aged couple talking about the problems with the Clinton plan. The big pharmaceutical companies backed away as well, fearing that the inclusion of prescription drugs in the plan would lead eventually to the regulation of drug prices. Even the automobile industry, which initially supported the Clinton proposal, came out against the plan when the details were revealed. Required to maintain their huge retiree benefit commitments, auto companies favored the cap the Clinton plan placed on any single firm's health-care costs and also supported lowering the age of eligibility for Medicare. But they soon found that Clinton's proposed health alliances were too comprehensive in scope and that the basic benefits package was too large. Moreover, employer premiums by 1994 had actually shrunk by 1.1 percent because of cost containment, after having increased by nearly 20 percent from 1990 to 1993.[12]

Conservative House Republicans led by Newt Gingrich (R-Georgia) also attacked the Clinton plan. Senate Republicans, however, waited to see which way the public winds blew. At first Senate Majority Leader Robert Dole (R-Kansas), who was the front-runner for the 1996 Republican presidential nomination, agreed to work with moderates in the Senate to improve the Clinton bill. Yet as public opinion began to shift away from Hillarycare, Dole and other Republicans distanced themselves from the Clinton health-care proposal. Hillary Clinton lashed back by attacking health insurance companies for "price gouging, cost shifting, and unconscionable profiteering," arguing that they had brought the country to the brink of bankruptcy.[13]

It did not matter that the five major private health insurers—Aetna, MetLife, Travelers, Cigna, and Prudential—were the major backers of Hillarycare. Mrs. Clinton and Ira Magaziner had brought them on board early in the process with the promise that they would be major beneficiaries of managed competition. The gang of five, as the big insurers became known, withdrew from HIAA over the issue.[14] Regardless, proponents of compulsory health care launched a campaign to paint "big insurance" as a special interest opposed to health-care reform. Instilling distrust of corporate America was an old trick among progressives.

Yet not all Democrats were happy with the attacks on the insurance industry. For example, Senator Christopher Dodd (D-Connecticut), who had received $375,000 from the political action committees of Aetna, Cigna, MetLife, Prudential, and Travelers, and another $24,000 from individual insurance officers, publicly criticized the Democratic National Committee for its attack on the insurance industry. The gang of five had contributed healthy sums to three other Connecticut incumbents, Senator Joseph Lieberman and Representatives Barbara Kennelly and Nancy Johnson. In 1994, Kennelly received $265,000 from health insurance companies. In addition, Representative Jim Cooper (D-Tennessee), who favored dropping the employer mandate, raised nearly $2.4 million in his reelection campaign, mostly from the big health insurers.[15]

Class warfare was not going to work this time around. By the summer, the White House's internal polling showed that the American people cared about one thing with health reform: "How is this going to affect me, my children, my parents?"[16] And Americans didn't like the answer one iota.

Meanwhile, within Clinton's own administration, economists from the Council of Economic Advisers, the Office of Management and Budget, and the Treasury Department informed the president that his health-care plan was unaffordable. Either taxes needed to be raised or benefits scaled back. This was exactly what Clinton had been told when he first proposed health care as president-elect. This time, however, it appears that the economists were leaking their complaints to key people in the Senate.

As opposition to national health care began to build, Clinton undertook his own lobbying campaign, appointing Harold Ickes, a union-connected Democratic Party insider, to head up the effort. As soon as he accepted the task, Ickes found himself bogged down by accusations that Bill Clinton and his wife had benefited from inside land deals in the Whitewater region in Arkansas when he was governor. Whitewater began to consume all of Ickes's time.

The progressive base that should have rallied to health care was experiencing problems of its own. Prior to the election, the aging president of the AFL-CIO, Lane Kirkland, had promised Clinton that the labor movement would provide foot soldiers for national health insurance. Yet by the time health care reached the legislative stage, the AFL-CIO was involved in a major campaign against the North American Free Trade Agreement (NAFTA), which the Clinton administration had brought to Congress. Organized labor opposed this free-trade agreement, which it saw as shipping jobs to Mexico.[17]

As the Clinton health-care proposal worked its way through the House, attempts to compromise by eliminating the employer mandate fell flat. Clinton refused to compromise. Small business was terrified of skyrocketing health-care costs, and the employer mandate leached support from more moderate Democratic congressmen. It quickly became apparent that Clinton was pressing a proposal for national health-care reform that lacked a consensus either among the American public or within the Democratic Party. In the summer of 1994, Senate Majority Leader George Mitchell announced that universal health care was dead for the time being.

Republicans swept the House, Senate, governorships, and state legislatures that fall. In 1997, Clinton was able to join a Republican Congress to enact the State Children's Health Insurance Program (SCHIP), which expanded health care for children through state-run programs. It was a small victory, but it did not provide Clinton with the historic achieve-ment he was seeking in bringing nationalized health care to America.

Progressives drew valuable lessons from the Clinton defeat. Next time they won the White House, they were not going to let the chance of enacting national health-care reform slip through their fingers. The failure of Hillarycare taught progressives to:

1. Involve Congress as a fundamental agency in drafting any future comprehensive-care legislation.
2. Take the planning of any future proposal out of the hands of the White House.
3. Present health-care reform as a measure to reduce rising health-care costs and save Medicare.
4. Tap into the humane instincts of the American people by selling the plan as a means of insuring the uninsured while protecting the existing health-care programs for the insured.
5. Make health-care reform the sole priority of the administration.
6. Unite the special interests by crafting a plan to win the endorsement of groups such as the AMA, the pharmaceuti-cal industry, and the American Association of Retired Per-sons (AARP).
7. Mobilize grassroots groups, unions, media, and special inter-ests on behalf of health-care reform.

Mobilizing Special Interests

A major blow to Clinton's health-care reform package was the lack of union support. Following the defeat of Hillarycare, progressives pledged not to let this happen again.

Organized labor was a natural ally for health-care reform, and not simply because it so heavily funded and supported the Democratic Party. By the twenty-first century, labor's interest in health-care reform was a matter of simple economics. For fifty years unionized American indus-tries had bought off labor through huge health-care and benefit pack-ages. By the late 1990s the rapidly growing number of retirees draining pension and health-care funds made these systems unsustainable. Worse, these costly commitments put American companies at a competitive disadvantage against international businesses that did not bear such huge expenses. Many large corporations and their unions supported shifting those costs to a nationalized health-care system. In fact, a close examination reveals that many corporations that capitulated to labor's demands for higher benefits and ever-expanding health-care programs did so on the assumption that the federal government ultimately would need to bail out a financially unsound system.[18]

The moment came with the financial crisis of 2008. When Barack Obama entered the White House, private-sector employers' pension funds were cumulatively $350 billion in deficit.[19] Companies from Sears to IBM had been forced to modify plans to keep them solvent. Especially hard hit were the automobile companies, which were collapsing under the weight of poor auto sales and escalating pension and retiree health costs.

The largest domestic automobile producer, General Motors (GM), had led the way. The result was a government bailout—a takeover—of GM in 2009.

From the mid-1980s through 2006, GM poured $55 billion into its workers' pension plan.[20] This extravagance can be traced to the years just after the Second World War when the United Auto Workers (UAW), under the leadership of Walter Reuther, envisioned an ever-expanding pension and health-care program for GM workers. Reuther was a social visionary who saw a broader role for the UAW as an agent of social change in the new liberal welfare state.[21] As he told a cheering UAW convention in Milwaukee in 1949, the union required from Big Auto nothing short of "a full welfare program," including "health care, a pension, death benefits, disability and the works."[22]

Reuther demanded that Ford Motor Company provide a monthly pension as well as a hospitalization plan equivalent to 5 percent of the payroll. UAW leadership understood that pension and health benefits offered tax advantages to both business and workers, because medical benefits were not taxed at all and taxes on pension benefits were deferred. By capitulating to the demand, Ford set the stage for a half century of rising pension and health-care costs in the auto industry. Only a few warned that Big Auto might not always enjoy the profits to cover the benefits liability it was taking on.

In 1961, Reuther led 255,000 GM workers in a strike. Although the strike resulted in only a 2.5 percent wage raise, pensions were boosted by 12 percent, and the UAW won full health insurance for employees and half the cost of hospital, medical, and surgical insurance for retirees. Then, in 1964, GM raised pension benefits an amazing 50 percent and gave retirees a boost from 50 percent to 100 percent of health-care costs. The list of treatments ran to nine pages, from X-rays and radiation therapy to in-hospital mental health treatments. By the time Reuther died in May 1970, GM was on the hook for millions of dollars in pension and health-care liabilities. In 1976, the UAW got vision care, hearing aids, and comprehensive substance abuse coverage.

Yet the flush times were coming to an end for American automakers. Foreign manufacturers were eroding their market share. Meanwhile, technological improvements were making workforces leaner. By 1984 the domestic auto industry had eliminated 300,000 union jobs, 100,000 at GM alone. These job cuts did not alleviate benefit costs, however. According to industry estimates, health-care costs accounted for $430 for every car produced. GM's health-care costs continued to grow at a staggering pace. By 2005, GM was spending at a rate of $5.3 billion a year and caring for about 1.1 million people, of whom only 140,000 were still on the job.[23] That year Delphi, GM's principal parts supplier, which had been spun off from the corporation a few years earlier, filed for bankruptcy primarily because of pension and retiree health-care costs. The bankruptcy left GM to make up lost benefits to Delphi employees to the tune of an estimated $5.5 billion.

GM management finally pushed back against organized labor. The automaker demanded radical downsizing of health coverage for active employees, as well as cutting of tuition assistance, insurance, and other benefits. Meeting with UAW leaders, GM head Rick Wagoner told them that the unfunded portion of GM's health-care obligations was about $60 billion.[24] He asked for $20 billion back.

In the end, UAW president Ron Gettelfinger agreed to the deal. Inserted into the joint GM-UAW agreement was this statement: "Given the fragmented and wasteful nature of the U.S. health care system, the parties recognize an issue-by-issue approach to reform . . . is no longer sufficient." The agreement stated that GM management and the UAW would "develop and/or support national proposals" that fostered "cost effective, quality health care." Noting that 47 million Americans were uninsured, GM and the UAW further pledged to support "public policies on the federal and state level that will enable all Americans to have health insurance."[25] UAW and GM leaders understood that their profligate health-care plans of the past needed to be passed on to the American taxpayer.

Rising pension and health-care costs were nailing other sectors of the economy too. By 2000, municipal and state governments realized that they were headed toward major financial crises. Neither enough taxes could be raised nor enough bonds sold to cover legacy liabilities and Medicaid obligations. By 2005, Starbucks reportedly spent more on health care for its employees than on coffee beans.

Hospitals found budgets stretched, especially as they began to take in more nonpaying patients, often illegal immigrants, and Medicaid patients, whom the government covered at low rates. Many inner-city hospitals, unable to cover the costs of caring for the poor, began closing their doors in the 1990s. Projections of escalating medical costs, hospital closings, and declining profits threatened the entire hospital industry. For unionized hospital workers, hospital closings and lower profit margins threatened the loss of jobs and declining wages and benefits. As a result, hospital workers within the Service Employees International Union (SEIU) joined the crusade for compulsory health insurance. The progressive SEIU provided the storm troops in electing Obama, as well as the ground troops in pushing national health-care reform.

SEIU's involvement in health care encapsulates the progressive-union alliance as it has evolved in modern America.[26] The history of SEIU, especially the hospital workers section of the union, itself reveals how Old Left prewar politics evolved into post-1960s New Progressive politics. Consider the hospital workers union: Local 1199 of United Public Workers of America (UPWA) in New York City was expelled from the Congress of Industrial Organizations (CIO) in the late 1940s because of its Communist Party affiliation. For a brief time the UPWA found refuge in the Teamsters union but was expelled for being "Red." Eventually, Local 1199, which continued to organize New York hospital workers, found a strange home in the Retail Drug Employees Union, one of a cluster of communist-led New York City unions that had been organized in the 1930s.

Local 1199 was an industrial union, a category that allowed it to organize all hospital workers, from janitors to nurses. Although investigated for its communist activity, Local 1199 survived the 1950s "Red Scare." It had organized Montefiore Hospital, one of New York City's largest medical complexes. In the 1960s municipal hospitals began to receive public funding from the city, which paid private medical colleges and hospitals to provide staff to city hospitals. The establishment of Medicare and Medicaid brought more government funds into the hospital system. Montefiore was able to increase its plant size and medical staff fourfold. By 1970, Montefiore Medical Center had become the largest employer in the Bronx. Enjoying the prosperity of Montefiore was Local 1199. Using Montefiore as a base, Local 1199 expanded its organizing efforts across the entire New York metro area and state.

In the following decades, hospital workers unions in New York City wrung huge concessions from the medical industry in the form of wages, pensions, and health benefits. The threat and use of strikes forced capitulation from New York public officials, Republican and Democrat. The 1980s brought internal divisions, as well as minor setbacks at the negotiating table, but new leader Georgianna Johnson promised to bring the union "back to where we used to be: number one in social activism."[27] In 1986 the union hosted the leftist Nicaraguan health minister and Chilean resistance leaders. It organized its members to support liberal governor Mario Cuomo's reelection bid. It backed the failed Senate race of consumer activist Mark Green. It sent a thousand-member delegation to demonstrations in Washington against South African apartheid and U.S. policy in Central America.

In 1989 longtime union activist Dennis Rivera was elected Local 1199 president. Almost immediately he was tested in contract negotiations. Through the use of rolling strikes, in which workers at various hospitals walked out in sequence, Rivera won huge concessions from hospitals, including 14 percent wage increases over two years, a 5 percent increase the third year, and a $500 bonus for each employee in 1991. Further agreements with New York hospitals allowed Rivera to institute a "Japanese workplace concept" in which unionized workers received a no-layoff promise and expanded free health care for themselves. Spencer Foreman, president of Montefiore Medical Center, remarked before the 1989 contract, "I don't have the foggiest idea how they think we can pay for this."[28]

The answer was that hospitals could not pay for it. Costs were rising, and Medicaid funds were being cut. Medicaid spending doubled in the 1980s; they doubled again between 1996 and 2006, reaching $300 billion. New York State had the largest Medicaid program in the country, while New York City had the largest proportion of Medicaid patients in the country. Rivera understood perfectly that if the system was going to be maintained, with a highly unionized workforce receiving high wages and benefits, hospital costs needed to be nationalized. To achieve this goal, Rivera knew he needed to get hospitals on board to support compulsory health insurance. He proclaimed that the union's biggest task was to "convince management that we're their greatest allies, not their biggest enemies, whether it is in financing, or be in operation of the institution."[29]

Rivera also realized that Local 1199, as a vanguard labor organization, needed to enter SEIU, which was equally committed to "social justice" in its politics. In 1998, Local 1199 joined SEIU to form a union with more than one million members in three locals. Rivera announced that with the merger, "we will have more money for politics, more money for organizing, more money for collective bargaining."[30] The union announced that it was prepared to spend $3 million on New York politics every two years. By 2007 the New York SEIU had established the largest union political action committee in any state. More than 125,000 union members contributed $5.5 million on top of their union dues in 2006.

At the same time, SEIU continued its drive for national health insurance. It collaborated with the Greater New York Hospital Association (GNYHA) to form the Health Care Education Project. Prevented from contributing directly to political campaigns, the GNYHA through this joint project sent out millions of mailings attacking public officials who called for hospital budget cuts. The project developed media ads, telephone calls, and house-to-house canvassing to fight cutting health-care expenditures for the poor. The activity forced politicians such as Governor George Pataki, a Republican, to back away from cutting state spending for health care.

In 2006, Dennis Rivera announced that he was stepping down as president of Local 1199 to head SEIU Health Care, an alliance of local health-care unions comprising nine million workers across the country. Rivera undertook a dual strategy of extending organizing across the country to bring more hospital workers into SEIU and campaigning for comprehensive health care for every American. He took to the road, traveling to New Jersey, Massachusetts, California, Maryland, and Washington State to encourage health-care-system owners and state government leaders to cooperate on the model his union had developed with the GNYHA. His efforts proved successful. In the early spring of 2007,

SEIU Health Care announced the establishment of the Partnership for Quality Care, a coalition that included the GNYHA, the Kaiser Foundation and Kaiser Hospitals, Catholic Health Care West, and SEIU. The purpose of this coalition was to press Congress to expand health-care entitlements.

The Partnership for Quality Care began lobbying Congress to expand SCHIP, which Congress had enacted in 1997. The union lobby called for extending coverage to young children's parents whose income was too high for Medicaid but who could not afford private insurance. Rivera made the larger goal explicit: this was the first step, he announced, in pursuit of "Quixote's dream of achieving . . . national health care reform, health care to every man, woman and child."[31] SEIU anticipated spending $100 million for new organizing efforts and another $40 million in the next national election cycle.

SEIU's program won the endorsement of Senator Ted Kennedy, who told a cheering union convention that labor was at the forefront in the struggle to bring in a "universal comprehensive health-care" system based on the "public, single-payer" principle." In typical rabble-rousing rhetoric, Kennedy exclaimed, "If it's good enough for U.S. senators, then it's good enough for you, and you, and you."[32] SEIU president Andy Stern told the convention in no uncertain terms of labor's commitment to nationalizing health care: "We are the ones who will write a new prescription for health care in America."[33]

In May 2008, SEIU, with a membership of 2 million, endorsed Barack Obama for president. Appearing via satellite before the SEIU convention in early June, Obama told the 3,500 delegates meeting in Puerto Rico that he stood shoulder to shoulder with "the purple-clad army of the SEIU" in the battle to bring nationalized health care to America.[34]

While labor was organizing its troops, other activists were rallying the base in support of nationalized health care. Especially important was the Association of Community Organizations for Reform Now (ACORN), a grassroots radical group closely aligned with SEIU. In Chicago, SEIU Local 880 *was* ACORN. They shared the same office and the same staff.

After Obama became president, ACORN would achieve national notoriety—and ultimately be forced to file for bankruptcy—when a conservative activist named James O'Keefe released undercover videos showing ACORN employees advising a couple whom the staffers believed to be a pimp and a prostitute on how to get away with illegal activity.[35] The scandal, and the spectacular collapse of ACORN that followed, obscured the fact that ACORN was, up to that point, one of the most powerful radical grassroots organizations in the country—one that played a key role in pushing national health care.

When ACORN advanced the cause of nationalized health care during the 2008 presidential campaign, it was a vast organization with an annual budget of $100 million, 103 offices operating across America, more than a thousand employees, and four hundred thousand dues-paying members. It had come a long way since its humble beginnings as a small community-organizing group. ACORN had grown out of the National Welfare Rights Organization (NWRO), a radical group organized in the 1960s to expand welfare benefits and protect the rights of welfare recipients. ACORN was the brainchild of NWRO organizer Wade Rathke, a Williams College dropout and former member of SDS. In 1970, Rathke received permission from NWRO to set up an organization of community activists in Little Rock, Arkansas. He envisioned a new populist movement that went beyond organizing welfare recipients, who were disproportionately African American. In Springfield, Massachusetts, where he had worked as an organizer for NWRO, his efforts led to a two-day riot that accomplished little except causing millions of dollars' worth of property damage in the inner city. Rathke concluded that welfare-rights organizing was a dead-end strategy; radically transforming American capitalist society could succeed only with middle-class support, he felt.[36] From his experience in SDS, Rathke believed that the New Left had too easily written off the white working class as an agent for change. While seeking to win middle-class support for his program, he believed that organizing needed to bring poor blacks, Hispanics, and whites together through local economic issues and then mobilize them into a multiracial, neighborhood-based national organization against the wealthy, financial, and corporate interests that he saw controlling America.

Within a year, Rathke had split from NWRO to form the Arkansas Community Organization for Reform Now, a title that quickly had to be broadened. Within five years, ACORN had chapters throughout Arkansas, as well as in Texas and South Dakota. ACORN became involved in campaigns to lower utility rates, reduce prices for generic drugs, and raise taxes on wealthy individuals and large corporations. Operating with a budget of $250,000, the association had a paid staff of twenty and owned two self-sustaining noncommercial FM radio stations in Arkansas.

ACORN became a training camp for young activists, many from Ivy League schools. These activists took their organizing skills to other states where ACORN formed chapters. Several of these organizers eventually entered the labor movement, including Mark Splain, who became organizing director for the AFL; Kirk Adams, who became chief of staff to Andy Stern, president of SEIU; and Myra Glassman, who became director of Chicago-based SEIU Local 880.[37]

In the years that followed, ACORN grew in membership and funding. For a community-organizing group, ACORN was unusual in that it charged membership dues. It also began to receive federal and state funding when, in the mid-1980s, it created the ACORN Housing Corporation, which sponsored community-redevelopment projects in New York, Philadelphia, Phoenix, St. Louis, and Little Rock. In the 1990s, ACORN used provisions of the Community Reinvestment Act (1977) to negotiate low-income housing loans from banks seeking mergers. Large banks began offering grants to ACORN to win its support. Critics saw this as a form of corporate blackmail. For example, Robert L. Woodson, president of the National Center for Neighborhood Enterprise, said that corporate America was "buying peace" so ACORN would not agitate against it.[38] ACORN also received grants from the Ford Foundation, the Carnegie Endowment, and the U.S. Council of Catholic Bishops.

Although ACORN professed to be nonpartisan, the organization developed close ties with progressives in the Democratic Party. Rathke saw that under the caucus rules the McGovern Commission had instituted, ACORN could influence the Democratic Party. As the 1980 election approached, ACORN pressured the Democratic National Committee to establish the ACORN Commission to increase participation for low- and moderate-income people. The ACORN Commission held hearings in six states, but little came from its recommendations beyond a seat at the Democratic Party table.

Following the close 2000 election, ACORN undertook an extensive voter-outreach program to register low-income voters. Heading ACORN's political operations was Zach Polett, a Harvard University graduate and a Stanford University School of Medicine dropout who had joined the organization in 1975, rising to the position of ACORN's political director. In 1982, Polett had helped found Project Vote, a nonprofit organization devoted to involving poor and minority voters. Not surprisingly, then, ACORN and Project Vote developed a close relationship, working together on voter outreach. Backing for the coordinated ACORN–Project Vote campaign came from billionaires such as George Soros and Herb and Marion Sandler, founders of Golden West Financial savings and loan, as well as left-leaning unions. The campaign mounted a massive mobilization effort in twenty-six states, targeting especially battleground states such as Florida, New Mexico, Colorado, and Arizona.

In the 2008 election these efforts intensified, as ACORN and Project Vote launched a $15.9 million campaign to sign up 1.2 million voters. There was little doubt about whom these organizations wanted to become president: Barack Obama had worked for Project Vote, running the Chicago voter-registration effort in 1992.[39] Although charges of voter registration fraud surfaced in the 2008 campaign, defenders claimed that the problems revealed mismanagement, not malfeasance.[40]

Soon it became clear that within ACORN there were problems of both mismanagement and malfeasance. Only Wade Rathke; his brother Dale, the business manager; and ACORN's attorney, Steve Bachman, understood the complex web of more than two hundred entities the organization had created—including radio stations; local chapters; for-profit and nonprofit financial services; community-redevelopment agencies; local, state, and national political action committees; and real estate holdings. In the summer of 2008 a whistleblower revealed that Dale Rathke had embezzled $1 million from ACORN and that a small group of executives, including Wade Rathke, had kept the information from the board and from the police.[41]

Although Wade Rathke was forced to resign, ACORN continued to press its progressive agenda throughout the 2008 campaign. Along with voter registration, ACORN had launched a vigorous campaign on behalf of national health insurance. Tamecka Pierce, a member of ACORN's national board, was a leader in the national Health Care for America Now (HCAN) campaign. HCAN endorsed national health insurance with a public option. This forty-six-state coalition was supported by more than a thousand organizations, including progressive unions, community activists, civil rights groups, feminists, pro-choice groups, health activists, church groups, and physician and nursing organizations. Following Obama's election in 2008, HCAN rallied to fulfill the long-sought dream of progressives: nationalized health insurance—that is, the federal government's takeover of the nation's health.

The New Progressive Leviathan

Why did the Left make national health insurance a cornerstone of its agenda, pushing to revamp the entire system, even though polls showed that most Americans were happy with the current system? Why did progressive activists want to create a governmental Leviathan, the inevitable result of nationalizing health insurance, with so little likelihood of success in reducing rising health-care costs or reducing the national debt?

The answer to this question is that New Progressives seek to control the everyday lives of Americans. Government regulation expands the power of political and corporate elites. By assuming control through regulation of health care, the progressive Left would gain control over 17 percent of the economy. Just as New Progressives sought to control the environment, population growth, and basic consumption of Americans, they required control over health care—all in the name of saving the people from the consequences of their own choices.

As the 1960s came to an end, New Progressives had recognized the ineffectiveness of mere protest. They learned to work within the political, legal, and corporate systems to remake the country. Forty years later they would have their greatest opportunity to extend government's power in the name of the progressive agenda when a fellow progressive, Barack Obama, emerged on the national scene.

6

The Long March Leads to the White House

I t had been a long march for the New Progressives. Beginning in the 1960s, this new breed had turned its back on the New Deal–Great Society tradition. The goal was to redefine liberalism and to work within the system to radically transform the United States. Although progressives had experienced setbacks along the way, their advances endured, especially their reforms of how the Democratic Party selected its presidential nominees and the legal victories they had achieved on behalf of progressive causes. Perhaps more important, the movement had built up a vast infrastructure of unions and environmental, health-care, feminist, and other activist groups. That infrastructure was firmly in place when, in 2008, the progressives finally had one of their own as a legitimate candidate for president of the United States: Barack Obama.

How the United States, a center-right nation in all polls, elected a leftist president is a fascinating story.

Out of Progressive Enclaves

Nothing is more frustrating to a child than looking through a window into a candy store. The glass barrier entices, but it also establishes that the goodies on the inside are beyond reach. For progressives, as they increasingly took to calling themselves after the 1960s, electoral politics was often like the proverbial candy store, with progressives on the out-side looking in. They did enjoy a few successes, mostly in college towns where idealistic, youthful voters could be mobilized to take control of local governments.

Thus, in Madison, Wisconsin, graduate-student activist Paul Soglin won a seat on the city council and then became mayor. He hired unemployed youth to keep State Street clean, which both pleased older voters and built a personal patronage machine. Except for flamboyant radical rhetoric, the new politics, it turned out, was not all that different from the politics of Tammany Hall.[1]

The progressive machine in Berkeley, California, was more problematic. Not only were the sidewalks filthy, but the city-funded Berkeley Peace and Justice Commission pursued its own foreign policy by sending radicals on global inspection junkets. Progressive rent-control wars were long and vicious, annihilating as many landlords as possible. One local ice cream parlor that refused to pay an $18,000 bribe to a city inspector could not occupy the vacant adjacent space on which it was paying rent for more than a year.[2]

The former student radical Tom Hayden settled down with Jane Fonda in Santa Monica and brought New Progressive government to that upscale Los Angeles seaside suburb. A majority of the residents were renters, and progressives used rent control to rally the tenant majority into installing a progressive city government. The "People's Republic of Santa Monica" pioneered other leftist innovations, including a ban on cigarette smoking in restaurants and the requirement that public buildings have only unisex restrooms. Hayden went to the California legislature as a progressive Democrat. He focused on racial and labor issues, pushed legislative Democrats to the left, and was so hated for having opposed the Vietnam War that some legislators tried to expel him.[3]

During the 1970s and 1980s, New Progressives demonstrated to themselves that progressive governance could be popular, at least in progressive enclaves. The 1990s proved more frustrating. Bill Clinton came out of the moderate Democratic Leadership Council wing of the Democratic Party, and then the Republican takeover of the Congress in 1994 stunned progressives. Incapable of seeing the public as conservative, progressives looked for scapegoats to blame for Democrats' failures. Progressives wanted to purge Rush Limbaugh and other conservatives from the airwaves. Oliver Stone, Martin Luther King III, Bill Moyers, and Jim Hightower saw various conspiracies. Perhaps a "vast right-wing conspiracy" controlled the country, Hillary Clinton once suggested.[4]

From the beginning of Bill Clinton's presidency, it was understood that Vice President Al Gore was to be the heir in 2000. For years, Gore had been regarded among mainstream politicians as a fervent supporter of the Green Revolution. Although Gore had certain moderate tendencies, including support for the North American Free Trade Agreement (NAFTA), and had cast votes in the House and Senate that did not upset his decidedly conservative Tennessee constituents, he balanced these votes by speaking out on the environment. For Gore, Ralph Nader's acquiescence in the 2000 campaign was a necessity. The election was expected to be close, and Gore needed all the support he could collect.

But Nader, like many progressives, had tired of the Reagan-Bush-Clinton years. "I can no longer stomach the systemic political decay that has weakened our democracy," he said. Urging progressives to stand up for their beliefs, Nader asserted that "big business is on a collision course with American democracy." He declared that Bush and Gore were "tweedledum and tweedledee" with "few major differences." Endorsing universal health care, antipoverty legislation, consumer protection, and environmentalism, he announced, "We are building a historic, progressive, political movement in America." Nader preferred the word *progressive* to *liberal*.[5]

Nader's third-party candidacy allowed George W. Bush, a friend of the oil industry, to win. But with Nader on the ballot, millions of progressives who had dropped out of politics had an incentive to vote, and their votes further down the ballot helped elect other progressive Democrats. In the future, Nader and his followers could hope, Democrats might nominate progressives rather than moderates like Clinton and Gore.[6]

Sure enough, in 2004, Democrats nominated John Kerry for president. The Massachusetts senator was no moderate, boasting one of the most liberal voting records in the Senate. Nader ran again, but he did poorly this time. Kerry lost, but the Naderites had helped push the Democrats away from Clinton's 1990s moderation to the left.[7]

Obama's Progressive Roots

In 2008 one candidate was uniquely positioned to appeal to New Progressives, and that candidate was Senator Barack Obama (D-Illinois). Even before learning his position on issues, progressives loved his biracial heritage and multicultural life experiences. Obama's white grandparents had liberal, populist views; his father was a self-proclaimed African socialist; and his mother held progressive views, had spent her life working on Third World poverty issues, and had taken Obama to live in Indonesia.[8] Going to high school in Hawaii exposed young Obama to America's most multicultural state. The state was known as liberal and tolerant, but Obama, who attended an elite prep school, was pained to see poverty side by side with wealth.[9] To give Obama an adult black male role model, Obama's grandfather introduced his grandson to Frank Marshall Davis, a communist poet.[10]

One student at Occidental College recalled Obama as a Marxist passionate about maldistribution of wealth.[11] After transferring to Columbia University, Obama attended at least one socialist scholars' conference, where it was explained that organizing the poor might hasten a socialist revolution in the United States.[12] He graduated in 1983 and went to work for New York PIRG, a Naderite activist group that had pressured banks to grant mortgages to low-income borrowers.[13] In 1985, Obama moved to Chicago to become a community organizer among poor blacks on the South Side. He worked for the Gamaliel Foundation, which had ties to progressive churches and unions. As an organizer, Obama used radical Saul Alinsky's confrontational methods. Conflict between poor residents and officials humiliated the government, enhanced participants' sense of self-worth, and produced favorable negotiated settlements.[14]

Eventually, Obama concluded that he could accomplish more for the poor by working inside government. He reached this conclusion when the progressive Harold Washington was Chicago's first black mayor. In 1983, Washington won by rallying poor blacks and Hispanics, progressive whites, and a portion of the business community. Business leaders hoped that Washington might turn the decaying city around. Having installed a number of progressives in his administration, the mayor proved adroit in using federal funds, city policies, and progressive foundation grants to push a left-wing agenda. Washington understood the limits beyond which progressive policies must not go to retain business support. Obama learned that progressives could make alliances with business or at least with certain favored corporations.[15]

Obama sought out elite training to advance his political career. At Harvard Law School, he served as president of the law review, a prestigious post that usually led to a lucrative job with a major law firm.[16]

Instead, Obama returned to Chicago to join a small progressive firm specializing in social justice issues and taught part-time at the University of Chicago Law School. He lived in the progressive enclave of Hyde Park, served on progressive foundation boards, and met leading wealthy progressives such as Penny Pritzker. Through Pritzker, he became acquainted with many business and society leaders, which proved useful when he later ran for office.[17]

In Chicago, Obama received early political support from the tainted real estate developer Tony Rezko. Also important were the African American real estate attorney Valerie Jarrett, a former appointee in the Harold Washington administration who became a close friend and later White House aide, and Rahm Emanuel, who had worked as a lobbyist for Goldman Sachs and had served in the Clinton White House. Andy McKenna, the Republican chair of McDonald's, called Obama "sensible" and not antibusiness. Another early enthusiast was Jamie Dimon, a liberal Democrat who was then CEO of Bank One in Chicago and who later became CEO of JPMorgan Chase. Through Chicago's elite social circles, Obama met George Soros, the leftist billionaire financier, who became a key early backer of Obama's presidential bid.[18]

At the same time, Obama continued to network among progressive-led groups with a mass base. Dating to his organizing days in the 1980s, he knew the ACORN crowd, which was closely linked in Chicago to SEIU Local 880.[19] He enjoyed mentorship and political support from many leaders at the Midwest Academy, a school for community organizers run by ex–SDS radicals Heather and Paul Booth.[20] ACORN, SEIU, and the Midwest Academy had a matrix of overlapping leaders, board members, occasional participants, and financial backers. It was this matrix that enabled Obama to meet Bill Ayers. Expressing an interest in urban school reform, Obama collaborated with Ayers, the former SDS radical turned college professor.[21]

Obama wanted to enter politics. Exploiting ties to ACORN, to SEIU Local 880, to the Midwest Academy, and to community organizers he knew from the 1980s, Obama ran a major voter-registration campaign in 1992. If large numbers of Chicago's poor, who were mostly black and Hispanic, could be registered and then turned out to vote, Democrats might win statewide on Election Day. Obama's Project Vote registered 150,000 new voters. One key to success was a poster that artfully invoked Malcolm X, who had been a hero among African Americans in Chicago.

Obama inspired the disaffected to become involved. The success of Project Vote brought Obama to the attention of powerful Illinois Democrats.[22]

When the local congressional seat suddenly opened in a special election in 1995, state senator Alice Palmer, an African American progressive Democrat from Hyde Park, announced that she would give up her seat to run for Congress. Toward the end of the Cold War, Palmer had had strong ties to the Communist Party. At one point she lavished praise on the Soviet Union in the *People's Daily World*, the party newspaper. Palmer raised eyebrows when she publicly backed Obama, a relative newcomer to the city, as her successor for the Illinois senate. She did so first at a small meeting at the house of Bill Ayers and Bernardine Dohrn and then in a more public setting.[23]

Other Chicago radicals became early Obama enthusiasts as well. Since the 1950s, Michael Harrington had advocated using the ballot box to bring socialism to America.[24] By the 1990s, prospects were poor for any openly socialist party in the United States. "Socialism," both as a concept and as a word, was unpopular. So socialists promoted "stealth socialism." In the 1960s, Frances Fox Piven and Richard Cloward had argued that expensive social programs could bankrupt the country and thereby ignite a socialist revolution. Socialists inside the Midwest Academy, ACORN, and other groups that organized the poor had borrowed the concept of stealth activism. Socialists in these groups agreed that they should never admit to their ultimate socialist goal among nonsocialists. Instead, they planned to use unions, community organizing, and third parties to take over the Democratic Party and turn it in a socialist direction.

In the early 1990s, Democratic Socialists of America (DSA), which Harrington had founded, joined other radicals willing to work within the political system, including former SDS radicals and current leaders in ACORN and SEIU, to form the New Party. DSA, ACORN, and the New Party favored redistribution of wealth and income. They wanted progressive taxes, easier unionization through "card check," and greater financial and business regulation. The New Party was created to enable socialists to pressure the Democratic Party to move left. Although some New Party members wanted government ownership of major industries, many believed that tight government regulation of business could force redistribution of wealth. For example, banks could be coerced into making loans to the poor, and government-subsidized health care would promote high wages for unionized health-care workers. Under "stealth socialism," elite control of governmental power could be used to pursue social justice.[25]

In 1996, the New Party stated in print that Obama was a member, and later that year another leftist publication, the *Progressive Populist*, identified Obama as a New Party member.[26] In 2008, when this issue arose in the presidential campaign, the Obama camp denied that he had ever been a member. In addition, a founder of the New Party denied that Obama could have been a member by claiming that the organization did not have formal memberships. But archival documents proved that there were memberships, and in 2012 the author Stanley Kurtz published proof that Obama had joined the New Party. The minutes of a meeting of the party's Chicago chapter on January 11, 1996, state that Obama joined the party that day. Kurtz discovered confirming documentation: a party roster from 1997 listed Obama as having been a member since January 11, 1996. At that early 1996 meeting, the minutes show, Obama also signed the New Party's "Candidate Contract," promising to support publicly and associate himself with the party while in office. According to the minutes, Obama asked for the New Party's endorsement that day; candidates seeking an endorsement were asked to support the party's official statement of principles, which called for an anticapitalist "peaceful revolution" and redistribution of wealth.[27] When Obama ran for the state senate that year, he was one of only five Democrats in Cook County, Illinois, to be endorsed by the New Party. The party's rules prohibited endorsements of any person who was not in an active relationship with the party. In addition, Obama was one of only four Democrats to be endorsed by the Chicago branch of DSA, Harrington's old group. All four of these candidates were among the five that the New Party also backed.[28]

Obama won the Illinois state senate seat. In Springfield he established a progressive voting record in keeping with public opinion in Hyde Park and the poorer neighborhoods in his district.[29] In 2004, when Obama decided to run for the U.S. Senate, he won a seven-way contest for the Democratic nomination by getting black votes, estimated to be 22 percent of the primary, as well as progressive votes. The Chicago machine backed another candidate because they regarded Obama as a newcomer who should wait his turn to run for a high post. David Axelrod, a progressive, ran Obama's campaign. One important Obama campaign issue was national health insurance. In the general election, he lucked out when scandal forced the main Republican candidate to quit.

As a U.S. senator, Obama continued his progressive voting record. In 2007 the *National Journal* ranked him the most liberal senator; Hillary Clinton ranked sixteenth.[30]

There was nothing in Obama's background, political actions, or positions to make progressives uneasy. His personal life story; his work as a community organizer; his ties to the Midwest Academy, ACORN, and SEIU; his consistent support of national health insurance and other progressive legislation; his votes for almost every spending bill in the legislature and the U.S. Senate—all affirmed his progressive values. Madeline Talbott, the head of Chicago ACORN, said it best in 1995: "We accept and respect him as a kindred spirit, a fellow organizer."[31]

Progressive Mobilization

In early 2007, Hillary Clinton was the favorite to receive the Democratic presidential nomination in 2008, holding 41 percent support in an otherwise weak field where other candidates were below 20 percent. But Clinton had a problem with progressives. Although she had a liberal voting record in the Senate and could claim feminist and African American backing, she lacked serious credentials among progressives, other than some ACORN ties that dated to Arkansas. Furthermore, she was married to Bill, the legendary centrist. Would a true progressive woman metaphorically and literally go to bed with a moderate like Bill? Despite long-standing rumors that Hillary was more liberal than Bill, progressives were suspicious of a woman who in 1964 had cheered for Barry Goldwater—and in 2003 had voted to make war in Iraq.[32]

The first Democratic candidate to calculate that progressive support might be the key to beating Hillary Clinton was John Edwards. The former senator and 2004 vice presidential nominee had long embraced economic populism, expressing working-class resentment against wealthy and powerful elites. It sounded radical, but it did not promise anything too specific that might frighten voters. It also appealed to ACORN and SEIU, which liked to focus on economic issues. Edwards knew that the only path to the nomination was to score an upset in Iowa. Because Clinton was weak in Iowa, and because Iowa was a caucus state where organization and activism mattered, Edwards shaped his message for Iowa party activists, including progressives, likely to attend caucuses.[33]

Barack Obama also could not get the nomination without winning Iowa. His staff knew from polls that Edwards, who was better known since he had been campaigning in Iowa off and on since 2004, would win the regular party progressives who had participated in past caucuses. Clinton would rally moderate rural voters and women. To win, Obama needed to register many new voters, concentrating on minorities and young people. Almost all of Obama's numerous appearances in Iowa in 2007 were designed to stimulate voter registration.[34]

In addition, Obama took progressive policy positions on health care, the environment, and taxation to cut into Edwards's support. He planned to run to the left of Edwards, whose vague economic populism sounded old-fashioned to many progressives. Obama's message was calculated to appeal both to progressive Iowa caucus attendees and to progressive enclaves across the country. The Obama campaign calculated that if it won Iowa, Edwards would be forced to withdraw, leaving Obama as the progressive alternative to Clinton.[35]

On January 3, 2008, Obama won the Iowa caucuses with 38 percent of the vote to Edwards's 30 percent and Clinton's 29 percent. Newly registered voters and whipped-up enthusiasm caused turnout to soar from 124,000 in 2004 to 240,000. Clinton, the front-runner, was shattered with a humiliating third-place finish. Edwards, who needed a strong win to stay in the contest, saw his funds dry up after his weak second-place finish. Suddenly, Clinton was short of funds as well. That month, Obama raised $32 million, much of it online, to Clinton's $13 million.[36]

Although Clinton recovered enough to win the New Hampshire primary, she was always behind and on the defensive after Iowa. In the end, she could never quite catch up.[37] Obama's positioning himself as the progressive alternative to Clinton rallied new voters, the old Naderites, and those suspicious of the Clintons' moderate past. Obama attracted the antiwar Left, having publicly denounced the Iraq war ("a dumb war") even before the fighting began, whereas Clinton and Edwards had cast votes in the Senate to authorize the war.[38] Obama also appealed to Christian progressives, especially black Protestant preachers interested in government welfare programs and white nonevangelical Protestant clergy, whose social gospel practices promoted urban soup kitchens and asylum for illegal immigrants. Progressives concerned with health care and the environment found Obama congenial as well. To pay for new programs,

Obama proposed raising taxes on the wealthy, an idea that sat well with many of Edwards's populist supporters.[39]

Obama's victory was truly a victory for progressives. It reflected the enduring impact of the McGovern Commission's reforms, especially the emphasis on precinct caucuses. Clinton actually outpolled Obama in primary votes in 2008, but Obama won the most delegates because he used money and organization to dominate the caucuses, where progressives were more likely to participate than were party moderates. Recall that in Texas, Obama lost the primary but won the caucus—and ended up claiming many more Texas delegates than did Clinton, even though the caucus drew only a fraction of the voters who turned out for the primary. It is hard to escape the conclusion that progressives gave Obama the nomination.[40]

Progressives remained important to Obama in the general election, especially the youthful progressives who volunteered for the campaign to register voters, get out the vote, and help with Obama's pioneering online and social-media efforts. But to win, Obama needed to expand his support. Moderates were lured to vote for Obama by the promise of no tax increases on the middle class, as well as a general exhaustion with George W. Bush and the Republican Party. Of voters who believed that Republican nominee John McCain represented continuity with Bush, 90 percent picked Obama. Most of Obama's speeches lacked specifics in order to reduce tension between moderate and progressive voters that he sought to win.[41]

In the fall, the media discovered that Obama had had a political connection since the 1990s with the former 1960s radical activist and domestic terrorist Bill Ayers. Obama noted that he was eight years old when Ayers was a terrorist. By the time the two met, Ayers was a respected college professor interested in the education of the poor, a topic that also concerned Obama. The Ayers story probably did not cost Obama votes. Conservatives upset by the story probably would not have voted for Obama in any case. Moderates showed little interest, and among progressives, Obama's acquaintance with Ayers might have been a plus.[42]

Riding the Health-Care Issue

After the spectacular failure of the Clintons' health-care reform in 1993–94, most Democrats avoided the divisive issue. But by 2008, the time was ripe. Escalating private insurance premiums had produced pressure for cost containment; financially pressed businesses were canceling employee coverage; even the insurance industry wanted change. John Edwards calculated that by reintroducing the idea of national health insurance, he could win progressive voters in the primaries, as well as support from SEIU, which represented many health-care workers. Polls suggested that the public might be amenable to passing such a bill. Polling on health care, however, was always tricky, because while a majority favored the idea of national health insurance, it was difficult to find a majority for any particular plan.[43]

Because Hillary Clinton had been burned on the health issue in 1993–94, she had little incentive to emphasize the idea. Still, she remained committed to national health insurance and proposed a plan building on the existing employer-based system. Obama needed a health-care proposal in the Democratic primaries that would give him credibility and could appeal to progressives. His proposal had to seem comprehensive enough to constitute national health insurance but also flexible enough that it would neither frighten moderates nor draw attacks from the powerful insurance industry.[44]

Throughout the campaign, Obama left details of his health proposal vague. Progressives preferred a socialist-style single-payer system with the government as the sole provider; Obama said that he agreed with that position philosophically but that such a plan could not pass Congress. Moderate Democrats, whose votes were needed to pass a bill, came from districts or states where opposition to a single-payer plan was intense. Furthermore, polling data showed that most Americans liked the health-care plans they had. So there was little reason to force people to change to something new and untested. "Under the plan," Obama promised over and over, "if you like your current health insurance, nothing changes."[45] In place of a single-payer government-run system, Obama proposed that private employers might continue to use private insurers but that there would also be a government-run insurance option, known as the "public option." This was one aspect of the plan that Obama did make clear: it required people to do what the government told them to do. Thus, large businesses were mandated to provide health coverage for employees and their family members or pay a fee to the government. The proposal, however, did not provide specific numbers about coverage or the fee.

Obama actually proposed two different health-care plans, one during the spring primaries, when he was wooing progressive voters, and the other during the fall campaign, when he pivoted to win moderate independents. There were two key differences between the plans. First, in the spring proposal, all employers had to provide insurance or pay a fee, but in the fall version, small businesses were exempt from this mandate, leaving many Americans uncovered. Second, in the fall plan, individuals who were not covered by small business, were self-employed, or were not employed could buy health insurance, but they were not required to do so. The spring plan, however, had promised that "every American will be covered" by "making health insurance universal."[46]

The lack of specifics helped Obama during the campaign. It made the proposal more difficult to attack, for one thing. It signaled, too, that Obama would avoid the mistake the Clintons had made in trying to dictate the details of the bill to Congress. From the beginning, Obama indicated that he would allow Congress to draft the bill. He also indicated to medical providers and the insurance industry that he would work with them to make sure the bill did not contain features they found unworkable.[47]

Obama's use of the health-care issue showed how his campaign masterfully appealed to progressives while also playing to the establishment, including the "special interests" progressives so often condemned. In laying out a plan (however vague) for a nationalized health-care system, Obama promised to fulfill the elusive dream of progressives. But he was careful not to scare off physicians, hospitals, insurance companies, or the pharmaceutical industry—mainly by signaling that under his plan, they would be able to feast at the honey pot. Thanks largely to this approach, the pharmaceutical industry contributed $8 million to Democratic candidates in 2008—twice as much as it gave in 2004—and $1 million to Obama alone.[48]

Going Green

Environmentalism can be tricky for a Democrat. As Ralph Nader proved in 2000, it was dangerous for a Democrat to ignore the Greens, even when polls showed that they were a small (although vocal and litigious) minority. But any Democrat who embraced the full green agenda ran the risk of a backlash among working-class Democrats whose jobs were threatened by ultra-green policies that forced manufacturers to move work offshore. Obama tried to redefine the issue so that being green (to get the "tree-hugger" vote) might be a way to create new jobs (to get the blue-collar logger vote). Once again, as in health care, Obama's vision depended on talking in vague generalities that were difficult to parse and on projecting faith in using the power of the federal government to reconcile all the clashing issues.[49]

Federal power was the key concept. Markets, Obama seemed to believe, had failed to solve environmental problems. Only political force controlled top-down by bureaucrats in Washington could impose solutions on private enterprise and individuals. One could see the mentality operating already at the local level within the progressive enclaves. Fast food restaurants were banned from serving food in throwaway containers that could not be recycled, and homeowners were required to separate garbage into three types: recyclables, yard and food waste, and true garbage, which was defined in very narrow terms. In Seattle, garbage police inspected containers and issued fines for mishandling materials. The city also pushed fluorescent lightbulbs by prohibiting the sale of certain standard lightbulbs and inspected the efficiency of private home furnaces.

At the pinnacle of Obama's environmental plan was "cap and trade." The concept was simple. Every originator of carbon pollution, primarily coal-burning electric utilities, was required to reduce emissions gradually to a point that approached nil over the next generation. Because some polluters were wealthy and could easily afford to shift from polluting coal to nuclear, wind, or solar energy, they could reduce their emissions beyond the immediate requirement (the cap, which the government set); they would then have "emission permits" available to sell to financially weak polluters, who could, in effect, buy the right to continue to pollute on a temporary basis. In theory, the system would lead to a more rapid reduction in carbon emissions than any other system.[50]

Proponents of cap and trade cited it as a market-based system, but the Obama version clearly emphasized the government's role. For one thing, the payments by the polluters who could not rapidly meet changing standards would go to the federal government. In turn, these payments would allow the federal government to invest in private companies to promote wind and solar energy, clean coal burned underground, and other new technologies. Although few objected to the government's funding of basic scientific research, here the government would be picking particular corporations for key investments. The odds of favoritism in allocating funds were high, while the odds that government bureaucrats would make successful investments were low. Governments almost always invest poorly, and the result would be a permanent misallocation of capital away from promising technology efficiently developed by the private sector into pet projects of little or no value.[51]

The emphasis on top-down control could be seen in other Obama environmental mandates: putting one million plug-in hybrid cars on the road by 2015, cutting carbon in fuels by 10 percent by 2020, producing 25 percent of electricity from renewable resources by 2025, and reducing greenhouse-gas emissions by 80 percent by 2050. As with health care, Obama proposed bringing the energy sector under federal control. Although private energy companies such as Exxon Mobil, Peabody Coal, Duke Power, and the Southern Companies might survive for a while, how long would it be before privileged or politically connected companies, relying heavily on government subsidies despite bad management and poor fundamentals, would use those very subsidies to push their competitors into bankruptcy?[52]

At the same time, cap and trade promised to deliver boatloads of cash—possibly $200 billion per year—to the government, and Obama proposed to spend some of the money on social programs. If that turned out to be true, the alternative energy sources would remain underdeveloped, but the price of energy would soar. One European expert calculated a double-digit increase in electricity prices within two years, and a Harvard study saw $7-a-gallon gasoline by 2020. As energy prices rose, Americans would have less money to buy anything else. The private sector would have to lay off large numbers of workers. Some jobs might leave the country, but a good many might simply cease to exist. Cap and trade promised to destroy jobs, reduce living standards, and shrink the economy.[53]

The Obama plan's top-down approach was also evident in its call for most Americans to drive all-electric automobiles within a generation. The plan ignored the fact that no such practical vehicle actually existed. The best current all-electric car, the California-based Tesla, would go up to 245 miles on a single charge. The catch was that it cost $109,000. For most consumers, the price was unrealistic, and the driving range ineffective. But with Obama's emphasis on governmental power, the big businesses that manufactured green technologies were sure to benefit. Indeed, once Obama took office, one of his biggest enthusiasts was Jeffrey

Immelt, CEO of General Electric (GE), which lobbied for, and received, government subsidies for its plug-in hybrid electric vehicle, the Chevy Volt. (The subsidies came in the form of a consumer tax credit of $7,500.) At headquarters, Immelt said, "We're all Democrats now" (though he later expressed second thoughts).[54] Consumers certainly were not lining up to buy the Volt: in the first two months of 2011, GM sold only 602.[55]

Obama also pushed high-speed rail. In most parts of the United States, the density of population was insufficient to make such rail feasible, and even in dense areas there were practical difficulties in obtaining rights of way and paying the construction and operation costs. But pushing for an expensive, tax-subsidized public rail system appealed to progressives and would mean more contributions from public service employee unions.[56]

Middle-Class Tax Cuts

In 1980 one of Ronald Reagan's major campaign promises was to cut income taxes. He did so in 1982 and again with a major tax-reform bill in 1986 that slashed the top rate to 28 percent. When the tax cuts were combined with Paul Volcker's Federal Reserve policy to squeeze inflation out of the economy, the result was a steep drop in interest rates, soaring business investment, and rising purchases of homes and automobiles. During the long boom that began in 1983 and lasted until 2007, the economy more than doubled in size, and living standards for most Americans dramatically increased.

In 1984, Walter Mondale lost the election when he promised to raise taxes. To increasing numbers of Americans, the idea seemed daft. In 1988, George H. W. Bush, attempting to follow in Reagan's footsteps, promised, "Read my lips. No new taxes." Senate Majority Leader George Mitchell, a Democrat, ruined Bush by making him agree to a bill increasing taxes. In 1992, Bush lost to Bill Clinton, who promptly signed a bill increasing taxes. Although Clinton's increases were modest, taxes helped defeat the Democrats in 1994. In 2000, George W. Bush, imitating Reagan, promised tax cuts. Bush both cut taxes and increased spending, but he lacked the political strength to make the tax cuts permanent.[57]

With the Bush tax cuts set to expire in December 2010, tax policy was bound to be an issue in the 2008 election. Republicans promised to make the Bush tax cuts permanent. As a candidate who appealed to liberals with an expensive domestic proposal like universal health care, Obama knew that he had to handle the tax issue carefully to be a credible candidate. Borrowing a page from John Edwards's populist playbook, he came up with the clever plan of retaining the Bush tax cuts for everyone except wealthy taxpayers, defined as families earning more than $250,000 per year. This tax plan would "spread the wealth around," Obama said in the campaign.[58] According to polls, the plan persuaded voters that Obama was better than John McCain on taxes, an issue that normally favored Republicans.[59]

It did not matter that his tax increases would choke small businesses. A majority of small businesses are taxed at the individual level. For many of these businesses, a sudden increase in individual income tax rates would be a jolt that would cause them not to hire new employees or perhaps even to lay off workers. Choking small businesses means choking the economy. Between 1995 and 2010, businesses with fewer than five hundred workers, employing half the private-sector workforce, created 64 percent of new jobs.[60]

Obama and his progressive followers ignored the fact that tax rates drive behavior. The federal government collected income tax on $140 billion a year in income that foreigners made inside the United States. At what point would Obama's plan to raise taxes simply lead foreigners to pull their money out of the United States?[61] And when would high-earning Americans decide that the risks of going for big earnings were not worth it? The record was clear: every time in the past fifty years that the government increased the capital-gains tax, the amount of capital-gains income fell as a percentage of gross domestic product; in every case the rate was cut, capital-gains income rose. When the top tax rate on capital gains was 39 percent from 1976 to 1978, revenues were $23.9 billion; when the rate was 20 percent from 1983 to 1985, revenues were $66.7 billion. It is easy to explain why. Wealthy people who sell real estate or stock pay most capital-gains taxes. If they perceive that the tax rate is higher than it will be later, they wait for the lower rate. With low rates, wealthy individuals pay the tax rather than hold the investment, meaning that capital is redeployed throughout the economy in more efficient ways. Much of the 1980s boom can be explained by lower tax rates.[62]

Diplomacy as a Form of Strategic Defense

In the eyes of the Left, as well as world leaders and people across the globe, the Bush administration had been trigger-happy, too quick to impose military solutions and too reluctant to engage in the slow process of diplomacy. Every Democrat running for president in 2008 promised a more balanced foreign policy that put a greater emphasis on diplomacy than on military might. As a woman, Hillary Clinton perhaps had a need to sound sufficiently bellicose that Americans would be reassured that she was tough enough to be commander in chief. Her service on the Armed Services Committee, where she asked hard, pointed questions, had helped shape an image of responsible military preparedness.[63]

Obama, by contrast, consistently played the peace card. Part of his sensibility came from his own multicultural background: an African father; a white Kansan mother; a Muslim stepfather; time in school in Indonesia; life in multicultural Hawaii; his own racial-identity crisis; his marriage to Michelle, who had a strong sense of blackness; the decision to help the poor black community on the South Side of Chicago; and exposure to the Reverend Jeremiah Wright's sermons. Obama could claim more diverse experiences than most Americans, and the variety of exposures made him determined to be a catalyst for reconciliation and change. One could see the reasoning in his widely admired speech on race in Philadelphia in March 2008.

After 9/11, Obama, like most Americans, had supported the war against the Taliban in Afghanistan. But from the beginning he opposed the Bush administration's decision to invade Iraq. He saw the war not only as unnecessary but also as destabilizing to the region. He wanted diplomacy to be given a chance. In the Senate, Obama served on the Foreign Relations Committee, another proof of his preference for diplomacy.

Because Obama had always opposed the Iraq war, he had an excellent chance to capture the antiwar progressives in the Democratic primaries and caucuses. To firm up this support, Obama pledged that, if elected, he would withdraw all American combat troops from Iraq by summer 2010. He also promised to close down the American detention facility at Guantánamo, Cuba, which had caused such enormous controversy. At the same time, Obama said that the United States had to remain in Afghanistan, which was showing increasing signs of instability during 2007 and 2008. In some ways, the pledge to leave Iraq but stay in

Afghanistan seemed an odd pairing, but Obama had to appeal to anti–Iraq War voters without suggesting that he was a pacifist. The long-term strategic implications of such a bifurcated foreign policy were difficult to sort out.[64]

During one of the primary debates, Obama said that if elected he would talk without preconditions to the dictators of such countries as Cuba, Iran, and Venezuela. Clinton called his position naive and suggested that it showed inexperience. The media declared that Obama had clearly misspoken. The rules of diplomacy required that one talked to repressive tyrants only after some useful preliminaries at a lower level had cleared away the underbrush. In diplomacy, even the willingness to talk was a bargaining chip that should not be given away lightly. Some advisers suggested that Obama issue a clarification saying that he had overlooked the preconditions that would have to precede any high-level talks. Obama refused. He really did offer to meet any high-level leaders for talks without preconditions.[65]

Progressives defended Obama, who, in their eyes, was acting as a man of peace. They cared little for the rules of diplomacy and tended to believe that the world had suffered so many wars because an older generation had played diplomatic games instead of pursuing peace. The yearning for peace after nearly a decade of war was palpable, especially on the left. Obama thought he could break down barriers. As the first African American president, he might be seen differently in many parts of the world, especially in the nonwhite Third World. As a onetime resident of a Muslim nation, Indonesia, he might be more admired than other American presidents in Muslim circles around the world.[66]

Obama held out the prospect of a "charm" offensive. As a device to reassure Americans that the government was doing all it could on the diplomatic front, such an offensive had great value. Whether it would actually lead any nation to recalibrate its relationship with the United States was far less certain. And the policy could be dangerous, if unfriendly nations exploited Obama's approach the way Adolf Hitler had exploited British prime minister Neville Chamberlain at Munich in 1938. The United States ran the risk of being forced either to accept groveling humiliations or to make a war that might have been avoided. It was hard to reconcile peace through strength with a charm offensive.

Media Euphoria

From the beginning of the 2008 campaign, Obama enjoyed a relationship with the media different from the other candidates'. John McCain had been something of a media darling in 2000, when he lost the Republican nomination to George W. Bush. Now McCain found that the press barely covered him because they were so enraptured by Obama. The other Republicans and most of the Democrats who had entered the contest in 2007 were totally ignored. As the Democratic front-runner, Hillary Clinton generated ample coverage, but much of it was critical. Reporters discussed her hairstyle and clothes rather than her policy proposals, or they repeated Obama talking points against Clinton.[67]

By contrast, reporters could not rhapsodize enough about Obama. They crowded around the candidate in record numbers, even in the early days in Iowa in 2007, seeking endless photo-ops, including autographed photographs for reporters' family members. The press hung on every word, giddy with appreciation, despite the vagueness of many of Obama's set speeches. In questioning Obama, reporters never deflated him or tripped him up, as the press usually does with candidates. Watching Obama, MSNBC's Chris Matthews recalled, "I felt this thrill going up my leg." Bill Clinton complained about the press corps, "They just want to cream in their jeans over this guy."[68]

More important than the personal favoritism was the failure of the media to investigate Obama's background. In early 2008, when Obama was still little known by the American people, audiotapes of the Reverend Jeremiah Wright's scurrilous anti-American sermons (e.g., "God-*damn* America!" and "U.S. of KKK A.") were being sold to the public at Wright's church. Obama did not hide the fact that he belonged to Wright's church, and Wright was present at Obama's presidential announcement in February 2007 in Springfield, Illinois, although the campaign at the last minute decided to stop Wright from giving the invocation. Reporters saw Wright at the event, but they made no inquiries. By the time ABC News broke the story in March 2008, Obama had such a strong lead for the nomination that he was unlikely to be stopped. Although ABC and Fox News covered the story for a while, most of the other media gave it only modest play.[69] In the fall campaign, McCain's team discussed raising the Wright issue. McCain's pollster concluded that the issue might enable McCain to win the election but that race relations would be so embittered that governance would be all but impossible. In the end, McCain ran no anti-Wright ads.[70]

Obama skillfully deflected the issue by giving a speech on race in Philadelphia on March 18. A masterpiece of artful construction, Obama stressed his own biracial persona, personalizing America's dilemma over race by discussing his white grandmother, who had played a significant role in raising him, and his African father. Many Americans found the speech moving. The speech pushed the racial discussion beyond the usual bromides (the brotherhood of man) and cant (Al Sharpton). It suggested, as many Americans believed, that Obama was postracial, and yet it rooted Obama's comfort with his own biracial identity in what appeared to be a deep empathy with all sides of the American racial past and present.[71]

The media raved about Obama's speech. Many reporters were happy to drop the race issue after that, except to continue to celebrate Obama as a postracial candidate, a theme that constantly boosted his campaign. Political rivals found it difficult to criticize Obama without having the media question whether the criticism was openly or subconsciously racist. Even Bill Clinton, campaigning for Hillary before the South Carolina primary, "kept tripping up on the racial front," as two veteran campaign reporters put it.[72]

The media seldom scrutinized Obama's proposals or plans. Thus, his health-care plan did not get the same close attention as other candidates' proposals, and his proposed cap-and-trade legislation was written about with cheerleading enthusiasm without addressing real concerns about costs, benefits, winners, and losers. Most of the press had long opposed the Iraq war. They were happy to endorse Obama's call for a quick pullout of American troops without questioning his larger Middle East strategy or, indeed, probing to see whether Obama had a real strategy.

The Obama campaign took advantage of the swooning media. The candidate used the media to transmit his spin on his campaign's meaning, the significance of his proposals, and his theme for hope and change. In the spring the campaign planted ideas that led to stories hostile to Clinton, and in the fall the campaign planted ideas that led to stories hostile to McCain. In one incident, Obama's campaign manager, David Axelrod, had suggested that Clinton was partly responsible for the assassination of Benazir Bhutto, the former prime minister of Pakistan. In the fall the Obama campaign encouraged the media's pursuit of Sarah Palin.[73]

At the dawn of the new progressivism in the 1970s, a new generation of journalists had aided the rise of environmentalists, feminists, anticorporate activists, public interest lawyers, and other progressive crusaders by helping challenge the established corporate and political order. The close relationship between the progressive movement and the media would reach its apotheosis in the campaign to elect a true progressive, Barack Obama, president of the United States.

Money and Votes

Obama was a little-known candidate who could be nominated only by starting his campaign early, at the beginning of 2007. The campaign knew that it would have to raise large amounts of money, partly because the front-runner, Hillary Clinton, was well funded, and partly because becoming known would be expensive. After Obama's impressive speech at the Democratic National Convention in 2004, he received thousands of invitations to speak at party fund-raisers. In early 2005 he was getting three hundred requests a week. These opportunities enabled Obama not only to help the party but also to acquire party donor lists in many states. In early 2007, Obama did many traditional high-price fund-raisers for himself, but he also worked in some low-cost events to try to broaden the party's donor base.[74]

Obama's early cultivation of Wall Street also mattered. For a relatively unknown Chicago politician, support from New York's bankers was important. Thus, even as he was using his progressive credentials to win over activists, in private meetings he was persuading Wall Street of his moderation and electability. Many bankers disliked Bush's wars, energy policies, and disdain for urban problems. They distrusted Hillary Clinton and hated John McCain, who hated Wall Street. In private dinners, Obama said he wanted to help the poor, contain health-care costs, and restore American prestige in the world. Larry Fink, CEO of BlackRock (and innovator of mortgage-backed securities), had many Arab clients, and he especially appreciated the latter point. Fink helped sell Obama to Wall Street. Big liberal government and Wall Street could have a mutually advantageous relationship, and the bankers always liked backing a winner. Obama won the support of major Wall Street players, including Jamie Dimon, head of JPMorgan Chase; Lloyd Blankfein,

CEO of Goldman Sachs; and John Mack, the Republican CEO at Morgan Stanley. Wall Street gave Obama $100 million, almost twice as much as McCain received. Most of the Wall Street contributions came in early, providing the essential seed money for Obama's campaign. Of the twenty corporations that bundled the most money for Obama, six were Wall Street banks.[75]

The Obama campaign's most important innovation was to develop an effective website that made it easy for donors to give small amounts online. In addition, Obama had a major Facebook site, and eventually the campaign developed powerful e-mail and text-messaging services, which could also be used for fund-raising. The new media staff included a key player from Howard Dean's 2004 website and a developer of the Orbitz travel site. Tech-savvy twentysomethings helped develop these electronic systems, which led other young voters to become Obama supporters.[76]

Obama targeted antiwar and anticorporate activists because they were skilled at mobilizing people quickly. (Never mind that anticorporate activists were lining up to support a campaign so heavily funded by corporate leaders.) To build a web-based community, the campaign applied community-organizing principles, including the use of local people to bond closely with other locals. Frequent personal communication provided much of the bonding. Obama collected cell phone numbers; McCain did not. By enabling the campaign to communicate rapidly with supporters using text messages, cell phones became a virtual phone bank. By June 2008, Obama had five million e-mail addresses. Forty percent were volunteers or donors. By Election Day, Obama had thirteen million e-mail addresses. Obama had four times as many Facebook friends as McCain, and viewers spent thirty times as many hours watching Obama's campaign videos as McCain's. By November, Obama had posted 1,820 videos on his YouTube site.[77]

The early development of a large youth network mattered a lot. Young voters proved to be a significant source of small donations, and many of the donors also became campaign volunteers. The Obama campaign was able to deploy volunteers to organize in almost every primary and caucus state. The early fund-raising dollars paid off too. Having raised so much more money than his rivals—during the primary season, Obama raised $414 million to Clinton's $224 million—Obama could afford the paid staff needed to supervise the volunteers' activities. Whereas Clinton struggled to pay staff members, Obama employed six thousand staffers,

95 percent under the age of thirty. From June to October 2008, Obama spent $56 million on paid staff, while McCain spent $22 million.[78]

As money rolled into the campaign in record amounts, Obama made a crucial decision. After the Watergate scandal in 1974, Congress had set up a program of federal financing for presidential campaigns. Every major candidate since 1976 had taken federal money for the general-election campaign. In return, each campaign had to cap spending at that same level. For 2008, federal financing offered each candidate $85 million. Candidates could supplement that amount with some funds from their parties, but rules about how party funds could be spent left the individual presidential candidates with little overall message control.[79]

Although Obama had earlier promised to take the federal money and the cap, the prowess of his fund-raising machine caused a reevaluation in June. Obama shocked some reformers by announcing that he would forgo federal money with its tight spending cap. In September alone, Obama raised $150 million. In the entire fall campaign, Obama raised and spent $336 million, almost four times McCain's entire $85 million in federal funds. Much of the extra campaign money went to register new voters, especially African Americans, Hispanics, and young people in battleground states. Because McCain could not legally coordinate his campaign with the Republican Party's effort, the result was a confused message.[80]

Obama, by contrast, had a coherent message ("change") as well as enough money to buy ads in all competitive states. The Democratic Party spent $255 million, partly coordinated with Obama's spending (which was legal, since Obama did not take federal funds) and partly promoting candidates further down the ballot. Thus, the decision to forgo public money enabled Obama to drive up Democratic turnout and elect Democrats from states where Democrats normally did not compete. Obama also used local cable and radio to target narrow groups of voters, such as disappointed Clinton supporters who might shift to McCain. Pro-abortion ads were played only on radio shows with liberal women listeners. Including the primaries, Obama and the Democrats spent $1 billion, nearly twice as much as McCain and the Republicans. Obama *alone* spent more money than *both* Kerry and Bush spent in 2004. Special interests, including unions, spent another $400 million. Including local contests, total political spending in 2008 amounted to $5.3 billion.[81]

Obama's money also helped with early voting, which by 2008 had become common in many states. Nationally, one-third of votes were cast before Election Day. In some states, anyone could request an absentee ballot. In Oregon, all ballots were by mail. In other states, voters could vote in person at special locations as much as a month before the election. The same campaign organization that registered voters made sure that new, inexperienced voters actually voted. Obama volunteers used e-mails to stimulate votes and pushed enthusiasts to get recalcitrant relatives to vote. Most states tallied the receipt of completed absentee ballots electronically as they were returned, so campaign staff could concentrate on identified supporters whose ballots had not yet been received at the counting place. Staff got out the early vote and then relocated to states that did not have early voting to get out the vote on Election Day.[82]

As a technical feat, the Obama campaign was a marvel. The voter registration drives, the tech savvy, the fund-raising prowess, and the rock-star quality of the candidate were all impressive, perhaps unprecedented. But disturbing questions might have been asked. Just where did all the money come from? No doubt much of it came from small donors caught up in Obama mania, but rumors circulated that some money came to the website from untraceable foreign e-mail addresses, perhaps tied to the Middle East, to Venezuela, to Colombia drug cartels, or to other unsavory elements.[83] The media did not investigate the allegations.

In the end, Obama's advantages in money, organization, media euphoria, and crowd enthusiasm, as well as the spike he received after the financial collapse in mid-September, allowed him to run away with the election. He won 53 percent of the popular vote and 365 electoral votes to 46 percent and 173 electoral votes for McCain.

For the first time, the New Progressive movement had elected one of its own. Here was a leader who had come up in progressive circles and who shared the progressive vision to use governmental power in pursuit of social justice. Unlike previous progressive leaders, Barack Obama had been able to harness the progressive spirit into a well-organized political movement—while not turning off moderates and the establishment.

Undeniably, Obama's election was a triumph for progressives. But a closer look at the election returns reveals that it was not a *mandate* for progressivism. The electorate, though bigger, remained surprisingly undifferentiated from the ones that had twice elected Bill Clinton and

George W. Bush, neither of whom had progressive credentials. There was neither a dramatic swing to the left nor any other sign that a progressive era had begun.

For all the talk about how Obama inspired young voters to action, voters under the age of thirty accounted for 18 percent of the electorate in 2008—barely up from the 17 percent they represented in 2004. Obama did, however, perform very well among these young voters, receiving 66 percent of their vote. By contrast, Kerry in 2004 won only 54 percent of young voters.[84]

Americans in 2008 did not turn to the left. Exit polls showed that 22 percent of voters called themselves liberals, another 34 percent were conservatives, and the remaining 44 percent moderates. These percentages had been almost identical in every election over the previous twenty years. Obama won 89 percent of Democrats, while McCain got 90 percent of Republicans. While Democratic turnout rose from 37 percent of the electorate to 39 percent, Republican turnout plummeted from 37 percent to 32 percent, indicating that some Republicans declined to turn out for McCain.

The election hinged, ultimately, on independent, African American, and Hispanic voters. Obama carried independents, who made up 29 percent of the electorate, with 52 percent to McCain's 44 percent. This was the first time that independents had voted Democratic since Lyndon Johnson's landslide in 1964. Obama's success with these voters showed the effectiveness of his campaign theme of postpartisanship. By downplaying his progressive proposals, which were published for the benefit of liberals on his website but rarely became television sound bites, Obama appeared nonthreatening to moderates and conservatives. At the same time, Obama benefited from the normal pendulum swing of politics. The country was ready for change and to abandon Bush's policies.[85]

Changes in the black and Hispanic votes marked a major difference between Kerry's loss and Obama's win. The white electorate split in almost the same proportions as in 2004. Obama won 43 percent of white voters, only 2 percent more than Kerry did. Yet Obama received nearly 10.5 million more votes than Kerry did in 2004. Of that increase, 42 percent came from African Americans and 20 percent from Hispanics. Both groups turned out in increased numbers in 2008, and both voted in higher percentages for Obama than they had for Kerry. The black vote increased from 11 percent of the total in 2004 to 13 percent in 2008, while the

Hispanic vote rose from 8 percent to 9 percent. In 2004, Bush received 11 percent of the African American vote and 40 percent of the Hispanic vote; in 2008, McCain won 4 percent and 31 percent, respectively.[86]

There was one curious aspect to Obama's winning coalition. In a number of states, Obama's greatest support came from a combination of well-educated voters and poorly educated voters; McCain ran strongest among high school graduates. In a parallel pattern, Obama performed well with voters with high and low incomes, while McCain's strength was concentrated among middle-income voters. Obama had created an odd coalition of the top and the bottom against the middle, matching strong support among elites, including Wall Street, with mass enthusiasm among the poor. Whether the administration could devise policies to sustain such an unstable and contradictory coalition remained to be seen.[87]

Exactly what Obama would do with his presidency remained doubtful even after his election in November 2008. What kind of change was possible? What kind of change was desirable? What kind of policies would be popular? Which followers would he please? Which would he disappoint? The problem with presidential elections won on euphoric excitement is that they predict little about governance.

Progressivism in Power

In 2008, Barack Obama won a historic victory as the first African American president. He registered many new voters, used new technology to motivate them to vote, got Wall Street support, spent tons of money, and benefited from the financial crisis. By campaigning on generalities in the mainstream media, he came across as hopeful and nonthreatening. He used targeted ads on radio or in the new media to cultivate voters with special concerns, such as feminists or gays, who were part of his coalition but whose issues he did not want to emphasize. Downplaying his progressive values in the fall campaign, he won 60 percent of moderates and even 20 percent of conservatives.[88]

Decades earlier, a new breed of progressives had set out to redefine liberalism, take over the Democratic Party, and use the transformed party to attain the political power necessary to remake the United States. Now, with the election of Barack Obama, New Progressives had an opportunity to fulfill those goals. They envisioned remaking the nation into a highly centralized, top-down, expert-planned, elite-managed, and bureaucratic state. Individual liberty, initiative, and enterprise would be stifled, and virtually all aspects of life would be controlled. Law, health-care rules, environmental regulation, consumption controls, and tax policy would discipline and coerce the public into obedience to the progressive elite.

7

The Heights of Power

Barack Obama's victory excited progressives. The winner's coattails enabled a dozen or more Democrats to win House seats in normally Republican districts and created a liberal majority in the House. In the Senate, the Democrats gained sixty members, enough to pass almost any bill Obama wanted. The United States was about to embark on its first New Progressive government.

As Obama took office, however, legislation concerning the environment, business regulation, health care, and other leftist social justice issues had to compete with the urgent management of an unfolding economic crisis. The new president had to confront this crisis. Rhetoric was no substitute for judgment and action.

Grappling with the Financial Crisis

In many ways, Obama's presidency began the day after the election. The timing of the financial crisis necessitated immediate action.

Even before the election, the federal government had moved to respond to the crisis. On September 7, with housing prices plummeting, the federal government had seized control of Fannie Mae and Freddie Mac, the two quasi-governmental agencies chartered by Congress that guaranteed or owned about half the nation's mortgages. Under government pressure, both had specialized in no-down-payment loans for low-income borrowers with poor credit histories. Losses on those loans were predicted to approach $400 billion.[1] As ubiquitous mortgage-backed securities hollowed out the financial system, the government seized Washington Mutual, which was heavily involved in real estate, and sold its business to JPMorgan Chase. Global investors attacked other investment banks that held mortgage-backed securities. After a run on Morgan Stanley, the Federal Reserve allowed that investment bank and Goldman Sachs to reorganize as commercial-bank holding companies so they would have access to Fed money, which was available to commercial banks but not to investment banks in the case of a run. Lehman Brothers failed; Bank of America rescued Merrill Lynch; and Wells Fargo bought Wachovia. In just a few days, two of the four largest investment banks, and the third and sixth largest commercial banks, ceased to exist.

The federal government's biggest move came when President Bush's treasury secretary, Henry Paulson, a former CEO of Goldman Sachs, asked Congress for an unprecedented special appropriation of $700 billion. The Troubled Assets Relief Program (TARP) faced fierce debate and was initially defeated in the House, but a revised bill passed Congress on October 3. As passed, TARP came with strings. Democrats, with Bush's acquiescence, insisted that TARP include assistance to the auto industry, which the Michigan delegation knew was heading off a cliff. Instead of pursuing the original plan to have the government buy the banks' toxic assets, which were hard to price fairly, the government used TARP to take an ownership stake in all the big banks in order to increase their capital so they could write off bad loans. Even before Obama's election, the government had become intimately involved in the financial sector.

As the financial disaster spread throughout the economy, the government stepped in to bail out AIG, the world's largest insurance company. Some holders of mortgage-backed securities, especially Goldman Sachs, had protected themselves by purchasing a form of insurance on the bonds, called credit default swaps. In return for a small premium, the insurer promised to buy the bonds from the bondholder at par in case of a default. AIG wrote many contracts for credit default swaps. When the mortgage securities failed, the insurer owed far more money than it had on hand. The government spent $150 billion to bail out AIG, knowing that its failure would have taken down other major insurance companies and myriad other interconnected businesses.

It is doubtful that Obama fully grasped the dimensions of the financial crisis at the time. True, he regularly communicated with Secretary Paulson, Federal Reserve chairman Benjamin Bernanke, and New York Federal Reserve head Timothy Geithner, devouring information from all three officials and asking questions on a daily basis. But few Americans understood how much Wall Street had to do with Main Street. Many observers expected a short, sharp V-shaped recession, as had been typical of post–World War II recessions. But interest rates were already low going into the downturn, so the Fed could reduce rates only slightly—typically the most important tool to kick-start the economy. As the economy continued to decline, unemployment rose sharply, tax revenues fell, and emergency government spending soared. The federal budget deficit reached shocking heights.

To prop up the shaky stock market, which had lost 14.1 percent of its value during October, Obama needed to put an economic team in place as quickly as possible. On November 24, Obama named Geithner to run the Treasury and Lawrence Summers to head the National Economic Council.[2] Although Geithner had never worked on Wall Street, he was close to Robert Rubin, Clinton's first treasury secretary and onetime CEO of Goldman Sachs.[3] During 2008, Rubin briefed Obama frequently about Wall Street.[4] Obama had been impressed with both Geithner and Bernanke at the height of the crisis, and he reappointed Bernanke to lead the Fed in 2009. Summers would be Obama's chief economic adviser. A prominent economist and moderate liberal, Summers had served in the Clinton administration in several posts, including treasury secretary, and had been for a time president of Harvard.[5] Summers wanted to come back to Treasury or replace Bernanke at the Fed, but Obama resisted both ideas and finally persuaded Summers to work inside the White House. He gave daily briefings to the president on the economy, and all economic policy proposals flowed through Summers's office.[6]

Obama's top White House advisers were David Axelrod and Robert Gibbs, who also served as press secretary. Both were progressives.[7] Rahm Emanuel, a protégé of Rubin from Goldman Sachs, became chief of staff.[8] While Emanuel had a few leftist ties in Chicago politics, he was better known for having gotten along with the Daley machine.[9] He had also worked in Clinton's White House and had won election to the U.S. House of Representatives from a Chicago district. Using Wall Street money, Emanuel had recruited and elected enough Democrats from moderate districts in 2006 and 2008 to create a new Democratic majority.[10] Bringing him into the White House enabled the administration to cultivate or cajole votes needed to pass important bills.

The Auto Bailout

Both Chrysler and General Motors ran out of money not long after Election Day. In consultation with Obama and the Democrats, the Bush administration injected $17.4 billion in TARP cash into both auto companies to keep them going until March. The final resolution would have to take place on Obama's watch. To handle these difficult issues, the new president named Wall Street insider Steven Rattner as the "auto czar." The most immediate headache was Chrysler. The only interested investor was the Italian auto manufacturer Fiat, headed by Sergio Marchionne. Rejecting a direct takeover of Chrysler, he proposed a major Fiat investment. In addition, Fiat could provide some new models, either through imports or through building Fiat designs inside the United States. In the end, Obama personally approved Rattner's deal with Marchionne.[11]

Chrysler filed for bankruptcy, which wiped out shareholders and, in theory, retiree claims. In the restructured company, its employees' union, United Auto Workers (UAW), got 55 percent ownership; Fiat, 35 percent; the federal government, 8 percent; and Canada, the remaining 2 percent. UAW retirees got reduced retirement benefits, including a less generous health plan. UAW workers also had to accept wage cuts, fewer vacation days, smaller pension promises, and reduced health plan coverage. Rattner pressured the bondholders, mostly Wall Street investors, to agree to a settlement that paid them about 29 cents on the dollar for their bonds. The outcome violated the normal legal ranking of claims in bankruptcy, under which bondholders would expect to take precedence over the UAW's shares, pension benefits, and retiree health claims. In a special expedited review, the U.S. Supreme Court upheld the settlement. The lesson was clear: never invest in a company in bed with a powerful, politically connected union.[12]

General Motors (GM) had likewise been in trouble for years, losing $80 billion from 2005 through 2008. Neither its management nor its union, again the UAW, had seemed to grasp the seriousness of the situation.[13] GM filed for prearranged bankruptcy, which wiped out shareholders and pension and retiree health-care obligations. The U.S. government, which had already invested $19.4 billion, put up another $30.1 billion to keep GM alive. The UAW gave concessions on retiree benefits, health coverage, and vacation pay for current workers. In return, the UAW retiree health-care fund got 17.5 percent of the shares in the reorganized company. The government held 60.8 percent; the old bondholders, 10 percent; and Canada, 11.7 percent. It was, some joked, now Government Motors. Again, the UAW was privileged over the bondholders. In a normal bankruptcy, bondholders would have a prior claim on the assets.

The Obama administration was heavily involved in the GM restructuring. The president personally approved the final deal, including favoring the UAW over the bondholders. Aligning the union and the company, however, seemed like a small price to pay to many observers. More people were alarmed by the size of the government stake and feared political interference. This was governmental power in its most blatant form. Sure enough, Barney Frank, the House finance chair, made so much noise about the threatened closing of a minor GM plant in his home state of Massachusetts that the new GM management announced it would stay open.[14]

Obama also decided that Rick Wagoner would have to resign as CEO of GM and insisted that corporate boards fire executives of other firms that the government assisted. The heads of Merrill Lynch and Bank of America were forced out. The president also became obsessed with executive pay. "I am angry," he said, about certain bonuses.[15] He seemed to agree with Senator Claire McCaskill of Missouri, who introduced a bill stating that no CEO could be paid more than the president of the United States. In the end, Obama lacked any power to cut pay for executives at most companies, but he controlled pay at any business that had taken TARP money, including healthy banks forced to take loans. Some banks, like Wells Fargo, quickly paid back the loans to get out from under the restrictions.[16]

In other cases, companies suffered a talent drain. Hordes of well-paid traders left Merrill Lynch for foreign banks or unregulated private equity firms not subject to U.S. regulation. Their departure greatly reduced the value of Merrill to Bank of America. AIG lost several divisions when their heads, previously paid far above the government cap, decamped with staff. The worst effect was on GM, which could not recruit talent from other auto companies. The pay cap stopped GM from paying these key leaders directly, and the lack of any stock options prevented offering the kind of future consideration that might have been an alternative.

The financial and auto bailouts together were unprecedented. Even in the 1930s, Franklin Roosevelt never meddled so personally in the business sector. The Obama administration's aggressive use of governmental power mixed a certain amount of necessity with considerable opportunism. It reflected the progressive faith in top-down authority. In the case of the auto industry, Obama's policy was politically calculated to curry favor with the UAW. The auto bailout enabled the New Progressives to embrace their holy trinity: social justice (giveaways to the UAW), elite control (their own), and governmental power (government ownership of stock).

The Stimulus Bill

The collapsing economy brought clamor for increased federal spending. In the 1930s the economist John Maynard Keynes had argued that the cure for a slumping economy was a massive and rapid increase in government spending. Congress had used temporary spending programs, often increasing highway construction, during the recessions that followed World War II. But federal spending often failed to get into the pipeline fast enough to affect the recession, and after John Kennedy successfully used tax cuts to stimulate the economy in the 1960s, cuts were generally preferred to treat recessions because they worked more rapidly.

The economic decline following the financial meltdown in late 2008 was so dramatic that it suggested a need for both tax cuts and spending increases. Government spending was music to the ears of the New Progressives. Here was a chance to expand Head Start, college subsidies, Medicaid, alternative energy, and welfare programs.[17] Experts disagreed about the size of the stimulus that was required. Some economists warned that the stimulus bill was poorly designed.[18] While liberals believed that the larger the package, the greater the impact on the economy, conservatives worried that unprecedented deficits would rattle financial markets and dry up private investment, as investors purchased enormous quantities of new government bonds.[19]

In January 2009, Christina Romer, head of the Council of Economic Advisers and an expert on the correlation of government spending and unemployment, suggested that to prevent a depression, the total stimulus package, about one-third tax cuts and two-thirds spending increases, needed to be $1.2 trillion. Larry Summers kept this proposal from reaching Obama.[20] Even big-spending Democrats in Congress resisted a trillion-dollar bill. Constituents were already calling for government retrenchment. "We got as much," said Summers, "as Congress was ever going to give us at that time."[21] Team Obama pushed for about $700 billion, divided roughly two to one in favor of spending. By the time the measure passed Congress, it became stuffed with pork and reached $787 billion. Tax cuts were now $212 billion and spending $575 billion.

Romer had predicted that the stimulus bill would keep the unemployment rate from rising above 8 percent in 2009 and that it would then fall to 7 percent by late 2010 or early 2011. In reality, unemployment reached 8.1 percent in February 2009 and peaked at 10.2 percent in October 2009; two years later it was still 9 percent.[22]

There was little controversy about the tax cuts in the stimulus bill, although some economists pointed out that mailing out checks created "income" that was more likely to be banked than spent.[23] State and local governments experienced a precipitous fall-off in revenue owing to the declining economy. Because these governments had to maintain balanced budgets, they faced major layoffs unless the federal government rescued them. In an unprecedented move, Congress temporarily bailed out states, counties, and cities with general revenue. Republicans fumed about this large federal subsidy of local government. The money propped up highly paid public employees whose unions were major Democratic donors.

The biggest problem with the stimulus bill was the high cost of the jobs it created. The bill saved around one million public-sector jobs and created close to two million private-sector jobs.[24] It cost more than $200,000 to create each private-sector job. What the economy needed was ten million jobs at $30,000 ($300 billion), not two million jobs at $200,000 ($400 billion). Why were these jobs so expensive? Much of the money to create each job went to governmental oversight, and some went to buy expensive materials. The real problem was the high price of labor in the types of jobs the stimulus bill supported. By contrast, federal employment projects in the Great Depression of the 1930s used cheap, low-skill workers, mostly with picks and shovels.

Much of the 2009 stimulus money went to public works projects. The authors of the stimulus bill promised to fund what Obama called "shovel-ready" projects rather than pay for construction that would take place years later, after the recession had ended. Few such projects existed, however. "There's no such thing as shovel-ready projects," Obama later lamented.[25] Public construction jobs were slow to materialize for many reasons. Contractors spent a lot of time training workers to use complex equipment. Low-end construction workers were out of work, but most could not qualify for high-end jobs, because it took six months or longer to be certified on the sophisticated equipment that high-end workers used.

Congress and the Obama administration made the problem worse by applying Davis-Bacon rules to the Stimulus Act. The 1931 Davis-Bacon law required contractors on federal projects to pay prevailing local construction wages, a phrase interpreted to mean that contractors had to pay union wages.[26] In previous recessions, federal stimulus money applied Davis-Bacon rules only to projects that would normally be subject to such rules, such as interstate highways, airports with substantial other federal funds, or federal facilities. The 2009 act's Davis-Bacon requirement slowed contracting, reduced employment, and produced exasperation. The whole tangle could have been avoided, but New Progressives were less interested in stimulating the economy and creating jobs than in playing power politics to benefit their favored constituencies.

The day the Stimulus Act passed Congress, the government-bond interest rate jumped one-quarter percent. The bond market disliked the stimulus, which struck many Americans as a boondoggle. The big spending of the New Progressives was not popular. As the stimulus played out, unemployment stayed high. "It's dead wrong," said New Jersey governor Chris Christie about the stimulus. "More spending with what? The federal government continuing to print money and leaving debt for our kids? It will only grind the economy down further."[27] The public increasingly turned against the Stimulus Act. "I'm not supposed to call it stimulus," said Representative Barney Frank, who faced a tough reelection. "The message experts in Washington have told us that we're supposed to call it the recovery plan."[28] Many Democrats running for reelection in 2010 found that the vote they had cast for that big spending bill put them on the defensive. So did the vote for Obamacare.

Obamacare: The Dream Becomes Grim Reality

On March 23, 2010, Barack Obama signed into law the Patient Protection and Affordable Care Act. No longer was compulsory health insurance an unmet promise; it was now the law of the land, upheld, 5–4, by the U.S. Supreme Court in most respects in June 2012. Called Obamacare by opponents, a term that eventually the administration accepted, the legislation extravagantly promised to reduce health-care costs, lower insurance premiums, eliminate waste and inefficiencies, cover every single uninsured individual, and, most important, save Medicare from impending bankruptcy. How Obamacare will work in practice remains to be seen.[29]

Obama rammed the bill through Congress along partisan lines. The bill won the support not only of ultraliberal Democrats but also of corporate interests that stood to benefit. The drug lobby Pharmaceutical Research and Manufacturers of America (PhRMA) spent more than $26 million lobbying in 2009 for health-care reform. Support for Obamacare also came from General Electric, AARP, the American Medical Association, and the American Hospital Association. Each was eager to shift health-care costs to the federal government. Obamacare linked the New Progressive agenda of expanding government control over American consumption, in this case health care, with corporate interests that benefit in the short run from government expansion.

In 2009, Democratic members of Congress faced angry town halls on health care. When Representative Russ Carnahan of Missouri told constituents that the bill would save money, they laughed. He narrowly won reelection in a heavily Democratic district. At a town hall meeting organized by Representative Brian Baird of Washington, a constituent said, "I heard you say that you are going to let us keep our health insurance. Well thank you! It's not your right to decide whether I keep my current plan or not, that's my decision." The crowd cheered. Baird did not seek reelection, and his district elected a Republican.[30] The bill never polled well with the public. On the eve of the vote on final passage in the House, in March 2010, CNN found the measure scored only 39 percent approval, to 59 percent disapproval.[31]

It is important to look at the details of Obamacare to understand why opponents saw this bill as a massive government takeover of health care. Proponents stressed that the new system "relies on private companies and free markets." Listening to them, one might believe that Obamacare was the vision of the libertarian economist Friedrich Hayek, as amended by House Speaker Ayn Rand.[32]

While Obamacare was not a British-type system, where the government owns the hospitals and doctors are public employees, the plan marked a vast expansion of federal control over the financing and delivery of health care. The law converted health insurers into government contractors by dictating the content of policies, sales techniques, and overhead costs. All citizens or their employers had to pay for mandated benefits regardless of individual needs or preferences. Obama claimed that the plan was "fully paid for" and would "bring down the cost of health care," but 81 percent of Americans believed that the plan would cost more than projected.[33] The public expected health-care costs to rise, patient choice to be reduced, and national fiscal disaster to ensue. Apart from the new entitlement spending necessitated by universal coverage, the Patient Protection and Affordable Care Act did not plausibly address Medicare's seventy-five-year unfunded liability of approximately $30.8 trillion.[34]

The complex Patient Protection and Affordable Care Act defies easy summary. Even after the yearlong debate on Obamacare, much remained unclear. It did not help that much of the voluminous bill was not available to lawmakers until the final days before passage. "We have to pass the bill so you can find out what is in it," said House Speaker Nancy Pelosi.[35] In its broad outlines, the act forces Americans to purchase insurance. Businesses are coerced into providing insurance to their employees. If they refuse, they will be fined, or, according to Chief Justice John Roberts, "taxed." Medicare and Medicare Advantage will be cut. If all the states sign on, Medicaid will be expanded to cover eighteen million of the additional thirty-four million people who will be insured. Childless adults will be eligible for taxpayer-subsidized coverage originally established to cover only impoverished children.

Health insurers will be extremely regulated, with the government telling them who must be covered, the premiums that can be charged, and how much they will pay in claims. The legislation called for the establishment of 159 new boards. The federal government will oversee the establishment of an array of state health insurance exchanges and medical coordinating committees. "Progressives are forever longing to replace the governance of people by the administration of things," observed the columnist George Will.[36]

The expansion of Medicaid forces heavy financial burdens onto state governments, most of which face huge costs already.[37]

Obamacare was projected to cost at least $1.05 trillion over a decade, and some experts projected double the cost.[38] Yet even with this expansion, an estimated twenty-three million people will remain uninsured by

2019, if the estimates of the nonpartisan Congressional Budget Office (CBO) are correct. It is also clear that Obamacare uses sticks and carrots. Subsidies will be provided to individuals and families to purchase insurance within newly erected American Health Benefits Exchanges if they fall within income guidelines established by the act. For individuals, subsidies will be provided for those earning from $14,403 to $43,320, while for families, income must fall between $29,326 and $88,200.

The punitive nature of Obamacare lies at the core of the system. Individuals who refuse to sign up for health insurance are required to pay a penalty of $695 or 2.5 percent of household income up to $2,085, whichever is higher. Employers of fifty or more workers who refuse to offer federally approved insurance are to be fined $2,000 per employee, with the first thirty workers exempted when calculating the fine. The CBO estimates that employers will drop coverage for fourteen million workers.[39] To enforce this compulsory system, the Internal Revenue Service will be expanded. An estimated sixteen thousand new agents will be assigned to track down individuals and businesses that fail to enlist in the program.

To cover the costs of the system, individuals making more than $200,000 and couples making more than $250,000 will face a Medicare tax increase from 1.45 to 2.35 percent of earned income. They will also have to pay a new 3.8 percent tax on unearned income, including partnership income, interest, dividends, capital gains, royalties, and rents. Insurance companies will pay $47.5 billion in new taxes between 2010 and 2018. Pharmaceutical companies will pay $16.7 billion in new taxes through 2019, and then another $2.8 billion a year afterward—on top of what they are already paying.

A 2.3 percent federal tax will be applied to medical devices such as pacemakers, medical scanners, and insulin pumps. Meanwhile, funds for Medicare will be reduced by at least $529 billion over ten years. Beginning in 2011, payments for Medicare Plus, which covers additional medical costs for seniors not covered in regular Medicare (about 20 percent of Medicare enrollees), were to be frozen at current levels. However, Congress postponed these cuts for 2011 and 2012. If Congress continued to resist these unpopular cuts, then Obamacare's drain on the budget would increase. This reduction to Medicare funding coincides with a planned expansion of Medicaid to include more than sixty million people, up from forty-three million currently covered by the program, although the Supreme Court ruled that the states had the option to decline to expand these programs. The costs of this expansion, if fully implemented, are estimated at $410 billion, much of it shifted to the states.

Assuming that all states participated, Medicaid enrollment was expected to rise 32 percent. California was projected to gain 2 million more recipients; Texas, 1.9 million; and Florida, 1 million. This expansion threatened to overwhelm already perilous state finances and to create huge logistical problems in managing the program. By 2011 nearly 70 percent of Medicaid enrollees had been outsourced to private companies managing state Medicaid programs. For large private health insurance companies such as United Health, WellPoint, Amerigroup, and Centene, this expansion presented a lucrative opportunity to manage state Medicaid funds. It was a rare bright spot for insurers. Despite the Obama administration's charged rhetoric against the profit-hungry insurance companies, the truth was that health insurance industry profits had been anemic in recent years. According to a *Fortune* magazine study in 2009, the health insurance industry made only 2.2 cents in profit for every dollar in revenue.[40] Under Obamacare, regulatory crackdowns on premiums for traditional programs would press profit margins even more.[41]

In late 2010, Health and Human Services Secretary Kathleen Sebelius warned that insurers asking unjustified rate increases would be excluded from participating in mandated state health-care exchanges. The feds were willing to exert governmental power to exclude insurers from managing state Medicaid programs if they refused to play ball. When Connecticut state insurance commissioner Tom Sullivan approved, based on an actuarial analysis, a rate increase for premiums offered by Anthem Blue Cross and Blue Shield, he came under attack from the Department of Health and Human Services. Sullivan responded, "I find myself in an unprecedented place and time, as do my counterparts throughout the country, in overseeing the implementation of one of the most far-reaching policy initiatives enacted by the federal government in recent history." State regulators, he continued, were being placed in "an unenviable position as we are required by Congress to approve richer benefit packages, while simultaneously being called upon . . . to reduce rates."[42] In the end, he resigned under political pressure from local labor unions.

Obamacare quickly provoked legal challenges. Could the government use the commerce clause to force an individual to buy private insurance? Virginia thought not, and a federal judge concurred. A majority on the Supreme Court upheld this point, but Chief Justice John Roberts joined four liberal justices to find the law constitutional. Roberts said the law could be justified under the right of Congress to tax. Attorneys general for twenty states argued that the imposition of increased Medicaid costs violated the Tenth Amendment. A federal judge in Florida agreed. Eventually, so did the Supreme Court. Incredibly, the statute had no severability clause clarifying that if any provision was unconstitutional, its invalidity would not require invalidation of the entire law.

Other legal issues concerned statutory vagueness about bureaucratic rule making, illegal executive discretion to give waivers to employers, and the requirement that employers provide insurance to nonemployees, including an employee's adult children aged eighteen to twenty-six and those children's children.[43] Within the bureaucratic rule-making apparatus, the Obama administration set off a firestorm of opposition from the Catholic bishops by requiring that all health plans, including church-sponsored ones, cover contraception. In previous bureaucratic decisions, the federal government had always shown deference to religious sensibilities. This action was yet another example of the New Progressive tendency toward aggressive top-down exercise of power, even at the expense of First Amendment rights.[44]

Experts—on both the Left and the Right—have predicted that the system will not work as advertised. Obamacare will not contain rising health-care costs. Even with its tax hikes, it is woefully underfunded, perhaps by 50 percent. Premiums will increase. The infrastructure of federal regulation, state health exchanges, and a myriad of oversight agencies is a bureaucratic nightmare in the making.

Even though Obamacare was sold as a debt-reducing measure, it is doubtful that its proponents actually believed such rhetoric. In fact, if the system collapses of its own weight, that could open an opportunity for progressives to push for the next step: a government-run, single-payer system, European-style.

Before he was elected president, Obama favored a single-payer system. In May 2007 he told a receptive audience of union workers, "We can have universal health care by the end of the next president's first term, by the end of my first term." A short time later he declared, "If I were designing a system from scratch I would probably set up a single-payer system."[45] If Obamacare proves as unworkable and expensive as its critics have predicted, inevitably New Progressives will push for further "reform" of health care through a single-payer system. The dream surely will not die.

"You Never Want a Serious Crisis to Go to Waste"

In the 2008 campaign, Obama had promised a soak-the-rich tax policy. Concerning the Bush tax cuts set to expire automatically at the end of 2010, he proposed keeping the cuts that affected the middle class but repealing those that favored the wealthy.[46] Team Obama in 2009 found little support in the Democratic Congress for the proposal. Economists both inside and outside the administration warned that raising taxes in a sinking economy would only depress the economy further and increase unemployment. Democrats from moderate districts, many of whom had first been elected in 2006 and 2008, also found little support among constituents for soaking the rich.[47] So Obama postponed any action on the Bush tax cuts until 2010.

If Congress failed to act, taxes on the wealthy in January 2011 would automatically rise from a maximum rate of 35 percent to 39.6 percent, and the capital gains rate, which was important to investors, would jump from 15 to 20 percent. At the same time, the lowest bracket would leap from 10 to 15 percent. Millions of Americans had benefited from the expanded Earned Income Tax Credit passed in 2001 and enhanced in 2003. If that credit expired at the end of 2010, these lower-income Americans would face large tax increases. Americans earning from $20,000 to $40,000 who had been removed permanently from the tax rolls might find themselves suddenly owing $1,000 or more of income tax. Their take-home pay might drop by $100 a month or more.

After failing to enact a long-term tax plan in 2009, Obama in December 2010, after Democrats had lost the House, was compelled to make a deal with the Republicans to stop the 2011 tax increases that threatened to push the weak economy into recession. To stop the increases on lower incomes, the president had to agree to extend all cuts through 2012. This was not simply a political mistake on Obama's part. The two-year extension of the Bush-era rates left the administration without a clear long-term tax policy. As a result, business investors faced uncertainty, which had the effect of retarding investment and economic growth.[48]

Another sign of weakness was the inability of the Democratic Congress in 2010 to pass any budget bills. In an unprecedented move, committees held no hearings and marked up no bills. When the federal fiscal year, FY2011, started in October 2010, all Congress could do was pass a continuing resolution to allow expenditures to continue temporarily at FY2010 levels, leaving nondefense discretionary spending 26 percent above the level for FY2008. Budget uncertainty adversely affected the larger economy. State and local governments and businesses hesitated to make plans because no one knew what the federal government was going to do.[49]

Democrats could not pass a budget because they were divided between progressives, who wanted to increase spending, and moderates, who came from districts that opposed higher spending. Because progressives never met a federal program they did not like, they were incapable of setting priorities. The failure to pass a budget helped Democrats lose the 2010 elections. Obama's presidency was on the verge of a meltdown. "With the exception of core Obama administration loyalists," wrote *Time* magazine's Mark Halperin, "most politically engaged elites have reached the same conclusion: The White House is in over its head, isolated, insular, arrogant and clueless about how to get along with or persuade members of Congress, the media, the business community or working-class voters."[50]

Despite these failures, Obama and other progressives charged forward with their plans to impose their vision on the country. After all, had they not won the 2008 election? Or they may have cynically believed, as White House chief of staff Rahm Emanuel put it, that "you never want a serious crisis to go to waste."[51] They were confident that they knew what was best for Americans. "The *point* of progressivism," wrote George Will, "is that the people must progress up from their backwardness."[52] Team Obama was determined to use governmental power in pursuit of their goals. "These are ideas," observed the economist Don Boudreaux, "about how one group of people (the politically successful) should engineer everyone else's contracts, social relations, diets, habits, and even moral sentiments."[53] Progressives paid no attention to objections, dismissing opponents as reactionaries.[54]

And so the New Progressives pursued their extreme leftist agenda. "The stereotype of Democrats as wild-eyed spenders and taxers has been resurrected," noted Senator Evan Bayh, a Democrat.[55] Liberals had piled onto the necessary TARP bailout bill a hefty increase in routine domestic government spending, and then they added the pork-laden Stimulus Act and Obamacare for good measure.

The financial crisis provided an opportunity to pursue another progressive objective: government regulation of business. Liberals, abetted by the media, chanted that deregulation had caused the crisis.[56] This was at best an overly simplistic explanation that overlooked the multiple, complex reasons the financial crisis came about—unprecedented imbalances in the global trading system, housing policies that lowered lending standards, mortgage-backed securities that spread throughout the international financial system, interest rates held artificially low, and more.[57] The progressive explanation also missed the fact that the U.S. economy had been regulated since the 1910s, and the financial system had been heavily regulated since the 1930s. Government was, in fact, heavily involved in the economy.

The problem was not *lack* of government regulation but *mediocre* regulation combined with political meddling. The Securities and Exchange Commission (SEC), for example, had done a poor job regulating the investment banks, reducing capital requirements just as the banks got swept up in risky mortgage-backed securities.[58] The weak SEC staff had also missed the Bernie Madoff fraud. Bad regulation was even more dangerous than no regulation.[59] The progressives failed to grasp a crucial point that political commentator Michael Barone made: "When government is small and deft, a little more of it may help folks. But when it is big and plodding . . . a lot more of it may just be a dead weight on the private sector economy."[60]

In another move toward increased regulation, Obama and the New Progressives were determined to impose severe new regulations on business.[61] They wanted to devise regulations to enhance social justice (as they saw it), expand elite control (Congress, bureaucrats, and trial lawyers), and advance governmental power (a new agency).[62] Thus, Senator Chris Dodd (D-Connecticut) and Congressman Barney Frank drafted a bill to create what they called a consumer protection agency. The new Bureau of Consumer Financial Protection, placed inside the Federal Reserve System, was to have broad powers and could choose to investigate almost any business practice.

This bill, and especially the proposal for a consumer protection agency, infuriated Wall Street. "The legislation has contributed to uncertainty," complained investor Henry Kaufman.[63] The bankers who had backed Obama and the Democrats in 2008 felt betrayed, especially as Obama attacked Wall Street as "fat cats."[64] When Harry Reid, the Democratic leader in the Senate, took Goldman Sachs money and then blasted Wall Street, Gary Cohn, the number two at Goldman Sachs and an early Obama supporter, told Reid, "We're sick of the bullshit!"[65]

Jamie Dimon, CEO of JPMorgan Chase and another early Obama enthusiast, was angry because the law would cost his company $3 billion a year, one-quarter of its profits. Dimon began to write checks to Republican candidates in 2010.[66] Dimon's woes increased in 2012, when it was disclosed that rogue traders inside the bank had lost billions of dollars. Dimon was skewered at congressional hearings, and calls for his resignation were heard. Perhaps banks were not so much too big to fail as too big to manage.[67]

The Dodd-Frank Act, which passed late in 2010, specified that the Bureau of Consumer Financial Protection was to monitor how well businesses served subsections of the public, including minorities, women, and the handicapped. The bill called for five hundred new rules, studies, and reports—in contrast with fourteen in the Sarbanes-Oxley Act.[68] Small businesses, already pressed by the IRS, environmental rules, health and safety concerns, labor standards, and compliance with the Americans with Disabilities Act, feared time-consuming reporting requirements as well as potential lawsuits. "The U.S. economy faces hurricane force headwinds," warned an economist for the National Federation of Independent Business, "and the government is at the center of the storm, making an economic recovery very difficult."[69]

Obama named Elizabeth Warren, one of Nader's raiders, to set up the new agency, recruit talent, and write its rules. The president could not appoint her to the official post to head the agency because the Senate signaled that she was too extreme to be confirmed. After organizing the operation along progressive lines, Warren left the administration to run against Senator Scott Brown (R-Massachusetts). As a candidate, she generated considerable controversy when it was revealed that she had gained affirmative action status as a Cherokee Indian while serving on the faculty of the Harvard Law School, although her connection to the tribe was decidedly remote.[70]

New Progressives were mystified at the public rejection of their unprecedented federal spending and other government interventions. When Franklin Roosevelt introduced massive government spending and aggressive regulation of business in the 1930s, he enhanced his popularity. But by 2010 the public saw how three generations of big government had favored entrenched elites and special interests and how regulators had destroyed businesses and jobs. "The progressive vision that resonated in the 1930s," observed former senator Phil Gramm, "foundered on the hard experience of the twentieth century, and it has no broad appeal in the twenty-first."[71] The high-tech revolution of the late twentieth century had only reinforced the American faith in entrepreneurship, innovation, creativity, and personal empowerment. These ideas conflicted with New Progressive statist ideology.

For all businesses, the regulations promised to raise costs, increase prices, cut profits, reduce efficiency, lower productivity, and destroy jobs. Home Depot cofounder Ken Langone offered a blunt take on the Obama administration's economic agenda: "If we tried to start Home Depot today under the kind of onerous regulatory controls that you [i.e., Obama] have advocated, it's a stonecold certainty that our business would never get off the ground." Langone cited rules barring stock options, the cost of regulatory compliance, and Obamacare.[72] In the name of consumer protection, progressives had embarked on another scheme to choke economic growth and personal freedom in the pursuit of "social justice."[73]

A Banana Republic with No Bananas

From George Washington through Bill Clinton, the U.S. government ran up a national debt of $5.7 trillion, a bit more than half of one year's gross domestic product (GDP) in 2001. Most debt has come from wars, especially World War II. In the single year of 1943, the deficit was $57 billion, or about 25 percent of GDP at that time. The government found it easy to borrow during the war because debt compared to GDP was comfortably low before the war. In 1946 the debt peaked at 120 percent of GDP.[74]

After George W. Bush's 2001 tax cuts, the United States faced a structural deficit of roughly $200 billion per year. In an economy of $10 trillion that grew 3 percent per year, the annual increase in the debt was manageable, because the debt was projected to grow at about the same rate as GDP. Bush did not count on 9/11. The resultant chaos cost the economy $500 billion, and Homeland Security added billions a year to expenses. Soon wars in Afghanistan and Iraq added more than a trillion dollars in spending during the rest of the decade. The economy grew somewhat sluggishly even before the housing slump hit in 2007.

Bush's eight deficits from FY2002 through FY2009 amounted to $6.1 trillion, which was more than all the debt run up from Washington through Clinton. Thus, by FY2009 the total debt was $12 trillion, while the economy had grown to more than $14 trillion. Perhaps one-fifth of Bush's debt increase could be attributed to the financial crisis. Spending rose from $3 trillion in FY2008, the last precrisis year, to $3.5 trillion in FY2010. For forty years federal spending averaged 20 percent of GDP and taxes 18 percent, with the deficit a manageable 2 percent. Now federal spending had soared to 24 percent of the $14.5 trillion economy, while sluggishness caused taxes to fall to 15 percent, leaving an unsustainable gap of 9 percent of GDP.[75]

Obama's first full budget year, FY2010, started in October 2009 and produced a staggering $1.3 trillion deficit. Part of this deficit came from TARP and part from the Stimulus Act, but a good bit of it came from continuing the explosion of regular spending passed by the new Democratic Congress in 2009. The spending "enchanted the left of the Democratic Party," observed the economic journalist Clive Crook, "and might have been calculated to infuriate moderate Republicans."[76] Energy, agriculture, education, health, and nutrition agencies got 20 to 30 percent increases, or even more.

In FY2011, which began in October 2010, the deficit was another $1.3 trillion. This was 8.7 percent of GDP, which was $15 trillion. Another way of putting it is that $3.6 trillion in federal spending, 24 percent of the economy, was being supported by $2.3 trillion in tax revenues. After the crash, revenues dropped; in FY2011 the government collected about 64 cents for every dollar it spent. To balance the budget meant either a 56 percent increase in taxes or a 36 percent reduction in expenditures, more than Social Security and Medicare combined.[77] "The nation," said Fed chairman Ben Bernanke, "will ultimately have to choose among more taxes, modifications to entitlement programs such as Social Security and Medicare, less spending on everything else from education to defense, or some combination of the above."[78]

Obama's spending was wanton and reckless. "The most fiscally irresponsible government in American history," declared the publisher and former Obama supporter Mortimer Zuckerman.[79] In four years Obama would come close to accumulating as much debt as Bush did in eight years, and in eight years it looked likely that Obama would nearly double the national debt, running up as much debt as Washington through Bush had in more than two hundred years. According to one calculation, once debt reaches 80 to 90 percent of GDP, interest payments become hard to bear, and growth slows. When debt reaches 90 percent of GDP, economic growth is only 1.7 percent per year. When debt is 30 percent of GDP, the growth rate is double.[80] While the drop-off in revenues resulting from the financial crisis played a role in the soaring deficit, the real problem was runaway spending.

The Obama administration's own projections foretold the dangers ahead. The administration estimated that in FY2016 the federal government would require $846 billion just to pay interest on the debt, more than double the amount in FY2009 ($383 billion). To put these numbers in perspective, note that in 2009 individuals paid $915 billion in income tax.[81] And those estimates were optimistic. In March 2011 the nonpartisan CBO predicted that the Obama deficits would exceed the numbers in the FY2012 Obama budget proposal by $270 billion *per year* over the next decade.[82]

Obama's huge deficits alarmed many on Wall Street, including supporters from 2008. Some of them blamed the president's poor grasp of finance and lack of budgetary experience. He had neither been a governor nor run a business, and few Obama advisers had business experience. Larry Fink, CEO of BlackRock, knew that borrowing had its limits. Jamie Dimon was appalled by the spending and felt betrayed. When Wall Street bankers complained to Representative Spencer Bachus (R-Alabama), he said, "If you get a pet rattlesnake, expect to be bitten."[83]

Obama's deficits, unlike all previous deficits, threatened the destruction of federal finances, borrowing capacity, government credibility, and ultimately the existence of the United States itself as a viable nation.[84] "For how much longer," asked Larry Summers, "can the world's top borrower carry on being the world's top power?"[85] By 2020 interest payments would exceed defense spending, and interest payments to China would finance China's military buildup.[86] If present trends continued, China by 2030 would have 70 percent of U.S. per capita GDP and an economy three times the size.[87]

In the spring of 2010 the International Monetary Fund (IMF) surveyed the world's major nations and their financial health. In a report that the American media virtually ignored, the IMF noted that all the major countries were running large, chronic, and unsustainable government deficits. When the global financial crisis hit, revenues plummeted, while routine expenditures continued and special expenditures linked to the crisis and the recession, including TARP and the Stimulus Act, were added. The temporary measures did not bother the IMF, but the organization noted that there was insufficient money in the entire world to finance all the existing levels of deficits in the decade ahead.[88] Accordingly, the IMF demanded that every nation adopt a plan to reach fiscal balance and solvency.[89] The Bank for International Settlements concurred and concluded, "Drastic measures are necessary."[90]

Germany's Angela Merkel was the first world leader to embrace austerity, and doing so cost her government its control of the upper house of the Bundestag. Nicolas Sarkozy decided to spend political capital to raise the retirement age in France, although voters later replaced him with the free-spending François Hollande. The French stock market promptly fell, and bond rating agencies warned Hollande of a possible downgrade. Silvio Berlusconi took budget-cutting measures in Italy, but he did not move fast enough to satisfy either the IMF or bond markets and was forced out. Stephen Harper, the prime minister of Canada, had already embraced the concept of limits, and the new British government under David Cameron announced a severe austerity plan. Even José Luis Zapatero, the socialist leader of Spain, gave in, as did new governments in Japan and Australia, although in both cases the prime ministers were forced to resign.[91]

Only one major nation in the G-20 group did not adopt an austerity program: the United States. Obama refused to face the financial realities that other global leaders and the IMF acknowledged. The result was increasing tensions among Obama, Merkel, and other leaders at the ongoing G-20 summits, as well as financial stress across the globe as worldwide austerity contrasted with drunken-sailor spending by the U.S. government.[92] The IMF estimated that U.S. debt would amount to more than 110 percent of GDP by 2015.[93] Even as late as Obama's State of the Union address in January 2011, the president continued to call for new spending programs.[94] So did the FY2012 budget proposal released not long after the speech.[95] Obama continued to push spending in the 2012 State of the Union, but the all-too-predictable message attracted little attention.[96] Obama seemed increasingly out of touch with economic reality.

Who will buy U.S. debt? In 2009, Americans saved only $465 billion. Today foreigners hold half of publicly traded debt, and the United States is the biggest debtor nation in history.[97] In 2010, U.S. government debt was 45 percent of all the public debt in the world.[98] Foreigners may not have the will or the money to roll over the U.S. bonds they already hold, much less buy more; interest rates may have to soar to entice purchases.

Exploding deficits will not only cause interest rates to rise but also crowd out private loans and dramatically increase the dollars needed for debt service. All will cripple the economy, producing a recession or depression. The Federal Reserve might print money, but that will cause inflation and a further increase in interest rates.[99] The gaping deficits have already led the Federal Reserve, for the first time since it was founded in 1913, to buy Treasury bonds and hold them on its balance sheet. The Fed called this policy "quantitative easing." Although the policy was marketed as a way to stimulate the economy, the real reason for the dollar balances was obvious: the Treasury could not have sold the bonds easily at a low interest rate in the open market in the quantity required. So Bernanke's Fed is now the enabler for Obama's profligate spending.[100]

Another option will be to double taxes to continue necessary services. That thought might thrill New Progressives, but such hikes would destroy economic growth, create rising permanent unemployment, and leave the United States as a has-been nation. According to one calculation, every increase in government spending equal to 1 percent of GDP is associated with a 1.8 percent decline in nongovernmental GDP. Eventually there will be no more dollars to be borrowed. The spending will have to cease—after Americans have become addicted to big-spending New Progressive government.[101]

For a time, the United States, like any addict, can get away with its refusal to face reality. That is because the dollar is the world's reserve currency. Obama's policies, however, have weakened the dollar, and while the administration hoped that this would improve American exports, the danger is that the dollar will implode, the world will be left without a trading currency, everyone will be forced to resort to barter, and the resultant shrinkage in trade will create a global depression.[102] The American position is not pretty. Because the U.S. economy runs on oil, 45 percent of which is imported, the inability to spend dollars abroad could cause the price of oil to soar or maybe even make it unobtainable at any price in unwanted dollars. Unlike Greece, the United States is not too big to fail. Instead, it is too big to bail.[103]

New Progressives, however, pay little attention to these facts. One reason is economic illiteracy: when a Zogby poll asked eight simple economic questions, conservatives missed one or two; liberals missed four or five.[104] The disaster of Greece ought to be a warning to all governments about the consequence of governance based on wild promises and financial profligacy.[105] Yet one sees little recognition of the hard truth in such liberal, hard-pressed states as New York, Illinois, and California. All three states have bloated budgets, huge deficits, and underfunded pensions.[106] In 2012, Stockton and San Bernardino, California, filed for bankruptcy, and San Jose came within twenty-four hours of defaulting on bond interest payments. Bond firms warned that if more California cities defaulted, interest rates on bonds from all California jurisdictions would soar.[107] Is bankruptcy the inevitable legacy of liberalism? Does the mindset devoted to social justice, elite rule, and governmental power invariably lead to folly? "The policy mindset," warns the financial expert Mohamed El-Erian, "really, really matters."[108]

Staying the Progressive Course

By mid-2009 the backlash against Obama's progressive policies had begun. The Tea Party was up and running. Looking back to the American Revolution, the Tea Partiers resolved to take back the country from the big spenders and their cronies.[109] They saw Obama, as one conservative put it, as "a revolutionary post-national progressive who seeks to establish a new liberal ruling class."[110] Borrowing a page from the Obama playbook of 2007, they held mass rallies with surprisingly large crowds, and when smeared in the mainstream media as racists, fascists, or kooks, the Tea Partiers launched their own social media to prove that they were ordinary Americans concerned about the well-being of their country. Surveys showed that they were older than the average American, better educated, and earned more money. They included Republicans, Democrats, and especially independents.[111]

The New Progressives mostly ignored the movement, except to issue occasional snickers and jabs.[112] Perhaps, over time, the Tea Party would have died out if Obama had let well enough alone. Instead, he pushed his plan for a government takeover of health care. In 2009, Vice President Joe Biden and domestic adviser David Axelrod recommended postponing the issue, owing to the financial crisis.[113] Also opposed was economic adviser Christina Romer, who worried that the economy was too fragile to handle an expensive new entitlement program. Rahm Emanuel had a different objection. Democrats elected to the House in 2006 and 2008 from moderate districts had already been damaged at home by casting votes for TARP and the stimulus bill. Another vote against their constituents' views might ensure their defeat in November 2010.[114]

Despite all the attempts to dissuade him, Obama moved forward with his push for an expensive health-care plan. He had been committed to the idea of national health insurance since his earliest days in politics. The idea was a part of his New Progressive roots, including his years operating among Chicago leftists. SEIU, the public-employees union that was one of his strongest supporters, also wanted a bill. In addition, Obama had made a personal promise to Senator Ted Kennedy to pursue the measure. Kennedy's illness during 2009 and his subsequent death led Obama to see a health-care bill as a memorial to the senator who more than any other had enabled Obama to beat Hillary Clinton and win the Democratic nomination.[115]

Obama, Emanuel, and the New Progressives were convinced that opposition to the health-care plan would subside once the bill passed.[116] The administration failed to see that an expensive health-care program would only increase rising public anger over the deficit, which had led to the creation of the Tea Party in the first place. The New Progressives also failed to understand that any bill that ordered people to buy health insurance would enrage libertarians as an affront to liberty. Nor did they comprehend the way Obamacare would upset ten million seniors on Medicare Advantage or up to thirty million Americans who faced possible loss of employer-provided insurance.[117] "Did the president and Congress," asked former New York City mayor Ed Koch, "have to terrify people who had insurance coverage in order to provide coverage for the additional thirty-two million Americans covered under the new law?"[118]

House Speaker Nancy Pelosi weakened the position of moderate House Democrats by insisting that they support cap-and-trade legislation. The moderates wanted to postpone this additional hard vote, following on the stimulus bill and health care, until after the Senate acted. If, as many suspected, the Senate never acted, House Democrats would be freed from having to take a stand that could only hurt them at home. Pelosi did not seem to care about either the Senate or her moderate members' plight, and she forced a vote. The Senate never acted on cap and trade, and House Democrats faced angry voters.[119] Bitten by Obama, Wall Street responded by financing Republicans in 2010 by a

2-to-1 margin.[120] Democrats lost sixty-three House seats and control of the House in November 2010. Moderates were hit especially hard, and twenty-two of twenty-six Democrats first elected in 2008 lost.

Exit polls show that the electorate in 2010 was similar to the electorate in 2008.[121] Although Republican turnout increased some, the real difference in the results came from independents. In 2008 they favored Democrats over Republicans by 64 to 30 percent; in 2010 they favored Republicans over Democrats by 56 to 38 percent, a swing of 26 percent.[122] Democrats had misread the 2008 election as a mandate for a leftist agenda. All that independents, most of whom were moderates, had been saying in 2008 was that they did not want more George W. Bush–style conservatism; they were not embracing liberalism, big spending, huge deficits, or a government takeover of the economy. Democrats blamed their poor showing on a bad economy, but polls showed that progressive policies were the problem.[123] An Ohio restaurateur, Karl Kissner, said, "The health care bill caused a breach with the public." He added that the Stimulus Act "created a false bottom" to the recession that made it hard to plan investments.[124]

Some progressives urged Obama to adopt a scorched-earth policy toward the new Congress, but the president had to run a government. In December 2010 he signaled a grudging acceptance of compromise by doing a tax deal with Republicans. Although some progressives charged that Obama had sold out, there were only minor differences between the final bill and what Obama had originally proposed. The Republicans won an extension of the lower Bush tax rates on the wealthy for two years, a continued low capital gains tax, and low estate taxes. In return, Obama got the tax issue settled for two years and ratification of the Strategic Arms Reduction Treaty (START). With lower taxes, he also won increased prospects for faster economic growth, lower unemployment, and a better chance to win reelection.[125]

Two days after the deal, Obama held a press conference in which he denounced the deal he had just made. He claimed that he had been the victim of Republican "hostage takers," that the tax bill was rotten, and that members of his own party were "sanctimonious." A savvy politician always takes credit for any deal that is made, promotes the notion of win-win, and heaps praise on deal-making partners to lay the groundwork for a future deal. Obama may have designed this strange tirade to protect himself from a left challenge in 2012, or he may have wanted to send a signal that such deals would be rare. Or perhaps the president was just emoting.[126] Successful presidents, the Democratic pollster Pat Caddell noted, know that "the country is bigger than their presidency. With Obama, it is always about him."[127]

Obama stayed true to his progressive roots throughout. He showed little inclination to move to the middle, as Bill Clinton had done after the 1994 elections. When forced to act in a moderate way, he did so reluctantly, in order to save his presidency. But he intended to resist as much as possible. In early 2011, David Axelrod said that Obama remained a true progressive: "I mean, there's no doubt he is progressive."[128] In February 2011 the moderate Democratic Leadership Council (DLC) folded.[129] With many moderate Democrats forced out of Congress and with the Obama administration's ongoing commitment to a leftist agenda, the DLC no longer mattered. In the 2012 campaign, Obama continued to call for taxing the rich and redistributing wealth. He even said, "If you've got a business, you didn't build that. Somebody else made that happen." He was praising neither saints nor leprechauns but the state.[130]

Time to Grow Up

Barack Obama's presidency proved profoundly disappointing to many Americans. The optimism of January 2009 faded quickly as Obama pursued unpopular policies. Although he bore no responsibility for the financial crisis, he exploited the crisis for narrow partisan purposes and refused to acknowledge its seriousness for public finances, present programs, or future plans. He seemed incapable of grasping the harsh truth about the economy, government expenditures, or the political system that produced the crisis. Like other progressives, he embraced big spending programs, including new initiatives, even when there was no way to pay for them.

Pursuing the progressive dream of national health care, he allowed Congress to produce a dysfunctional bill that the public disliked. He devised the Dodd-Frank Act, which raised business costs, reduced lending, slowed economic growth, failed to prevent future financial meltdowns, and gave politicians, not financial experts, the right to allocate capital. He did nothing for Main Street to spur job creation. He failed to put in place a long-term tax policy, to cut excessive regulations, to work on deficit reduction, or to embrace entitlement reform. Indulging in outbursts that mocked the claim of postpartisanship, he embraced leftist schemes, wild spending, and huge deficits.

To be a New Progressive is to refuse to be an adult. Americans desperately need a leader who will tell the truth about the hard choices the country faces, the high price of self-indulgence, and the delusion of believing that you can have anything you want. But such truths are not likely to be heard from the progressive elite that has come of age over the past several decades. The progressive plans to use governmental power to pursue absurd and destructive dreams of social justice require a flood of nonexistent government revenue and can be realized only with unsustainable deficits. As a result, inflation, increased taxes, slower growth, higher unemployment, and poorer government services will be the New Progressive legacy.

Notes

Introduction: The New Progressives

1   See, e.g., "American Progressivism," GlennBeck.com, April 16, 2009, http://www.glennbeck.com/content/articles/article/198/23936/; Jonah Goldberg, *Liberal Fascism: The Secret History of the American Left, from Mussolini to the Politics of Meaning* (New York: Doubleday, 2008); Ronald J. Pestritto, *Woodrow Wilson and the Roots of Modern Liberalism* (Lanham, MD: Rowman and Littlefield, 2005); and Ronald J. Pestritto, "Glenn Beck, Progressives, and Me," *Wall Street Journal*, September 15, 2010.

2   Sarah Weddington, *A Question of Choice* (New York: Penguin, 1993), 44.

3   For a discussion of the shift in political affiliations of law students, see Laura Kalman, *Yale Law School and the Sixties: Revolt and Reverberations* (Chapel Hill: University of North Carolina Press, 2005) and Steven M. Teles, *The Rise of the Conservative Legal Movement: The Battle for Control of the Law* (Princeton, NJ: Princeton University Press, 2008).

4   Teles, *Rise of the Conservative Legal Movement*, 52.

Chapter 1: Legacies of the Sixties

1   On Kennedy, see Arthur M. Schlesinger Jr., *A Thousand Days: John F. Kennedy in the White House* (Boston: Houghton Mifflin, 1965); Theodore C. Sorensen, *Kennedy* (New York: Harper & Row, 1965); Henry Fairlie, *The Kennedy Promise: The Politics of Expectation* (Garden City, NY: Doubleday, 1973).

2   Bill Haddad in Scott Stossel, *Sarge: The Life and Times of Sargent Shriver* (Washington, DC: Smithsonian, 2004), 191.

3   George Smathers U.S. Senate Oral History, 132–33 (online at http://www.senate.gov).

4   On Johnson, see Robert Dallek, *Lyndon Johnson and His Times, 1908–1973*, 2 vols. (New York: Oxford University Press, 1991–98).

5   On the Civil Rights Act (1964), see Hugh D. Graham, *The Civil Rights Era: Origins and Development of National Policy* (New York: Oxford University Press, 1990).

6   Sheri I. David, *With Dignity: The Search for Medicare and Medicaid* (Westport, CT: Greenwood, 1985); Hugh D. Graham, *The Uncertain Triumph: Federal Education Policy in the Kennedy and Johnson Years* (Chapel Hill: University of North Carolina Press, 1984); Edward D. Berkowitz, *Mr. Social Security: The Life of Wilbur J. Cohen* (Lawrence: University Press of Kansas, 1995).

7   Jaap Kooijman, *And the Pursuit of National Health: The Incremental Strategy toward National Health Insurance in the United States of America* (Amsterdam: Rodopi, 1999), 182–83 (quote at 183).

8   Ho chant in Todd Gitlin, *The Sixties: Years of Hope, Days of Rage* (New York: Bantam, 1987), 261; Brown quoted in Clayborne Carson, *In Struggle: SNCC and the Black Awakening of the 1960s* (Cambridge, MA: Harvard University Press, 1981), 260.

9   A good overview is John H. Franklin, *From Slavery to Freedom: A History of African Americans*, 8th ed. (New York: Knopf, 2000). See also Nicholas Lemann, *The Promised Land: The Great Black Migration and How It Changed America* (New York: Knopf, 1991).

10 An excellent biography is David L. Lewis, *King: A Biography*, 2nd ed. (Urbana: University of Illinois Press, 1978). See also David J. Garrow, *Bearing the Cross: Martin Luther King Jr. and the Southern Christian Leadership Conference* (New York: Morrow, 1986).

11 On King's social justice views, see Michael K. Honey, *Going Down Jericho Road: The Memphis Strike, Martin Luther King's Last Campaign* (New York: Norton, 2007).

12 On CORE, see August Meier and Elliott Rudwick, *CORE: A Study in the Civil Rights Movement, 1942–1968* (New York: Oxford University Press, 1973). On SNCC, see Carson, *In Struggle*. On the grass roots, see Charles M. Payne, *I've Got the Light of Freedom* (Berkeley: University of California Press, 1995), and John Dittmer, *Local People: The Struggle for Civil Rights in Mississippi* (Urbana: University of Illinois Press, 1994).

13 An early expression of the moral basis of the movement is Martin Luther King Jr., *Stride toward Freedom: The Montgomery Story* (New York: Harper & Bros., 1958).

14 Gitlin, *Sixties*, 81–126; Mary King, *Freedom Song: A Personal Story of the 1960s Civil Rights Movement* (New York: Morrow, 1987), 33–78; Tom Hayden, *Reunion: A Memoir* (New York: Random House, 1988), 25–52.

15 Among the first to write about the civil rights grass roots was Howard Zinn, *SNCC: The New Abolitionists* (Boston: Beacon Press, 1964). Zinn's notes of civil rights meetings, which are in his papers at the Wisconsin Historical Society, show the length, intensity, and detail at the grassroots level.

16 For examples of leaders who respected collective decision making, see Andrew

Young, *An Easy Burden: The Civil Rights Movement and the Transformation of America* (New York: HarperCollins, 1996), and Ralph D. Abernathy, *And the Walls Came Tumbling Down: An Autobiography* (New York: Harper & Row, 1989).

17 For a shrewd analysis, see King, *Freedom Song*, 525.

18 Jules Witcover, *Marathon: The Pursuit of the Presidency, 1972–1976* (New York: Viking, 1976), quoted in Steven F. Hayward, *The Age of Reagan: The Fall of the Old Liberal Order, 1964–1980* (Roseville, CA: Prima Forum, 2001), 494.

19 Richard C. Cortner, *The Apportionment Cases* (Knoxville: University of Tennessee Press, 1970).

20 On quotas, see Stephan Thernstrom and Abigail Thernstrom, *America in Black and White: One Nation, Indivisible* (New York: Simon & Schuster, 1997), and Shelby Steele, *White Guilt: How Blacks and Whites Together Destroyed the Promise of the Civil Rights Era* (New York: HarperCollins, 2006).

21 On felons, see Jeff Manza and Christopher Uggen, *Locked Out: Felon Disenfranchisement and American Democracy* (New York: Oxford University Press, 2006). On the Willie Horton incident, see John J. Brady, *Bad Boy: The Life and Politics of Lee Atwater* (Reading, MA: Addison-Wesley, 1997).

22 On the voter-registration projects, see Carson, *In Struggle*, 40. See also Steven F. Lawson, *Black Ballots: Voting Rights in the South, 1944–1969* (New York: Columbia University Press, 1976).

23 William H. Chafe, *Never Stop Running: Allard Lowenstein and the Struggle to Save American Liberalism* (New York: Basic Books, 1993), 180–86, 195–201; Theodore H. White, *The Making of the President, 1964* (New York: Atheneum, 1965), 182, 242.

24 Chana K. Lee, *For Freedom's Sake: The Life of Fannie Lou Hamer* (Urbana: University of Illinois Press, 1999), 86–102. See also White, *Making of the President*, 277–82.

25 On the Cold War, see H. W. Brands, *The Devil We Knew: The Making of the Cold War* (New York: Oxford University Press, 1993).

26 On culture, see Morris Dickstein, *Gates of Eden: American Culture in the Sixties* (New York: Basic Books, 1977), and Gitlin, *Sixties*, 31–54.

27 James Miller, *Democracy Is in the Streets: From Port Huron to the Siege of Chicago* (New York: Simon & Schuster, 1987), 112–17; Kirkpatrick Sale, *SDS* (New York: Random House, 1973), 56–57; Maurice Isserman, *If I Had a Hammer: The Death of the Old Left and the Birth of the New Left* (New York: Basic Books, 1987), 180–203.

28 C. Wright Mills, "Letter to the New Left," *New Left Review* (September–October 1960). Publishing history is in Paul Jacobs and Saul Landau, eds., *The New Radicals: A Report with Documents* (New York: Random House, 1966), especially 101. In general, see W. J. Rorabaugh, "Challenging Authority, Seeking Community, and Empowerment in the New Left, Black Power, and Feminism," *Journal of Policy History* 8 (1996): 110–18.

29 The best survey of SDS is Sale, *SDS*. The Port Huron Statement is reprinted in Miller, *Democracy*, 329–74. See also Hayden, *Reunion*, 84–102.

30 Miller, *Democracy*, 49–50, 57–61, 121; Sale, *SDS*, 35–36, 82–84.

31 Miller, *Democracy*, 23, 31–32, 111–17, 120–22, 127–35, 224–25 (Hayden at 31).

32 Miller, *Democracy*, 73–74, 116–17, 135–37; Sara Evans, *Personal Politics: The Roots of Women's Liberation in the Civil Rights Movement and the New Left* (New York: Knopf, 1979), 120–24; Gitlin, *Sixties*, 72–76.

33 Isserman, *Hammer*.

34 Sale, *SDS*, 60–68; Wini Breines, *Community and Organization in the New Left, 1962–1968* (New York: Praeger, 1982), 13–17.

35 Miller, *Democracy*, 169, 172–74, 182; Sale, *SDS*, 155–56, 219, 318–19.

36 Miller, *Democracy*, 94–95, 142–48, 152–54.

37 On ERAP, see Miller, *Democracy*, 182–217; Evans, *Personal Politics*, 129–55; Sale, *SDS*, 102–15, 131–50; Hayden, *Reunion*, 124–32.

38 On Columbia, see Dotson Rader, *I Ain't Marchin' Anymore!* (New York: David McKay, 1969).

39 On Peace and Freedom Party ties to the Black Panthers, see Carson, *In Struggle*, 279–80.

40 King, *Freedom Song*, 535–36; Charles Evers, *Evers* (New York: World, 1971). On black votes, see Earl Black and Merle Black, *Politics and Society in the South* (Cambridge, MA: Harvard University Press, 1987), 138. See also Frank R. Parker, *Black Votes Count: Political Empowerment in Mississippi* (Chapel Hill: University of North Carolina Press, 1990).

41 Barry M. Goldwater, *With No Apologies: The Personal and Political Memoirs of United States Senator Barry M. Goldwater* (New York: Morrow, 1979), 180–81, 193.

42 On the rights agenda, see Steven F. Lawson, *In Pursuit of Power: Southern Blacks and Electoral Politics, 1965–1982* (New York: Columbia University Press, 1985).

43 Marguerite R. Barnett, "The Congressional Black Caucus: Illusions and Reality of Power," in Michael B. Preston, Lenneal J. Henderson Jr., and Paul Puryear, eds., *The New Black Politics: The Search for Political Power* (New York: Longman, 1982); William E. Nelson Jr. and Philip J. Meranto, *Electing Black Mayors: Political Action in the Black Community* (Columbus: Ohio State University Press, 1977).

44 Dick Cluster, ed., *They Should Have Served That Cup of Coffee* (Boston: South End Press, 1979), 181–258; Jo Freeman, *The Politics of Women's Liberation: A Case Study of an Emerging Social Movement and Its Relation to the Policy Process* (New York: McKay, 1975). Freeman had been active in the civil rights movement and the Free Speech Movement. Jo Freeman, *At Berkeley in the Sixties: The Education of an Activist, 1961–1965* (Bloomington: Indiana University Press, 2004). See also Leila J. Rupp and Verta Taylor, *Survival in the Doldrums: The American Women's Rights Movement, 1945 to the 1960s* (New York: Oxford University Press, 1987). On the Equal Pay Act, see Cynthia Harrison, *On Account of Sex: The Politics of Women's Issues, 1945–1968* (Berkeley: University of California Press, 1988), 87, 89–105.

45 King, *Freedom Song*, 261–62, 444–70 (quote at 452). See also Evans, *Personal Politics*, and Paula Giddings, *When and Where I Enter: The Impact of Black Women on Race and Sex in America* (New York: Morrow, 1984), 278–81, 285–87.

46 On Smith, see Carl M. Brauer, "Women Activists, Southern Conservatives, and the Prohibition of Sex Discrimination in Title VII of the 1964 Civil Rights Act," *Journal of Southern History*, 49 (1983): 37–56. On NOW, see Betty Friedan, *It Changed My Life: Writings on the Women's Movement* (New York: Norton, 1976), 93–144.

47 Susan M. Hartmann, *From Margin to Mainstream: American Women and Politics since 1960* (New York: Knopf, 1989).

48 On San Francisco State, see William Barlow and Peter Shapiro, *An End to Silence: The San Francisco State Student Movement in the '60s* (New York: Pegasus, 1971). On Berkeley, see W. J. Rorabaugh, *Berkeley at War: The 1960s* (New York: Oxford University Press, 1989), 85–86, 154.

49 On AIM, see Dennis Banks and Richard Erdoes, *Ojibwa Warrior: Dennis Banks and the Rise of the American Indian Movement* (Norman: University of Oklahoma Press, 2004), and Russell Means, *Where White Men Fear to Tread: The Autobiography of Russell Means* (New York: St. Martin's Press, 1995).

50 Martin B. Duberman, *Stonewall* (New York: Dutton, 1993); Randy Shiltz, *The Mayor of Castro Street: The Life and Times of Harvey Milk* (New York: St. Martin's Press, 1982). See also John D'Emilio, *Sexual Politics, Sexual Communities: The Making of a Homosexual Minority in the United States, 1940–1970* (Chicago: University of Chicago Press, 1983), and John D'Emilio, William B. Turner, and Urvashi Vaid, eds., *Creating Change: Sexuality, Public Policy, and Civil Rights* (New York: St. Martin's Press, 2000).

51 Quote from inaugural address is in W. J. Rorabaugh, *The Real Making of the President: Kennedy, Nixon, and the 1960 Election* (Lawrence: University Press of Kansas, 2009), 212.

52 On the coup against Diem, see Ellen J. Hammer, *A Death in November: America in Vietnam, 1963* (New York: Dutton, 1987). On Johnson's war plans, see Larry Berman, *Planning a Tragedy: The Americanization of the War in Vietnam* (New York: Norton, 1982).

53 Charles DeBenedetti, *An American Ordeal: The Antiwar Movement of the Vietnam Era* (Syracuse: Syracuse University Press, 1990); Amy Swerdlow, *Women Strike for Peace: Traditional Motherhood and Radical Politics in the 1960s* (Chicago: University of Chicago Press, 1993); Milton S. Katz, *Ban the Bomb: A History of SANE, the Committee for a Sane Nuclear Policy, 1957–1985* (Westport, CT: Greenwood, 1986). On the SDS march, see Miller, *Democracy*, 226–34.

54 On the draft, see Lawrence M. Baskir and William Strauss, *Chance and Circumstance: The Draft, the War, and the Vietnam Generation* (New York: Knopf, 1978).

55 On the VDC, see Rorabaugh, *Berkeley*, 91–99.

56 Statistics in Rorabaugh, *Berkeley*, 103, 176.

57 Rorabaugh, *Berkeley*, 111, 165–66, 179.

58 Robert Scheer, *How the United States Got Involved in Vietnam: A Report of the Center for the Study of Democratic Institutions* (Santa Barbara, CA: CSDI, 1965).

59 On the PFP, see Rorabaugh, *Berkeley*, 83, 110; James M. Elden and David R. Schweitzer, "New Third Party Radicalism: The Case of the California Peace and Freedom Party," *Western Political Quarterly* 24 (1971): 761–74.

60 On the NCNP, see Alice Widener, *U.S.A.* (New York: U.S.A., 1968), 20–26 (council at 21). This book is a digest of issues of *U.S.A.* magazine.

61 Widener, *U.S.A.*, 23–24.

62 King in Garrow, *Bearing the Cross*, 551–62, 577.

63 Quoted in Sale, *SDS*, 478.

64 Widener, *U.S.A.*, 29–30.

65 Widener, *U.S.A.*, 53. See also Michael Harrington, *The Other America: Poverty in the United States* (New York: Macmillan, 1962).

66 Widener, *U.S.A.*, 54.

67 Stanley Kurtz, *Radical-in-Chief: Barack Obama and the Untold Story of American Socialism* (New York: Threshold Editions, 2010), 131–49, 160, 174–77, 180–86.

68 Chafe, *Never Stop Running*, 262–69.

69 Chafe, *Never Stop Running*, 270–71; George S. McGovern, *Grassroots: The Autobiography of George McGovern* (New York: Random House, 1977), 110–11.

70 Chafe, *Never Stop Running*, 271–72; Eugene J. McCarthy, *Up 'til Now: A Memoir* (San Diego: Harcourt Brace Jovanovich, 1987), 155–62, 182–85. See also Dominic Sandbrook, *Eugene McCarthy: The Rise and Fall of Postwar American Liberalism* (New York: Knopf, 2004).

71 On the campaign, see Eugene J. McCarthy, *The Year of the People* (Garden City, NY: Doubleday, 1969); Arthur Herzog, *McCarthy for President* (New York: Viking, 1969); George Rising, *Clean for Gene: Eugene McCarthy's 1968 Presidential Campaign* (Westport, CT: Praeger, 1997).

72 On New Hampshire, see Lewis Chester, Godfrey Hodgson, and Bruce Page, *An American Melodrama: The Presidential Campaign of 1968* (New York: Viking, 1969), 78–100.

73 Arthur M. Schlesinger Jr., *Robert Kennedy and His Times* (Boston: Houghton Mifflin, 1978), 849–57; Chester, Hodgson, and Page, *American Melodrama*, 105–26, 134–37.

74 Chester, Hodgson, and Page, *American Melodrama*, 4–5, 139–45, 297–307, 312–55.

75 Data in Chester, Hodgson, and Page, *American Melodrama*, 524, 357.

76 "Democrats: Humphrey's Bandwagon," *Newsweek*, June 10, 1968, 18, 25–28 (quote at 28); "Nation: Democratic Countdown," *Time*, June 7, 1968, 23–24; "After Oregon—HHH and Nixon?" *U.S. News & World Report*, June 10, 1968, 39–40; McGovern, *Grassroots*, 118; Chester, Hodgson, and Page, *American Melodrama*, 310, 403.

77 McGovern, *Grassroots*, 118–22, 127.

78 Hubert H. Humphrey, *The Education of a Public Man: My Life in Politics*, 2nd ed.

ed. (Minneapolis: University of Minnesota Press, 1991), 290–93; Chester, Hodgson, and Page, *American Melodrama*, 527–37, 579–81.

79 Hayden, *Reunion*, 293–326.

80 Jerry Rubin, *Growing (Up) at 37* (New York: Evans, 1976), 81–82; Jack Hoffman and Daniel Simon, *Run, Run, Run: The Lives of Abbie Hoffman* (New York: Putnam's, 1994), 89, 96–103; Marty Jezer, *Abbie Hoffman, American Rebel* (New Brunswick, NJ: Rutgers University Press, 1992), 137–71; Jonah Raskin, *For the Hell of It: The Life and Times of Abbie Hoffman* (Berkeley: University of California Press, 1996), 143–71.

81 Todd Gitlin, *The Whole World Is Watching: Mass Media in the Making and Unmaking of the New Left* (Berkeley: University of California Press, 1980); Jezer, *Hoffman*, 166–68 (quote at 167); Raskin, *For the Hell of It*, 165–67.

82 Hayden in David R. Farber, *Chicago '68* (Chicago: University of Chicago Press, 1988), 171.

83 On the Chicago Seven, see Tom Hayden, *Trial* (New York: Holt, Rinehart and Winston, 1970).

84 Hayden, *Reunion*, 420–26.

85 On the breakup of SDS, see Sale, *SDS*, 557–66.

86 On Weatherman, see Harold Jacobs, ed., *Weatherman* (Berkeley: Ramparts Press, 1970). See also Bill Ayers, *Fugitive Days: A Memoir* (Boston: Beacon Press, 2001). On Ayers and Obama, see Kurtz, *Radical-in-Chief*, 261–62.

87 To appreciate the resentment, see publications like *New Times*, *High Times*, and *In These Times*.

88 The best study of Wallace is Dan T. Carter, *The Politics of Rage: George Wallace, the Origins of the New Conservatism, and the Transformation of American Politics* (New York: Simon & Schuster, 1995). See also McGovern, *Grassroots*, 182–83.

89 McGovern, *Grassroots*, 118, 130–34; Bruce Miroff, *The Liberals' Moment: The McGovern Insurgency and the Identity Crisis of the Democratic Party* (Lawrence: University Press of Kansas, 2007), 19–20; Andrew E. Busch, *Outsiders and Openness in the Presidential Nominating System* (Pittsburgh: University of Pittsburgh Press, 1997), 1–2, 7–9.

90 Miroff, *Liberals' Moment*, 20–21, 43–45, 183–85; McGovern, *Grassroots*, 134–39; Busch, *Outsiders*, 10–11; Mark Strickertz, *Why the Democrats Are Blue: How Secular Liberals Hijacked the People's Party* (New York: Encounter Books, 2007), 87–91.

91 Steven S. Smith and Melanie J. Springer, "Choosing Presidential Candidates," in Smith and Springer, eds., *Reforming the Presidential Nominating Process* (Washington, DC: Brookings Institution Press, 2009), 5–6; McGovern, *Grassroots*, 141; Miroff, *Liberals' Moment*, 21; Stricherz, *Why the Democrats*, 83–85.

92 McGovern, *Grassroots*, 139–41, 143, 149–51 (Dutton at 150); Miroff, *Liberals' Moment*, 21, 74.

93 McGovern, *Grassroots*, 143–45, 148–49; Miroff, *Liberals' Moment*, 21–23, 185–86; Stricherz, *Why the Democrats*, 111–17, 156–58, 163–68.

94 Busch, *Outsiders*, 12–13; McGovern, *Grassroots*, 139, 153; Miroff, *Liberals' Moment*, 23–24.

95 Busch, *Outsiders*, 87–88, 90–92; McGovern, *Grassroots*, 153; Miroff, *Liberals' Moment*, 44–46, 52–55, 57–59, 64–68, 177–80, 204–6; Stricherz, *Why the Democrats*, 95–97.

96 Busch, *Outsiders*, 89–90, 96, 102; McGovern, *Grassroots*, 158–61, 172, 184–86, 231; Miroff, *Liberals' Moment*, 49, 62, 76, 81, 183–84.

97 Miroff, *Liberals' Moment*, 88, 97, 104–6, 187 (quote), 235–39, 243, 251–57. See also Stricherz, *Why the Democrats*. On Watergate babies, see Jay Nordlinger, "Watergate Babies," *National Review*, December 31, 1998, 30.

98 Busch, *Outsiders*, 107; Miroff, *Liberals' Moment*, 198, 266–67; Stricherz, *Why the Democrats*, 209–23.

99 Karen Brooks and Emily Ramshaw, "An Embarrassment of Riches?" *Dallas Morning News*, March 6, 2008, A1; Lisa Sandberg, "Campaign 2008: Dems Seek Simpler Dance for the Party," *Houston Chronicle*, March 8, 2008, B1; Sarah Wheaton, "Still Counting in Texas," *New York Times*, March 12, 2008, A22; CNN Election Center 2008, http://www.cnn.com/ELECTION/2008/primaries/results/state/#TX.

Chapter 2: From the Streets into the Courtroom and the Neighborhoods

1 Joshua Green, "John Edwards, Esq.," *Washington Monthly*, October 2001; "The 1998 Election: The Discontented: Rejecting Negative Advertising and the Candidate," *New York Times*, October 16, 1998; Adam Hochberg, "Senate Race Marked Edwards as Rising Political Star," NPR, October 1, 2007.

2 Green, "John Edwards, Esq."

3 Quoted in Charles McCarry, *Citizen Nader* (New York: Saturday Review Press, 1972), 199.

4 Ralph Nader, "Introduction to *The Company State*," in Barbara Ehrenreich, ed., *The Ralph Nader Reader* (New York: Seven Stories Press, 2000), 128–44, especially 134. In this same volume on Nader's anticorporatism, see Nader, Mark Green, and Joel Seligman, "Who Rules the Giant Corporation?" 114–27.

5 Biographical information about Nader is found in McCarry, *Citizen Nader*; Justin Martin, *Nader: Crusader, Spoiler, Icon* (Cambridge, MA: Basic Books, 2002); Patricia Cronin Marcello, *Ralph Nader: A Biography* (Westport, CT: Greenwood Press, 2004); and Dan M. Burt, *Abuse of Trust: A Report on Ralph Nader's Network* (Chicago: Regnery Gateway, 1982).

6 Ralph Nader, *Unsafe at Any Speed* (New York: Grossman, 1965).

7 The Corvair was involved in 2.44 single-car crashes per million miles driven on average for 1961–63, compared with 1.61 for the Volkswagen, 1.109 for the Falcon, and 1.0 for the Valiant. By 1964, however, the Corvair stood lower than any of its competitors, with 0.16 crashes per million miles, compared with 0.56 for Volkswagen, 0.55 for Falcon, and 0.24 for Valiant. McCarry, *Citizen Nader*, 9–13.

8 Quoted in McCarry, *Citizen Nader*, 25. The description of the hearings is drawn primarily from pages 21–28.

9   Quoted in Marcello, *Ralph Nader*, 39. For Nader's involvement in more successful issues, see pages 37–39.

10 Burt, *Abuse of Trust*, 84–85.

11 Teles, *Rise of the Conservative Legal Movement*, 53.

12 Martin, *Nader*, 74–77 (quote at 76).

13 These groups and their funding are described in Burt, *Abuse of Trust*, 51–71.

14 Martin, *Nader*, 203.

15 Quoted in Martin, *Nader*, 172–73.

16 Martin, *Nader*, 202–3.

17 Nader's shift is discussed by Stanley Kurtz, *Radical-in-Chief: Barack Obama and the Untold Story of American Socialism* (New York: Threshold, 2010), 79–93. In explaining this shift, Kurtz draws from Harry C. Boyte, *The Backyard Revolution: Understanding the New Citizen Movement* (Philadelphia: Temple University Press, 1980), 87–91.

18 Boyte, *Backyard Revolution*, 209–22. An excellent historical survey of community organizing, written from a sympathetic view, is Robert Fisher, *Let the People Decide: Neighborhood Organizing in America* (New York: Twayne Publishers, 1994).

19 Quoted in McCarry, *Citizen Nader*, 206.

20 Martin, *Nader*, 122.

21 Material on PIRGs is drawn primarily from Martin, *Nader*, 119–37.

22 Quoted in Martin, *Nader*, 133.

23 Kurtz, *Radical-in-Chief*, 38–42, 49–56, 189.

24 For a discussion of Nader's involvement in the anti-nuclear-energy campaign, see Martin, *Nader*, 172–80; Marcello, *Ralph Nader*, 78–79.

25 Quoted in Martin, *Nader*, 180.

26 Among them was Mike Pertschuk, who had worked closely with Nader as staff director of the Senate Commerce Committee. Carter selected Esther Peterson to be his consumer adviser; she selected as her assistant Nancy Chasen, who had worked for Nader's Congress Watch. Former head of the Consumer Federation of America Carol Tucker became assistant secretary of agriculture.

27 Only gradually would fences be mended. Nader later appointed her to head Public Citizen. In the meantime, the Carter administration turned out to be the golden years for Nader's influence on Congress.

28 Martin, *Nader*, 226.

29 The declining political fortunes of Nader within the Democratic Party are found in Martin, *Nader*, 226–29.

30 Robert Borosage et al., "The New Public Interest," *Yale Law Journal* 79 (1969–70): 1069–52 (quotes at 1104, 1105).

31 For an overview of the decade, see Stanley Lebergott, *Pursuing Happiness: American Consumers in the Twentieth Century* (Princeton, NJ: Princeton University Press, 1993); Melita Podesta, "1960s Family," http://economicadventure.org/family.

32 Quoted in Borosage et al., "The New Public Interest," 1077.

33 Borosage et al., "The New Public Interest," 1102, 1105–6.

34 Teles, *Rise of the Conservative Legal Movement*, 30.

35 Teles, *Rise of the Conservative Legal Movement*, 42–43. See also Heather Mac Donald, "This Is the Legal Mainstream?" *City Journal*, Winter 2006.

36 Quoted in Laura Kalman, *Yale Law School and the Sixties*, 89.

37 Teles, *Rise of the Conservative Legal Movement*, 41–43.

38 Kalman, *Yale Law School and the Sixties*, 284.

39 Quoted in Kalman, *Yale Law School and the Sixties*, 203.

40 David Schoenbrod, "Confessions of an Ex-Elitist," *Commentary*, November 1999, 37–38.

41 Quoted in Green, "John Edwards, Esq."

42 Teles, *Rise of the Conservative Legal Movement*, 53.

43 Ralph Nader and Mark Green, eds., *Verdict on Lawyers* (New York: Thomas Y. Crowell Company, 1976).

44 Peter W. Huber and Robert E. Litan, eds., *The Liability Maze: The Impact of Liability Law on Safety and Innovation* (Washington, DC: Brookings Institution, 1991), 1–2.

45 This discussion of liability draws from Walker K. Olson, *The Rule of Lawyers: How the New Litigation Elite Threatens America's Rule of Law* (New York: St. Martin's Press, 2003).

46 Quoted in Martin, *Nader*, 220.

47 Quoted in Marcello, *Ralph Nader*, 111. See also Martin, *Nader*, 207.

48 Huber and Litan, eds., *Liability Maze*, 15, 18, 30.

49 Jim Copland, "Trial Lawyers, Inc. Run for President," *National Review Online*, July 8, 2004.

50 The Center for Responsive Politics provides an excellent chart of contributions by trial lawyers and their firms at http://opensecrets.org/industries.

51 Olson, *Rule of Lawyers*, 69–89.

52 Discussion of the Scruggs case draws from Alan Lange and Tom Dawson, *Kings of Tort* (Battle Ground, WA: Pediment Publishing, 2009), especially 21–33.

53 Lange and Dawson, *Kings of Tort*, 35–43.

54 Lange and Dawson, *Kings of Tort*; Joseph B. Treaster, "A Lawyer Like a Hurricane," *New York Times*, March 16, 2007.

55 Treaster, "A Lawyer Like a Hurricane."

56 Scott Horton from *Harper's* magazine reported that Trent Lott had improperly intervened to help his brother-in-law Dickie Scruggs with his legal problems in the DeLaughter case. He portrayed Paul Minor as a political victim.

57 Adam Liptak and Michael Moss, "In Trial Work, Edwards Left a Trademark," *New York Times*, January 31, 2004. See also Green, "John Edwards, Esq."

58 Liptak and Moss, "In Trial Work, Edwards Left a Trademark."

59 Hochberg, "Senate Race Marked Edwards as Rising Political Star."

60 Jim Copland, "Kerry-Edwards & Company," *National Review Online*, July 8, 2004.

61 Green, "John Edwards, Esq."

62 Quoted in Andrew Young, *The Politician* (New York: Thomas Dunne Books, 2010), 19.

63 Hochberg, "Senate Race Marked Edwards as Rising Political Star."

64 Quoted in Young, *Politician*, 25.

65 Young, *Politician*, 132.

66 Liptak and Moss, "In Trial Work, Edwards Left a Trademark."

67 Robert Novak, "Ethanol and Politics," Syndicated Column, October 9, 2004.

68 Alec MacGillis, "Edwards to 'Rescue' on Foreclosures," *Washington Post*, September 14, 2007.

69 Young, *Politician*, 175.

Chapter 3: Brave Green World

1 Al Gore, "Foreword," in Bill McKibben, ed., *American Earth: Environmental Writing Since Thoreau* (New York: Literary Classics of the United States, 2008), xix.

2 Al Gore, *An Inconvenient Truth* (Emmaus, PA: Rodale Press, 2006), 220.

3 Alan Durning, "The Dubious Rewards of Consumption," in McKibben, *American Earth*, 770–80 (quote at 770).

4 President Barack Obama, Inaugural Address, January 20, 2009, http://whitehouse.gov/blog/inaugural-address.

5 Barack Obama, Remarks Delivered in St. Paul, Minn., June 3, 2008.

6 Ted Nordhaus and Michael Shellenberger, *Break Through: From the Death of Environmentalism to the Politics of Possibility* (Boston: Houghton Mifflin, 2007), 6.

7 Ronald T. Libby, *Eco-Wars: Political Campaigns and Social Movements* (New York: Columbia University Press, 1998), 22.

8 The results of this survey, and subsequent surveys cited, are found in Nordhaus and Shellenberger, *Break Through*, 32–33.

9 The Obama-Biden Plan, http://change.gov/agenda/energy_and_environment_agenda.

10 This discussion of the liberal tradition draws from Adam Rome, "Give Earth a Chance: The Environmental Movement and the Sixties," *Journal of American History*, September 2003, 525–54.

11 See Arthur M. Schlesinger Jr., "The Future of Liberalism: The Challenge of Abundance," *Reporter*, May 3, 1956, 8–11; "Where Does the Liberal Go From Here?" *New York Times Magazine*, August 4, 1957, 7, 36, 38, quoted in Rome, "Give Earth a Chance."

12 John Kenneth Galbraith, *The Affluent Society* (Boston: Houghton Mifflin, 1958), 253, quoted in Rome, "Give Earth a Chance."

13 *New York Times*, March 13, 1960, 4.

14 Vance Packard, *The Waste Makers* (New York: D. McKay, 1960), 294–313. See also Vance Packard, *The Hidden Persuaders* (New York: D. McKay, 1957), and Vance Packard, *The Status Seekers: An Exploration of Class Behavior in America and the Hidden Barriers that Affect You, Your Community, Your Future* (New York: D. McKay, 1959).

15 Quoted in Michael Egan, *Barry Commoner and the Science of Survival: The Remaking of American Environmentalism* (Cambridge, MA: Massachusetts Institute of Technology, 2007), 7.

16 Barry Commoner, *The Closing Circle: Nature, Man, and Technology* (New York: Knopf, 1971).

17 Quoted in Egan, *Barry Commoner*, 20. See also Mitchell Goodman, *The End of It* (New York: New American Library, 1963).

18 Quoted in Egan, *Barry Commoner*, 13.

19 Commoner's involvement in this group is described in Egan, *Barry Commoner*, 20, and "Oral Interview with Barry Commoner," April 24, 1973, transcript, Center for the Study of History and Memory, Indiana University, 73–001.

20 Barry Commoner to E. U. Condon, August 5, 1953, Barry Commoner Papers, Library of Congress, Box 343, quoted in Michael Egan, "Barry Commoner and the Science of Survival" (doctoral dissertation, Washington State University, 2004), 46. Condon, a well-known physicist and director of the National Bureau of Standards, had come under criticism from the House Committee on Un-American Activities in 1948 for his membership in the American-Soviet Science Society. He became a cause célèbre in progressive scientific circles. For background on Condon, see Jessica Wang, *American Science in an Age of Anxiety: Scientists, Anticommunism, and the Cold War* (Chapel Hill: University of North Carolina Press, 1998).

21 Quotations in Egan, *Barry Commoner*, 61.

22 Quoted in Egan, *Barry Commoner*, 48.

23 The Committee for Nuclear Information is discussed by Kelly Moore, *Disrupting Science: Social Movements, American Scientists, and the Politics of the Military, 1945–1975* (Princeton, NJ: Princeton University Press, 2008), 96–129.

24 Rachel Carson, *Silent Spring* (Boston: Houghton Mifflin, 1962), 2–4. Nordhaus and Shellenberger, two environmentalists, offer a pointed critique of Carson's view of nature in *Break Through*, 132–35.

25 Richard White, *Land Use, Environment, and Social Change: The Shaping of Island County, Washington* (Seattle: University of Washington Press, 1992).

26 This observation relies on Nordhaus and Shellenberger, *Break Through*, 132–33.

27 Carson, *Silent Spring*. For a short overview of the influence of Carson's work on the modern environmental movement, see Benjamin Kline, *First along the River: A Brief History of the U.S. Environmental Movement* (San Francisco: Acada Books, 1997), 76–79.

28 Samuel Hayes, *Beauty, Health, and Permanence* (New York: Cambridge University Press, 1987), 4–22.

29 Kline, *First Along the River*, 74–75; Andrew G. Kirk, *Counterculture Green: The Whole Earth Catalog and American Environmentalism* (Lawrence: University Press of Kansas, 2007), 19–22; Robert Gottlieb, *Forcing the Spring: The Transformation of the American Environmental Movement* (Washington, DC: Island Press, 1993); and Rik Scarce, *Eco-Warriors: Understanding the Radical Environmental Movement* (Chicago: Noble Press, 1990).

30 For a discussion of Kennedy's and Johnson's environmental policies, see Rome, "Give Earth a Chance," 525–54.

31 Environmental legislation in the 1960s included the Clean Air Act (1963); the creation of the National Wilderness Preservation System (1964); the Water Quality Act (1965); the Noise Control Act (1965); the Solid Waste Disposal Act (1965); the Air Quality Act (1967); the Wild and Scenic Rivers Act (1968); and the National Trails System Act (1968).

32 Egan, *Barry Commoner*, 102–35.

33 Rome, "Give Earth a Chance"; Kirk, *Counterculture Green*.

34 Tom Hayden, *Reunion: A Memoir* (New York: Random House, 1988), 418.

35 Hayden, *Reunion*, 419.

36 Hayden, *Reunion*, 415–39.

37 Editors of *Ramparts*, *Eco-Catastrophe* (New York: Harper & Row, 1970), v.

38 Robert Easton, *Black Tide: The Santa Barbara Oil Spill and Its Consequences* (New York: Delacorte Press, 1972). For the liberal take on environmental issues, see Martin Melosi, "Lyndon Johnson and Environmental Policy," in Robert A. Divine, ed., *The Johnson Years: Vietnam, the Environment, and Science* (Lawrence: University Press of Kansas, 1987); Lewis L. Gould, *Lady Bird Johnson and the Environment* (Lawrence: University Press of Kansas, 1988).

39 Denis Hayes, "The Beginning," in Environmental Action, ed., *Earth Day—The Beginning* (New York: Bantam Books, 1970), xv. See also Philip Shabecoff, *A Fierce Green Fire: The American Environmental Movement* (New York: Hill & Wang, 1993).

40 For a good overview, see Scarce, *Eco-Warriors*.

41 Scarce lists six principles of deep ecology: all nature has intrinsic worth; accept simple material needs over economic growth for growing human population; nature is limited; reject progress for nondominating science; reject consumerism in favor of making do with enough; and reject nationalism for "bioregion." Scarce, *Eco-Warriors*, 37, 39.

42 The claim that African American communities suffered from worse pollution is dismantled in great statistical detail by Christopher H. Foreman Jr., *The Promise and Peril of Environmental Justice* (Washington, DC: Brookings Institution, 1998).

43 Hayden, *Reunion*, 435.

44 Hayden, *Reunion*, 471–72.

45 For a full account of the Big Green campaign, see Libby, *Eco-Wars*, 89–129. The following discussion of Big Green draws heavily from this excellent history of the crusade. See also DRI, "Proposed Reductions in Carbon Dioxide Emissions: Consequences for the California Economy," September 1990; California Senate Toxic and Public Safety Management Committee, "Proposition 128: Environmental Protection Act of 1990" (Sacramento: California Senate, 1990); Larry B. Stammer, "Propositions 128, 130: Campaign Strategy Links 2 Environmental Initiatives," *Los Angeles Times*, November 30, 1990. An excellent summary of the legislation is found in Robert Guskind, "Big Green Light," *National Journal*, October 6, 1990.

46 Richard C. Paddock, "Hayden Says He Won't Run for Environmental Post," *Los Angeles Times*, October 28, 1990.

47 The entertainment industry's support of Big Green is found in Libby, *Eco-Wars*, 101–4.

48 Stars included Jeff Bridges, Chevy Chase, Jamie Lee Curtis, Robert Downey Jr., Michael Landon, Jack Lemmon, Demi Moore, Gregory Peck, Susan Sarandon, Cybill Shepherd, Jimmy Smits, Oliver Stone, Bruce Willis, Jane Fonda, and Bonnie Raitt. Hayden served as executive producer for the ad. See Libby, *Eco-Wars*, 101.

49 Quoted in Libby, *Eco-Wars*, 99.

50 R. Clayton Mansfield, "The Great Green Hope," *Yodeler*, September 1990, 1, 3–4.

51 Libby, *Eco-Wars*, 105.

52 Libby, *Eco-Wars*, 106.

53 Susan Reed, "Hollywood Heavyweights Turn Out in Force to Urge California Voters to Give the Green Light to Big Green," *People*, November 5, 1990.

54 Libby, *Eco-Wars*, 106.

55 Chip Jacobs, "Big Fight Brews over Big Green Ballot Measure," *Los Angeles Business Journal*, September 10, 1990.

56 Quoted in Libby, *Eco-Wars*, 121.

57 Maura Dolan, "Big Green Reached Too Far, Backers Say," *Los Angeles Times*, November 8, 1990.

58 Environmental progress is traced in superb detail by Seymour Garte, *Where We Stand: A Surprising Look at the Real State of Our Planet* (New York: AMACOM, 2008), on which the following discussion is based.

59 Garte, *Where We Stand*, 213–21.

60 Statistics are from Garte, *Where We Stand*, 104–19.

61 Garte, *Where We Stand*, xii.

62 Bill McKibben, *Deep Economy: The Wealth of Communities and the Durable Future* (New York: Times Books, 2007), 2, 4, 11, 221–24.

63 David Shearman and Joseph Wayne Smith, *The Climate Change Challenge and the Failure of Democracy* (Westport, CT: Praeger, 2007).

64 Shearman and Smith, *Climate Change Challenge*, 96,108, 136.

65 Robyn Eckersley, *The Green State: Rethinking Democracy and Sovereignty* (Cambridge, MA: MIT, 2004), 2, 12, 87, 91, 95, 120–21.

66 See Foreman, *Promise and Peril*.

67 http://yosemite.epa.gov/opa/admpress.nsf/6427a6b7538955c585257359003f02 30/cd2d72a02dda6281852579b100516ff3!OpenDocument.

Chapter 4: Controlling Life and Death

1 Ron Weddington to President-elect Clinton, circa January 6, 1993. This letter can be viewed at http://judicialwatch.org, A Judicial Watch Special Report:

"The Clinton RU-486 Files." These letters were procured through a Freedom of Information request by Judicial Watch, a conservative organization.

2   Ian Dowbiggin, *A Merciful End: The Euthanasia Movement in Modern America* (New York: Oxford University Press, 2003).

3   See Matthew Connelly, *Fatal Misconception: The Struggle to Control World Population* (Cambridge, MA: Harvard University Press, 2008), 7–8.

4   Quoted in Connelly, *Fatal Misconception*, 160. For the eugenic impetus for the council, see 161–63.

5   Connelly, *Fatal Misconception*, 159–60.

6   Connelly, *Fatal Misconception*, 188.

7   Quoted in Donald T. Critchlow, *Intended Consequences: Birth Control, Abortion, and the Federal Government in Modern America* (New York: Oxford University Press, 1999), 47. This discussion of the population movement draws heavily from this study.

8   Canfield's connection with the Kennedy family was close. Canfield's son Michael was then married to Jackie Kennedy's sister, Lee Bouvier, which is how Cass got to be JFK's publisher.

9   Quoted in Critchlow, *Intended Consequences*, 70.

10   Quoted in Critchlow, *Intended Consequences*, 55–56.

11   Quoted in Critchlow, *Intended Consequences*, 154–55.

12   Quoted in Critchlow, *Intended Consequences*, 155.

13   Connelly, *Fatal Misconception*, 240.

14   Quoted in Robert G. Weisbord, "Birth Control and the Black American: A Matter of Genocide?" *Demography* 10, no. 4 (November 1973): 580.

15   Connelly, *Fatal Misconception*, 244–45.

16   Connelly, *Fatal Misconception*, details these coercive programs, 276–326.

17   Quoted in Connelly, *Fatal Misconception*, 323. Sterilization numbers are at 323.

18   Quoted in Connelly, *Fatal Misconception*, 315.

19   Quoted in Connelly, *Fatal Misconception*, 315.

20   Quoted in Critchlow, *Intended Consequences*, 177.

21   See Critchlow, *Intended Consequences*, 133.

22   Quoted in Critchlow, *Intended Consequences*, 147.

23   Weddington, *Question of Choice*, 18.

24   Weddington, *Question of Choice*, 11.

25   Doug Rossinow, *The Politics of Authenticity: Liberalism, Christianity, and the New Left in America* (New York: Columbia University Press, 1998), 224, 260.

26   Rossinow, *Politics of Authenticity*, 307–10.

27   The best sympathetic account of the movement to overturn state abortion laws remains David Garrow, *Liberty and Sexuality: The Right to Privacy and the Making of* Roe v. Wade (Berkeley: University of California, 1998).

28   Weddington, *Question of Choice*, 45.

29   Weddington, *Question of Choice*, 49–53.

30   Weddington, *Question of Choice*, 64.

31   Harriet Pilpel, "The Right of Abortion," *Atlantic Monthly*, June 1969.

32 Quoted in Critchlow, *Intended Consequences*, 165.

33 Quoted in Critchlow, *Intended Consequences*, 194.

34 The best account of the history of euthanasia in America is Dowbiggin, *Merciful End*. This discussion of euthanasia and assisted suicide draws heavily on Dowbiggin's work.

35 This law is quoted in Dowbiggin, *Merciful End*, 18.

36 Quoted in Dowbiggin, *Merciful End*, 43.

37 Quoted in Dowbiggin, *Merciful End*, 44.

38 Olive Ruth Russell, *Freedom to Die: Moral and Legal Aspects of Euthanasia* (New York: Human Sciences Press, 1975); Russell quotation is in Dowbiggin, *Merciful End*, 130.

39 Derek Humphry, *Good Life, Good Death: Memoir of an Investigative Reporter and Pro-Choice Advocate* (Junction City, OR: Norris Lane Press, 2007).

40 Quoted in Timothy Appleby, "Suicide Law Falls Short, Activist Says 'Does Not Help People Who Need It Most,'" *Globe and Mail*, December 7, 1994.

41 Tom Bates, "Write to Die," *Sunday Oregonian*, December 18, 1994.

42 Barbara Coombs Lee quoted in "Death Stalks the Oregon Ballot Box," *Oregonian*, October 27, 1994.

43 Mark O'Keefe, "Analyzing the Ads Measure 16," *Oregonian*, October 12, 1994.

44 Mark O'Keefe, "Catholics Keep Up Lonely Vigil on Suicide," *Oregonian*, September, 25, 1994.

45 Derek Humphry, "Dr. Death Has It Right," *Oregonian*, September 27, 1996.

46 Barbara Coombs Lee, "Death with Dignity Act Really Isn't 'All about Money' in My Opinion," *Oregonian*, April 6, 1995.

47 Mark O'Keefe, "Assisted-Suicide Measure Survives Heavy Opposition," *Oregonian*, November 10, 1994.

48 "2nd Circuit Court Decision: A Landmark Right to Die Victory, States Hemlock's Founder," Public Radio Newswire, April 2, 1996.

49 James Long, "Churches Denounce Suicide Bill," *Oregonian*, September 19, 1994.

50 O'Keefe, "Assisted-Suicide Measure Survives Heavy Opposition."

51 Anne Muellens, "A Landmark Vote on Assisted Suicide," *Toronto Star*, October 20, 1994.

52 Ian Dowbiggin, *A Merciful End*, 151.

53 See Measure 51 election results, November 4, 1997, http://oregonvotes.org/pages/history/archive/nov497/other.info/m51abst.htm.

Chapter 5: The Dream of National Health Insurance

1 Quoted in David Blumenthal and James A. Morone, *The Heart of Power: Health and Politics in the Oval Office* (Berkeley: University of California Press, 2009), 68.

2 Quoted in Blumenthal and Morone, *Heart of Power*, 68–69.

3 Quotations in Blumenthal and Morone, *Heart of Power*, 76–77.

4 Quoted in Blumenthal and Morone, *Heart of Power*, 81.

5 Quotations in Blumenthal and Morone, *Heart of Power*, 84–85.

6 Quoted in Blumenthal and Morone, *Heart of Power*, 90–91.

7 George W. Bachman and Lewis Meriam, *The Issue of Compulsory Health Insurance* (Washington, DC: Brookings Institution, 1948), 41–46.

8 Quoted in Blumenthal and Morone, *Heart of Power*, 89.

9 Quoted in Blumenthal and Morone, *Heart of Power*, 181.

10 Quoted in Blumenthal and Morone, *Heart of Power*, 191.

11 Blumenthal and Morone, *Heart of Power*, 104.

12 Jill Quadagno, *One Nation, Uninsured: Why the U.S. Has No National Health Insurance* (New York: Oxford University Press, 2005), 191.

13 Quoted in Quadagno, *One Nation, Uninsured*, 188.

14 Quadagno, *One Nation, Uninsured*, 188, 190.

15 Quadagno, *One Nation, Uninsured*, 193.

16 Blumenthal and Morone, *Heart of Power*, 357.

17 Quadagno, *One Nation, Uninsured*, 186.

18 For example, General Motors executives, in expanding medical benefits to their employees, knew that ultimately the system could not be sustained without government assistance. See Roger Lowenstein, *While America Aged* (New York: Penguin Books, 2008). This was also understood by Walter Reuther as explained by Nelson Lichtenstein, *The Most Dangerous Man in Detroit: Walter Reuther and the Fate of American Labor* (New York: Basic Books, 1995).

19 Cited in Roger Lowenstein, *While America Aged* (New York: Penguin Books, 2008), 2.

20 The following discussion of General Motors relies on Lowenstein, *While America Aged*.

21 Reuther's social vision is detailed by his sympathetic biographer, Lichtenstein, *The Most Dangerous Man in Detroit*.

22 Quoted in Lowenstein, *While America Aged*, 20.

23 Lowenstein, *While America Aged*, 40–79.

24 Lowenstein, *While America Aged*, 74.

25 Quoted in Lowenstein, *While America Aged*, 76.

26 The following history of the SEIU is drawn from Leon Fink and Brian Greenberg, *Upheaval in the Quiet Zone: 1199 SEIU and the Politics of Health Care Unionism* (Urbana: University of Illinois Press, 2009).

27 Quoted in Fink and Greenberg, *Upheaval in the Quiet Zone*, 231.

28 Fink and Greenberg, *Upheaval in the Quiet Zone*, 251.

29 Quoted in Fink and Greenberg, *Upheaval in the Quiet Zone*, 253.

30 Quoted in Fink and Greenberg, *Upheaval in the Quiet Zone*, 256.

31 Quoted in Fink and Greenberg, *Upheaval in the Quiet Zone*, 290.

32 Quoted in Fink and Greenberg, *Upheaval in the Quiet Zone*.

33 Quoted in Fink and Greenberg, *Upheaval in the Quiet Zone*.

34 Fink and Greenberg, *Upheaval in the Quiet Zone*, 295.

35 See, e.g., Darryl Fears and Carol D. Leonnig, "Duo in ACORN Videos Say

Effort Was Independent," *Washington Post*, September 18, 2009; Michael A. Memoli, "ACORN Filing for Chapter 7 Bankruptcy," *Los Angeles Times*, November 2, 2010.

36 Quoted in John Atlas, *Seeds of Change: The Story of ACORN: America's Most Controversial Antipoverty Community Organizing Group* (Nashville, TN: Vanderbilt University Press, 2010), 14–18 (quote at 17). Atlas provides a sympathetic history of ACORN that is full of detailed information about the origins and growth of this organization.

37 Atlas, *Seeds of Change*, 57.

38 Quoted in Atlas, *Seeds of Change*, 70.

39 Gretchen Reynolds, "Vote of Confidence," *Chicago Magazine*, January 1993, http://www.chicagomag.com/Chicago-Magazine/January-1993/Vote-of-Confidence. For ACORN's relationship to Project Vote, see Atlas, *Seeds of Change*, 206; and although polemical, David Horowitz and Richard Poe, *The Shadow Party: How George Soros, Hillary Clinton, and Sixties Radicals Seiz ed Control of the Democratic Party* (Boston, 2006), 126.

40 Atlas, *Seeds of Change*, 205–19.

41 Voter-registration fraud and financial scandals within ACORN are discussed by Atlas, *Seeds of Change*, 219–49.

Chapter 6: The Long March Leads to the White House

1 For details, see http://psoglin.com/bio/php.

2 On the Berkeley Peace and Justice Commission, see http://cityofberkeley.info/ContentDisplay.aspx?id=13054. On rent control, see Charles Wollenberg, "Berkeley, a City in History," chap. 9, at http://berkeleypubliclibrary.org/system/Chapter9.html; bpoa.org.

3 On Santa Monica, see Mark E. Kann, *Middle Class Radicalism in Santa Monica* (Philadelphia: Temple University Press, 1986). On Hayden's near-expulsion, see Jennifer Warren and Carl Ingram, "State Senate Gives Hayden a Sentimental Send-Off," *Los Angeles Times*, August 24, 2000, 1. See also Tom Hayden, *The Long Sixties: From 1960 to Barack Obama* (Boulder, CO: Paradigm Publishers, 2009).

4 On the so-called Fairness Doctrine, see Fred W. Friendly, *The Good Guys, the Bad Guys, and the First Amendment: Free Speech vs. Fairness in Broadcasting* (New York: Random House, 1976); Marin Cogan, "Bum Rush: Obama's Secret Plan to Muzzle Talk Radio," *New Republic*, December 3, 2008; "Senate Backs Amendment to Prevent Fairness Doctrine Revival," Fox News, February 26, 2009. Clinton quote in David Maraniss, "First Lady Launches Counterattack," *Washington Post*, January 28, 1998, A1.

5 Nader quotes in Lizette Alvarez, "Vowing to Restore Confidence, Nader Joins Race," *New York Times*, February 22, 2000, A18; James Dao, "Nader Runs Again," *New York Times*, April 15, 2000, A1; Adam Clymer, "Green Horse

Candidate," *New York Times Book Review*, October 15, 2000, 26; "Nader Supporters Fill Madison," *New York Times*, October 14, 2000, A16.

6 On helping progressive Democrats, see Sam H. Verhovek, "Unlike '96, Nader Runs Hard in '00," *New York Times*, July 1, 2000, A8; James Dao, "Under Fire from Democrats," *New York Times*, October 26, 2000, A32; James Dao, "10,000 Turn Out to Hear Nader Urge Shift in Power," *New York Times*, November 6, 2000, A28. On polls, see Michael Janofsky, "Nader, Nominated by the Greens, Attacks Politics as Usual," *New York Times*, June 26, 2000, A14; James Dao, "Nader Fades in Polls but Draws Crowds," *New York Times*, September 24, 2000, 32; David W. Chen, "In Nader Supporters' Math, Gore Equals Bush," *New York Times*, October 15, 2000, 28; Barbara Ehrenreich, "Third Party, Mainstream Hopes," *New York Times*, October 26, 2000, A35; Janet Elder, "4 New Polls Show Bush with Advantage," *New York Times*, November 2, 2000, A25.

7 Kerry was rated the most liberal senator in "2003 Vote Rankings," *National Journal*, February 28, 2004. The American Conservative Union ranked him tied for fourth most liberal: http://conservative.org/ratings/ratingsarchive/2004/2004Senate. htm. Americans for Democratic Action ranked him tied for tenth most liberal: http://web.archive.org/web/20041220165812/http://www.adaction.org/sen.htm.

8 On Obama's background, see David Remnick, *The Bridge: The Life and Times of Barack Obama* (New York: Knopf, 2010), 41–70; Stanley Kurtz, *Radical-in-Chief: Barack Obama and the Untold Story of American Socialism* (New York: Threshold Editions, 2010), 91.

9 On Hawaii, see Remnick, *Bridge*, 70–82, 92.

10 On Davis, see Remnick, *Bridge*, 94–97.

11 On Occidental, see Remnick, *Bridge*, 98–111; Kurtz, *Radical-in-Chief*, 88–90.

12 On the 1983 conference, see Kurtz, *Radical-in-Chief*, 25–30, 34–36, 44–46.

13 On NY PIRG, see Kurtz, *Radical-in-Chief*, 79–80.

14 On Chicago, see Kurtz, *Radical-in-Chief*, 94–124; Remnick, *Bridge*, 134–42, 162–69.

15 On Washington, see Kurtz, *Radical-in-Chief*, 38–43, 49; Remnick, *Bridge*, 156–60.

16 On Harvard, see Remnick, *Bridge*, 182–200, 205–11.

17 On business, see Remnick, *Bridge*, 357–60.

18 Charles Gasparino, *Bought and Paid For: The Unholy Alliance between Barack Obama and Wall Street* (New York: Penguin Sentinel, 2010), 25–26 (quote at 26), 34–35, 60, 75–77.

19 On ACORN/SEIU, see Kurtz, *Radical-in-Chief*, 191–235.

20 On Midwest Academy, see Kurtz, *Radical-in-Chief*, 132–90, especially 135.

21 On Ayers, see Kurtz, *Radical-in-Chief*, 284–91, 345.

22 On Project Vote, see Remnick, *Bridge*, 220–26 (statistic at 223).

23 On Palmer, see Kurtz, *Radical-in-Chief*, 284, 335–36; Remnick, *Bridge*, 277–92.

24 On Harrington, see Kurtz, *Radical-in-Chief*, 31–36, 39–40.

25 On the New Party, see Kurtz, *Radical-in-Chief*, 236–45.

26 Kurtz, *Radical-in-Chief*, 257, 445–46.

27 Stanley Kurtz, "Obama's Third-Party History," *National Review Online*, June 7, 2012.

28 On Obama and the New Party, see Kurtz, *Radical-in-Chief*, 237–38, 246–49, 256–58, 333–34.

29 On the state senate, see Kurtz, *Radical-in-Chief*, 330, 338–339, 348–351; Remnick, *Bridge*, 296–306.

30 On the 2004 campaign, see Kurtz, *Radical-in-Chief*, 339; Remnick, *Bridge*, 345, 357–83 (statistic at 374); *National Journal* in Gasparino, *Bought and Paid For*, 38.

31 Quoted in Kurtz, *Radical-in-Chief*, 258.

32 On Hillary Clinton in 1964, see Dan Balz and Haynes Johnson, *The Battle for America: The Story of an Extraordinary Election* (New York: Penguin, 2010), 13. Poll in Dan Balz, "Hillary Clinton Opens Presidential Bid," *Washington Post*, January 21, 2007. On Hillary Clinton as an ambivalent progressive, see Balz and Johnson, *Battle for America*, 47, 50–51.

33 On Edwards, see Chuck Todd and Sheldon Gawiser, *How Barack Obama Won: A State-by-State Guide to the Historic 2008 Presidential Election* (New York: Vintage Books, 2009), 10–11; Balz and Johnson, *Battle for America*, 30, 51, 96, 113; David Plouffe, *The Audacity to Win: The Inside Story and Lessons of Barack Obama's Historic Victory* (New York: Viking, 2009), 12.

34 Plouffe, *Audacity to Win*, 17–21, 33–34, 43, 63–65, 91–92, 123, 126, 128–29; Balz and Johnson, *Battle for America*, 100–107, 109; John Heilemann and Mark Halperin, *Game Change: Obama and the Clintons, McCain and Palin, and the Race of a Lifetime* (New York: HarperCollins, 2010), 152–53.

35 Plouffe, *Audacity to Win*, 11–13, 32, 74; Balz and Johnson, *Battle for America*, 104, 117, 304.

36 Results in Balz and Johnson, *Battle for America*, 105, 125; funds in Heilemann and Halperin, *Game Change*, 224.

37 Balz and Johnson, *Battle for America*, 125–27, 134, 142, 144; Heilemann and Halperin, *Game Change*, 224. On the black shift, see Todd and Gawiser, *How Barack Obama Won*, 13–14; Balz and Johnson, *Battle for America*, 62–63; Plouffe, *Audacity to Win*, 117–18, 137–38, 140, 151.

38 Senate vote in Balz and Johnson, *Battle for America*, 52, 76–78; Obama speech in Plouffe, *Audacity to Win*, 104–5; Balz and Johnson, *Battle for America*, 21–22 (quote at 21).

39 Obama won 44 percent of the white nonevangelical Protestant vote and 94 percent of the black Protestant vote. Todd and Gawiser, *How Barack Obama Won*, 34.

40 Todd and Gawiser, *How Barack Obama Won*, 14–15; Balz and Johnson, *Battle for America*, 179–98; Plouffe, *Audacity to Win*, 92–94, 164–65, 167, 170, 176. On the rules change, see Justin Sizemore, "Conventions: The Contemporary Significance of a Great American Institution," in Larry J. Sabato, ed., *The Year of Obama: How Barack Obama Won the White House* (New York: Longman, 2010), 4–11, 16.

41 Balz and Johnson, *Battle for America*, 304. On linking McCain to Bush, see Kate Kenski, Bruce W. Hardy, and Kathleen H. Jamieson, *The Obama Victory:*

How Media, Money, and Message Shaped the 2008 Election (New York: Oxford University Press, 2010), 39, 41, 43; Plouffe, *Audacity to Win*, 333. Statistic in Todd and Gawiser, *How Barack Obama Won*, 39.

42 Kenski, Hardy, and Jamieson, *Obama Victory*, 93, 95, 97–98; Plouffe, *Audacity to Win*, 353–57; Heilemann and Halperin, *Game Change*, 408. Scott Shane, "Obama and '60s Bomber," *New York Times*, October 4, 2008, broke the story. Balz and Johnson, *Battle for America*, 360–61. See also Bill Ayers's unrepentant memoir, *Fugitive Days: A Memoir* (Boston: Beacon Press, 2001).

43 Plouffe, *Audacity to Win*, 75.

44 The Clinton plan is in Balz and Johnson, *Battle for America*, 86. The Obama plan is in Plouffe, *Audacity to Win*, 47, 55, 74–76.

45 Quote from the fall plan can be found at http://barackobama.com/pdf/issues/HealthCareFullPlan.pdf.

46 Quotes from two spring campaign documents: http://barackobama.com/pdf/Obama08_HealthcareFAQ.pdf and http://barackobama.com/pdf/HealthPlanFull.pdf.

47 Obama's fall campaign plan can be found here: http://barackobama.com/pdf/issues/HealthCareFullPlan.pdf. McCain's plan is in Kenski, Hardy, and Jamieson, *Obama Victory*, 208–11.

48 Jay Cost, "The Soul of the Democratic Party Machine," *Wall Street Journal*, June 22, 2012.

49 Obama's environmental policy can be found at http://barackobama.com/pdf/issues/EnvironmentFactSheet.pdf. See also Dan Shapley, "Sen. Barack Obama Green the Vote 2008," *Daily Green*, October 25, 2007.

50 On cap and trade as a concept, see http://epa.gov/capandtrade/documents/ctessentials.pdf; John M. Broder, "Cap and Trade," *New York Times*, March 26, 2010, A13.

51 On Obama's version, see William L. Watts, "Obama Calls for Cap-and-Trade Program," *MarketWatch*, October 8, 2007; http://my.barackobama.com/page/content/newenergy.more.

52 Details from Obama's plan at http://my.barackobama.com.

53 On economic consequences of cap and trade, see "An Inconvenient Tax," editorial, *Wall Street Journal*, February 27, 2009, A16; Kevin Bullis, "The Real Price of Obama's Cap-and-Trade Plan," *Technology Review*, March 4, 2009; Ben Lieberman, "$7-a-Gallon Gas?" *New York Post*, June 19, 2010. The $200 billion figure is in Declan McCullagh, "Obama Admin: Cap and Trade Could Cost Families $1,761 a Year," CBS News, September 15, 2009.

54 Gasparino, *Bought and Paid For*, 30, 211–12 (quote at 212), 239–40.

55 On electric cars, see http://hybridcars.com/electric-car. On Tesla, see http://teslamotors.com/roadster and /own. On the Volt, see Patrick Michaels, "Chevy Volt," *Forbes*, March 16, 2011.

56 On high-speed rail, see David Roberts, "Obama Loves High-Speed Rail," *Grist*, August 7, 2008; http://fra.dot.gov/Pages/203.shtml; ushsr.com. See also Robert Samuelson, "High Speed Pork," *Newsweek*, November 1, 2010.

57 George H. W. Bush, August 18, 1988, quote in http://americanrhetoric.com/speeches/georgehbush1988rnc.htm.

58 Obama quote in Balz and Johnson, *Battle for America*, 365.

59 The Obama tax plan is in http://barackobama.com/taxes. See also Kenski, Hardy, and Jamieson, *Obama Victory*, 203–6; Plouffe, *Audacity to Win*, 359, 363. The Obama and McCain tax plans are compared in http://taxpolicycenter.org/taxtopics/election_issues_matrix.cfm.

60 Gasparino, *Bought and Paid For*, 10–13, 117–20, 185; Curtis Dubay in Ed Feulner, "Stop Squeezing Small Business," *Orange County Register*, September 6, 2010.

61 The $140 billion in taxable U.S. income earned by foreigners is in http://irs.gov/businesses/article/0,,id=180219,00.html. Foreign rates can be found here: http://taxpolicycenter.org/taxfacts/Content/PDF/oecd_historical_toprate.pdf.

62 See http://taxpolicycenter.org/taxfacts/content/PDF/source_historical_cg.pdf and http://taxtopics/encyclopedia/Capital-Gains-Taxation.cfm.

63 Balz and Johnson, *Battle for America*, 46.

64 On Iraq, see http://barackobama.com/issues/iraq/index_campaign.php. On Afghanistan, see Barack Obama, "The War We Need to Win," http://barackobama.com, August 1, 2007.

65 Plouffe, *Audacity to Win*, 84–85, 89.

66 Balz and Johnson, *Battle for America*, 26–27.

67 Heilemann and Halperin, *Game Change*, 149, 155, 265; Plouffe, *Audacity to Win*, 108–9; Diana Owen, "Media in the 2008 Election," in Sabato, *Year of Obama*, 168, 173, 176.

68 Balz and Johnson, *Battle for America*, 31–32; Heilemann and Halperin, *Game Change*, 161; Kenski, Hardy, and Jamieson, *Obama Victory*, 98–99, 137, 142; Owen, "Media in the 2008 Election," 174, 178. Matthews quote in Goldberg, *Liberal Fascism*, 414; Clinton quote in Heilemann and Halperin, *Game Change*, 228.

69 Plouffe, *Audacity to Win*, 206, 224–25; Balz and Johnson, *Battle for America*, 200, 211, 289; Heilemann and Halperin, *Game Change*, 75, 234–36, 239, 246–49 (sermon titles at 234).

70 Kenski, Hardy, and Jamieson, *Obama Victory*, 87. See also Todd and Gawiser, *How Barack Obama Won*, 12, 25.

71 Kenski, Hardy, and Jamieson, *Obama Victory*, 101–2; Heilemann and Halperin, *Game Change*, 237–38. "Barack Obama's Speech on Race" (transcript), *New York Times*, March 18, 2008.

72 On Obama as postracial, see Plouffe, *Audacity to Win*, 214; Heilemann and Halperin, *Game Change*, 72; Todd and Gawiser, *How Barack Obama Won*, 12. Clarence Page disagreed with this term on the *McLaughlin Report*, September 5, 2010. On Bill Clinton's South Carolina campaign, see Todd and Gawiser, *How Barack Obama Won*, 13; Balz and Johnson, *Battle for America*, 156–60.

73 On the media, see Kenski, Hardy, and Jamieson, *Obama Victory*, 180, 183; Heilemann and Halperin, *Game Change*, 155, 265, 328; Goldberg, *Liberal Fascism*, 413–14; Susan MacManus, "Presidential Election 2008," in Sabato, *Year*

of Obama, 266–67. On exploiting the media, see Balz and Johnson, *Battle for America*, 174, 338–42.

74 Plouffe, *Audacity to Win*, 22, 28, 33, 43, 49, 52–53, 70–71, 77–78; Balz and Johnson, *Battle for America*, 26.

75 Gasparino, *Bought and Paid For*, ix–xi, 10–12, 17–25, 32–33, 36–50, 52–55, 60-61, 95–101, 107, 247–55.

76 Plouffe, *Audacity to Win*, 21, 32, 48, 51–52, 76; Heilemann and Halperin, *Game Change*, 107.

77 Michael Cornfield, "Game Changers," in Sabato, *Year of Obama*, 221–25; Plouffe, *Audacity to Win*, 237; Michael Toner, "The Impact of Federal Election Laws," in Sabato, *Year of Obama*, 159–60; Girish Gulati, "No Laughing Matter: The Role of New Media in the 2008 Election," in Sabato, *Year of Obama*, 194.

78 Plouffe, *Audacity to Win*, 370; Toner, "The Impact of Federal Election Laws," 154.

79 Toner, "The Impact of Federal Election Laws," 150–51; Plouffe, *Audacity to Win*, 259.

80 Heilemann and Halperin, *Game Change*, 327; Kenski, Hardy, and Jamieson, *Obama Victory*, 37, 266–67, 309; Plouffe, *Audacity to Win*, 259–60; Toner, "The Impact of Federal Election Laws," 152.

81 Heilemann and Halperin, *Game Change*, 418; Kenski, Hardy, and Jamieson, *Obama Victory*, 6, 9, 25, 265–67; Toner, "The Impact of Federal Election Laws," 155–56. The $1 billion figure is in Todd and Gawiser, *How Barack Obama Won*, 17.

82 Plouffe, *Audacity to Win*, 350–51; Kenski, Hardy, and Jamieson, *Obama Victory*, 251, 255–62; Todd and Gawiser, *How Barack Obama Won*, 27.

83 On foreign money, see Pamela Geller, "Obama's Foreign Donors: The Media Averts Its Eyes," *American Thinker*, August 14, 2008; Matthew Mosk, "RNC to File FEC Complaint on Obama Fundraising Practices," *Washington Post*, October 5, 2008; John Fund, "Speaking of Foreign Money, What about Obama's?" *Wall Street Journal*, October 19, 2010.

84 Todd and Gawiser, *How Barack Obama Won*, 31.

85 Larry Sabato, "The Election of Our Lifetime," in Sabato, *Year of Obama*, 47; Todd and Gawiser, *How Barack Obama Won*, 20.

86 Todd and Gawiser, *How Barack Obama Won*, 29, 142.

87 Some data is in Todd and Gawiser, *How Barack Obama Won*, 52, 58, 76–77, 81–82, 87, 93, 114, 120, 125–26, 142–43, 157.

88 Todd and Gawiser, *How Barack Obama Won*, 34.

Chapter 7: The Heights of Power

1 Jim Puzzanghera, "Fannie Mae, Freddie Mac Bailouts," *Los Angeles Times*, October 21, 2010.

2 On Geithner, see Jonathan Alter, *The Promise: President Obama, Year One* (New York: Simon & Schuster, 2010), 49–53, 94–95, 193–95.

3 Charles Gasparino, *Bought and Paid For: The Unholy Alliance between Barack Obama and Wall Street* (New York: Penguin Sentinel, 2010), 99.

4 Gasparino, *Bought and Paid For*, 100.

5 Gasparino, *Bought and Paid For*, 80.

6 On Summers, see Alter, *Promise*, 29, 189–91, 197–98.

7 On Axelrod, see Alter, *Promise*, 18–19; Stanley Kurtz, *Radical-in-Chief: Barack Obama and the Untold Story of American Socialism* (New York: Threshold Editions, 2010), 187; on Gibbs, see Alter, *Promise*, 19, 69, 135, 276, 333.

8 Gasparino, *Bought and Paid For*, 78.

9 On Emanuel, see Alter, *Promise*, 20–24, 159–68; Kurtz, *Radical-in-Chief*, 165, 360.

10 On using Wall Street money, see Gasparino, *Bought and Paid For*, 101–2.

11 For an overview of the auto bailout, see Alter, *Promise*, 174–88. A useful narrative is the series in the *Detroit Free Press*, December 13–18, 2009.

12 On the bondholders and 29 percent, see Jake Tapper, "Political Punch," http://blogs.abcnews.com/politicalpunch/2009/05/bankruptcy-atto.html, May 2, 2009; Allan H. Meltzer, "Why Obamanomics Failed," *Wall Street Journal*, June 30, 2010. See also Mike Ramsey, "Chrysler Plans," Bloomberg, February 12, 2009, http://www.bloomberg.com/apps/news?pid=newsarchive&sid=abE 6IcH41yEQ&refer=us; Daniel Howes, "Commentary," *Detroit News*, May 1, 2009; Todd Zywicki, "The Auto Bailout and the Rule of Law," *National Affairs*, no. 7 (Spring 2011).

13 The $80 billion is in http://financialedge.investopedia.com/financial-edge/ 0211/1-CEOs-And-What-They-Make-Now.aspx. See also Daniel Howes, "Commentary," *Detroit News*, April 29, 2009; Paul Ingrassia, "How GM Lost Its Way," *Wall Street Journal*, June 3, 2009.

14 Frank: http://house.gov/frank/pressreleases/2009/06–04–09-gm-norton-gets-extension.html.

15 Quoted in Peggy Noonan, "Neither a Hedgehog Nor a Fox," *Wall Street Journal*, March 20, 2009.

16 On pay, see Steven Pearlstein, "Blaming Wall Street on Bonuses Is Hypocritical," *Washington Post*, January 15, 2010, A17; Charles Krauthammer, "Bonfire of the Trivialities," *Washington Post*, March 20, 2009; Alter, *Promise*, 309–14.

17 Matthew Continetti, "The Age of Irresponsibility," *Weekly Standard*, March 2, 2009.

18 Gary S. Becker and Kevin M. Murphy, "There's No Stimulus Free Lunch," *Wall Street Journal*, February 10, 2009.

19 John B. Taylor, "A Two-Trick Plan to Restore Growth," *Wall Street Journal*, January 28, 2011.

20 On Romer's $1.2 trillion, see Ryan Lizza, "Inside the Crisis," *New Yorker*, October 12, 2009.

21 Quoted in Peter Baker, "Education of a President," *New York Times Magazine*, October 17, 2010.

22 Romer cited in Darrell Issa, "Obama's Keynesian Failures Must Never Be Repeated," *Financial Times*, February 7, 2011. See also Ross Douthat, "Off the Chart," *New York Times*, November 16, 2009.

23 On the poorly structured tax cuts, see Meltzer, "Why Obamanomics Failed"; Alter, *Promise*, 116.

24 Robert Samuelson estimated 2.8 million total jobs in "Economics Unhinged," *Washington Post*, June 28, 2010.

25 Quoted in Baker, "Education of a President."

26 On Davis-Bacon, see *Wall Street Journal* editorial, "How to Save $40 Billion," January 21, 2009; Charles Lane, "Kill These Job-Killers," *Washington Post*, December 14, 2009; Amity Shlaes, "Depression Fear Mongers Obscure the True Concerns," Bloomberg, July 7, 2010, http://www.bloomberg.com/news/2010–07–08/depression-fear-mongers-obscure-the-true-concerns-amity-shlaes.html.

27 Quoted in Peggy Noonan, "Try a Little Tenderness," *Wall Street Journal*, July 30, 2010.

28 Quoted in Michael Barone, "Economic Doldrums Leave Americans in No Mood for Obama's Liberal Agenda," *Washington Examiner*, August 23, 2010.

29 See in general Sally Pipes, *The Truth about ObamaCare* (Washington, DC: Regnery, 2010); Alter, *Promise*, 244–66, 395–421, 431–34. On the Supreme Court decision, see Adam Liptak, "Justices, by 5–4, Uphold Health-Care Law," *New York Times*, June 29, 1912, A1.

30 Peggy Noonan, "The Town Hall Revolt, One Year Later," *Wall Street Journal*, July 10, 2010.

31 CNN Opinion Research Poll, March 19–21, 2010.

32 "PolitiFiction," *Wall Street Journal*, December 22, 2010.

33 Obama quoted in Peggy Noonan, "What a Disaster Looks Like," *Wall Street Journal*, March 4, 2010; poll in Scott Rasmussen and Doug Schoen, "Why Obama Can't Move the Health-Care Numbers," *Wall Street Journal*, March 9, 2010. See also Robert Samuelson, "Obama's Malpractice," *Washington Post*, November 16, 2009.

34 Timothy Carney, "Tick, Tick, Tick," *Washington Examiner*, January 16, 2011.

35 Pelosi quoted in Caroline Baum, "McDonald's Gets Taste of Obama Sausage-Making," Bloomberg, October 7, 2010.

36 George Will, "Obama in the Wilsonian Tradition," *Washington Post*, March 11, 2010.

37 This description of Obamacare, and following description, relies heavily upon Pipes, *Truth*, as well as a wide survey of existing literature on the subject.

38 For a detailed cost analysis, see Douglas Holtz-Eakin and Paul Howard, "Will Spending under Obamacare Trigger the Next Financial Crisis?" *Investor's Business Daily*, April 1, 2010. In 2011 the nonpartisan CBO raised the ten-year cost to $1.4 trillion. Nina Easton on *Fox News Sunday*, March 27, 2010.

39 Cited in Pipes, *Truth*, 41.

40 Cited in Pipes, *Truth*, 154.

41 "Insurers Bid for State Medicaid Plans," *Wall Street Journal*, December 29, 2010.

42 "Sebelius's Price Controls," *Wall Street Journal*, December 22, 2010.

43 On the Virginia case, see Ken Cuccinelli, "Virginia's Suit against Obamacare," *Wall Street Journal*, November 24, 2010. On the Florida case, see Kevin Sack, "Second Judge Deals Blow to Health Care Law," *New York Times*, February 1, 2011, A1. On waivers, see Philip Hamburger, "Are Health-Care Waivers Unconstitutional?" *National Review*, February 8, 2011; Philip Hamburger, "Can Health-Care Waivers Be Justified?" *National Review*, February 18, 2011.

44 Elise Viebeck, "Healthwatch," *The Hill*, July 22, 2012.

45 Quoted in Pipes, *Truth*, 9.

46 Campaign tax policy is in Kate Kenski, Bruce W. Hardy, and Kathleen H. Jamieson, *The Obama Victory: How Media, Money, and Message Shaped the 2008 Election* (New York: Oxford University Press, 2010), 50, 240–42, 244.

47 On tax policy and the budget, see Alter, *Promise*, 89, 93, 98n, 113, 116, 118, 130–31, 135–37, 246, 255, 268–69, 424. See also Daniel Henninger, "The Obama Rosetta Stone," *Wall Street Journal*, March 12, 2009.

48 On the importance of low rates, see Arthur B. Laffer, "Reaganomics: What We Learned," *Wall Street Journal*, February 10, 2011.

49 $522 billion in FY2008 vs. $655 billion in FY2011. Office of Management and Budget, FY2012 Budget Proposal, Historical Tables, 145. Available at budget .gov. Gary Andres, "The Democrats and the 2010 Budget Fiasco," *Weekly Standard*, September 30, 2010; Charles Krauthammer, "It's about His Policies," *Orange County Register*, October 7, 2010.

50 Mark Halperin, "Why Obama Is Losing the Political War," *Time*, October 11, 2010.

51 Quoted in Jason Horowitz, "Hotheaded Emanuel May Be White House Voice of Reason," *Washington Post*, March 2, 2010.

52 George Will, "A Recoil against Liberalism," *Washington Post*, November 4, 2010.

53 Quoted in Will, "A Recoil against Liberalism."

54 In general, see R. Emmett Tyrrell Jr., "Out of the Wilderness," *American Spectator*, November 12, 2010; Joel Kotkin, "How Liberalism Self-Destructed," *Politico*, November 19, 2010; Walter R. Mead, "The Crisis of the American Intellectual," *American Interest*, December 8, 2010.

55 Evan Bayh, "Where Do Democrats Go Next?" *New York Times*, November 2, 2010.

56 For a typical, shallow media interpretation, see Michael Hiltzik, "A Damning Post-Mortem of the Financial Meltdown," *Los Angeles Times*, February 6, 2011.

57 See, e.g., Jeremy Warner, "Jobless America Threatens to Bring Us All Down," *Telegraph*, October 11, 2010; Kenneth Rogoff, "Globalisation at the Crossroads," *Guardian*, November 7, 2010; Mortimer B. Zuckerman, "Obama's Anti-Business Policies Are Our Economic Katrina," *U.S. News & World Report*, July 16, 2010.

58 Zuckerman, "Obama's Anti-Business Policies."

59 Andrew R. Sorkin, "Wall St. Joins SEC in Plea for Bigger Budget," *New York Times*, February 7, 2011.

60 Michael Barone, "The Trouble with Big Bossy Government," *Washington Examiner*, October 25, 2010.

61 Alter, *Promise*, 196, 322.

62 On progressive ideology, see Henry Olsen, "Day of the Democratic Dead," *National Review*, November 1, 2010.

63 Henry Kaufman, "How to Fix the Economy," *Business Week*, September 16, 2010.

64 Gasparino, *Bought and Paid For*, 152.

65 Gasparino, *Bought and Paid For*, 142.

66 Gasparino, *Bought and Paid For*, 176, 206, 208.

67 Peter Eavis, "Parsing Jamie Dimon's Testimony," *New York Times*, June 12, 2012.

68 Five hundred rules in Zuckerman, "Obama's Anti-Business Policies." See also Gasparino, *Bought and Paid For*, 235.

69 William Dunkelberg in Zuckerman, "Obama's Anti-Business Policies."

70 Jennifer Liberto, "Elizabeth Warren in the Hot Seat," CNN Money, March 16, 2011; James Surowiecki, "The Warren Court," *New Yorker*, June 13, 2011; Aaron Blake, "Elizabeth Warren Controversy," *Washington Post*, May 25, 2012.

71 Phil Gramm, "Echoes of the Great Depression," *Wall Street Journal*, October 1, 2010.

72 Ken Langone, "Stop Bashing Business," *Wall Street Journal*, October 15, 2010.

73 On Obama as antibusiness, see Mike Allen and Jim VandeHei, "Obama Isolated Ahead of 2012," *Politico*, November 8, 2010, http://www.politico.com/news/stories/1110/44812.html.

74 Throughout this section, statistics are drawn from the FY2012 Budget Proposal. On the 1930s and 1946 debt, see Michael Pento, "Why the Greater Depression Still Lies Ahead," *Forbes*, June 30, 2010. The best study of the fiscal crises that invariably follow financial crises is Carmen Reinhart and Kenneth S. Rogoff, *This Time Is Different: Eight Centuries of Financial Folly* (Princeton: Princeton University Press, 2009). Much of what follows is from this important book. See also Jason Thomas, "Managing the Federal Debt," *National Affairs*, no. 5 (Fall 2010).

75 Statistics in Evan Thomas, "Truth or Consequences," *Newsweek*, November 13, 2010.

76 The Democratic Congress did not pass the FY2009 budget on time in fall 2008 because George Bush was still in office. Congress used continuing resolutions until spring 2009. Clive Crook, "How Obama Can Avoid a Policy Jam," *Financial Times*, March 15, 2009.

77 Thomas B. Edsall, "Limited War," *New Republic*, October 20, 2010. FY2011 data is at http://www.whitehouse.gov/omb/budget/Historicals, especially tables 1.1 and 1.2.

78 Bernanke quoted in Matt Welch, "We Are Out of Money," *Reason*, June 2010.

79 Mortimer B. Zuckerman, "The Most Fiscally Irresponsible Government in U.S. History," *U.S. News & World Report*, August 26, 2010.

80 Rogoff cited in Bill Gross, "Three Will Get You Two, or Two Will Get You Three," Investment Outlook, Pimco, June 2010, http://www.pimco.com/EN/Insights/Pages/Bill%20Gross%20June%202010%20Investment%20Outlook.aspx. The statistics are in Carmen Reinhart and Kenneth Rogoff, "Debt and Growth Revisited," MPRA Paper No. 24376, August 2010, http://mpra.ub.uni-muenchen.de/24376.

81 For a shrewd analysis, see Robert Rubin, "America Must Cut Its Deficit but Not in Haste," *Financial Times*, January 24, 2011. On the heroin analogy, see David Stockman, "Our Failed National Economy," Minyanville, November 4, 2010, http://www.minyanville.com/businessmarkets/articles/midterm-elections-quantitative-easing-qe2-fomc/11/4/2010/id/30936?page=full. See also BIS report cited in John Mauldin, "The Future of Public Debt," Safe Haven, May 1, 2010, http://www.safehaven.com/article/16621/the-future-of-public-debt; Sheila C. Bair, "Will the Next Fiscal Crisis Start in Washington?" *Washington Post*, November 26, 2010; Robert Samuelson, "Obama's Empty Evasion," *Newsweek*, January 27, 2011.

82 Editorial, *Washington Times*, March 18, 2011.

83 Gasparino, *Bought and Paid For*, 159–60, 165, 173 (quote), 177, 185, 228.

84 Robert Samuelson, "The Politics of Avoidance," *Newsweek*, November 22, 2010.

85 Quoted in Jeremy Warner, "Fed's $600 Billion Gamble," *Telegraph*, November 3, 2010.

86 On China, see Mark Steyn, "Dependence Day," *New Criterion*, January 2011.

87 Martin Wolf, "In the Grip of a Great Convergence," *Financial Times*, January 4, 2011.

88 On insufficient funding, see Michael Pento, "U.S. Solvency Hinges on Low Rates," Real Clear Markets, May 14, 2010, http://www.realclearmarkets.com/articles/2010/05/14/us_solvency_hinges_on_low_interest_rates_98466.html.

89 International Monetary Fund, "Global Financial Stability Report," April 2010. For the press release and links, see imf.org/external/pubs/ft/survey/so/2010/res042010a.htm. IMF data is summarized in Edmund Conway, "U.S. Faces One of the Biggest Budget Crunches in the World," *Telegraph*, May 14, 2010. See "Get Ready for Austerity Plan," *Toronto Star*, May 24, 2010. For another IMF report, see Randall W. Forsyth, "Why Americans Are Angry," *Barron's*, November 2, 2010. See also Mohamed El-Erian, "Navigating the New Normal in Industrial Countries," International Monetary Fund, October 2010, http://www.imf.org/external/np/speeches/2010/101010.htm.

90 BIS quoted in John Mauldin, "The Center Cannot Hold," Frontline Weekly Newsletter, May 7, 2010.

91 Robert Samuelson, "The Age of Austerity," *Newsweek*, October 11, 2010; Geoff Colvin, "As Europe Cuts, America Spends," *Economist*, November 2, 2010; Christopher Caldwell, "The Germany That Said No," *Weekly Standard*, Novem-

ber 8, 2010; Carol Matlack, "French Bonds Suddenly Look Shaky," *Business Week*, June 26, 2012.

92 William H. Gross, "Allentown," Investment Outlook, Pimco, December 2010, http://www.pimco.com/EN/Insights/Pages/AllentownDecember2010.aspx; Dylan Grice, "The Three Stages of Delusion," quoted in John Mauldin, InvestorsInsight.com, December 6, 2010, http://www.investorsinsight.com/blogs/john_mauldins_outside_the_box/archive/2010/12/06/the-three-stages-of-delusion.aspx; Alter, *Promise*, 228.

93 Jeremy Warner, "Jobless America," *Telegraph*, October 11, 2010.

94 On reaction to State of the Union, see Ruth Marcus, "The State of the Union Is Leaderless," *Washington Post*, January 28, 2011; John B. Taylor, "A Two-Track Plan to Restore Growth," *Wall Street Journal*, January 28, 2011; David A. Patten, "David Stockman: Obama Oblivious to Deficit," Newsmax, January 26, 2011, http://www.newsmax.com/InsideCover/obama-stockman-budget-details/2011/01/26/id/384047.

95 FY2012 Budget Proposal. Reaction was uniformly negative. See, for example, Megan McArdle, "Time to Get Serious about the Deficit," *Atlantic*, February 14, 2011; Dana Milbank, "In His New Budget, Obama Kicks the Can One More Time," *Washington Post*, February 15, 2011; Charles Krauthammer, "Obama's Louis XV Budget," *Washington Post*, February 18, 2011.

96 Sardya Somashekher, "Republican Reaction," *Washington Post*, January 24, 2012.

97 Pento, "U.S. Solvency Hinges on Low Interest Rates."

98 Daniel Fisher, "The Global Debt Bomb," *Forbes*, February 2, 2010.

99 John Mauldin, "Is This a Recovery?" Business Insider, April 3, 2010, http://articles.businessinsider.com/2010–04–03/markets/30080724_1_dividend-yields-recovery-stock-market.

100 Taylor, "Two-Track Plan"; Bill Gross, "Staying Rich in the New Normal," Investment Outlook, Pimco, June 2009, http://www.pimco.com/EN/Insights/Pages/IO%20June%202009%20Staying%20Rich%20in%20the%20New%20Normal%20Gross.aspx; Jon Markham, "Fed's Course Calls All Hands on Deck," MarketWatch, November 18, 2010, http://articles.marketwatch.com/2010–11–18/investing/30697850_1_fed-officials-treasury-rates-yuan; John Hussman, "Misquoting Keynes," Hussman Funds, February 7, 2011, http://www.hussmanfunds.com/wmc/wmc110207.htm; Joseph Y. Calhoun III, "Weekly Economic and Market Review," Contrarian Musings, Alhambra Investments, February 6, 2011, http://alhambrainvestments.com/blog/2011/01/23/weekly-economic-and-market-review-43/.

101 Robert Arnott, "What's Gross about Our GDP?" Real Clear Markets, March 10, 2010, http://www.realclearmarkets.com/articles/2010/03/10/whats_gross_about_our_gross_domestic_product_98378.html.

102 See Stephen G. Cecchetti, Madhusudan Mohanty, and Fabrizio Zampolli, "The Future of Public Debt," Bank for International Settlements, March 2010, which made ominous calculations. For a summary, see John

Mauldin, "The Future of Public Debt Is Terrifying ," Business Insider, February 12, 2011, http://articles.businessinsider.com/2011–02–12/markets/29988138_1_public-debt-endgame-international-settlements. See also Matt Miller, "A Fiscal Mess Our Leaders Won't Face," *Washington Post*, December 1, 2010.

103 Meltzer, "Why Obamanomics Failed." On oil imports see Neela Banerjee, "U.S. Report," *Los Angeles Times*, March 12, 2012.

104 Daniel B. Klein, "Are You Smarter Than a Fifth Grader?" *Wall Street Journal*, June 8, 2010.

105 Steven Pearlstein, "Greece and the Myth of the Easy Economic Fix," *Washington Post*, May 3, 2010, A16; Jim Jubak, "Jubak's Journal," MSN Money, May 24, 2010.

106 On states, see Michael Gerson, "The Blue State Budget Crisis," *Washington Post*, November 12, 2010; Mortimer Zuckerman, "Public Employee Union Benefits Are a Fiscal Disaster," *U.S. News & World Report*, January 21, 2011; James Pethokoukis, "When States Go Bust," *Weekly Standard*, February 14, 2011.

107 Eli Segall, "San Jose, County Dispute Leads to Bond Downgrading," *BizJournals*, June 8, 2012; Joel Kotkin, "Is Perestroika Coming in California?" *Forbes*, June 11, 2012; Catherine Saillant and Dan Weikel, "Stockton Bankruptcy," *Los Angeles Times*, June 27, 2012; Jim Christie, "San Bernardino 3rd California City to Seek Bankruptcy," Reuters, July 11, 2012.

108 Mohamed El-Erian, "Waiting for Better Times Is No Substitute for Action," *Telegraph*, January 10, 2010.

109 Barone, "The Trouble with Big Bossy Government."

110 Jeffrey T. Kuhner, "Demolishing the Democrats," *Washington Times*, October 14, 2010.

111 The best essay on the Tea Party is Paul A. Rahe, "How to Think about the Tea Party," *Commentary*, February 2011. See also Alter, *Promise*, 263–64, 408.

112 See Daniel Henninger, "Why the Left Lost It," *Wall Street Journal*, January 12, 2011.

113 On the debate inside the White House, see Alter, *Promise*, 115–16, 244–46, 395–96, 407. See also Ruth Marcus, "Clueless on a Shellacking," *Washington Post*, November 10, 2010; Peggy Noonan, "Obama's Gifts to the GOP," *Wall Street Journal*, November 12, 2010.

114 On Emanuel, see Dana Milbank, "Why Obama Needs Rahm at the Top," *Washington Post*, February 21, 2010, A3; Horowitz, "Hotheaded Emanuel May Be White House Voice of Reason."

115 Alter, *Promise*, 400–401.

116 For a skeptic, see Peter Wehner, "An Ideologue Instead of a Statesman," *Commentary*, November 12, 2009.

117 Charles Krauthammer, "A Return to the Norm," *Washington Post*, November 5, 2010.

118 Ed Koch, "The Coming Political Tsunami," Real Clear Politics, October 26, 2010, http://www.realclearpolitics.com/articles/2010/10/26/the_coming_political_tsunami_107726.html.

119 On cap and trade, see Michael Barone, "In 2010 Sweep, Even the Finns Voted Republican," *Washington Examiner*, November 25, 2010.

120 Gasparino, *Bought and Paid For*, 176, 192, 217, 226–32.

121 On polls, see Liz Sidoti and Jennifer Agiesta, "2010 Elections Highlight Obama's Eroding Base," AP, November 13, 2010; Karlyn Bowman, "What the Voters Actually Said on Election Day," *American*, November 16, 2010.

122 Statistics in Karl Rove, "Obama Has a Listening Problem," *Wall Street Journal*, November 11, 2010.

123 Charles Krauthammer, "The Great Campaign of 2010," *Washington Post*, October 28, 2010.

124 Quoted in Ron Radosh, "The Disappearance of the Emerging Democratic Majority," Pajamas Media, October 29, 2010, http://pjmedia.com/ronradosh/2010/10/29/the-disappearance-of-the-the-emerging-democratic-majority-the-failure-of-a-thesis/.

125 "Pimco Raises U.S. Growth Forecast after Tax Deal," CNBC, December 10, 2010; Simon Schama, "An America Lost in Fantasy Must Recover Its Dream," *Financial Times*, December 23, 2010.

126 Quotes in Peggy Noonan, "From Audacity to Animosity," *Wall Street Journal*, December 10, 2010.

127 Robert Costa, "Caddell on the Midterm Elections," *National Review*, September 12, 2010.

128 Greg Sargent, "David Axelrod," Plum Line, January 27, 2011, voices.washingtonpost.com/plum-line.

129 John Fund, "Dems Show Centrists the Door," *Wall Street Journal*, February 8, 2011.

130 "Obama to Business Owners: You Didn't Build That," Fox News, July 15, 2012.

Acknowledgments

T he authors want to thank three people in particular who were crucial in producing this book: Jed Donahue, editor in chief of ISI Books, made an early commitment to this project, and through his hands-on editing he pushed us to clarify our arguments, strengthen our narrative, and make sure our facts were right. In our opinion he is one of the ablest editors in publishing today. We also want to acknowledge the important role Liza Forshaw had in the process. She read chapters in draft and then copyedited the book for the press. She brought to her editing her fine eye as a professional lawyer who loves words. In addition, the authors appreciate the research assistance provided by Joshua Mather, a graduate student in history. Although, we suspect, he does not agree with the politics of this book, he provided objective and timely research. Finally, Donald Critchlow wants to acknowledge the early intellectual contribution by Jeffrey Paul, the codirector of the Social Philosophy and Policy Center at Bowling Green State University. This book grew out of many conversations with Jeff about the history of American liberalism when Critchlow was a fellow at the center.

Index